THE
DEPRESSED
WOMAN

THE DEPRESSED WOMAN

a study of social relationships

Myrna M. Weissman and Eugene S. Paykel

with a foreword by Gerald L. Klerman

The University of Chicago Press   Chicago and London

International Standard Book Number: 0–226–89160–7
Library of Congress Catalog Card Number: 73–90944

Portions of this book first appeared, sometimes in different form, in the
journal articles indicated below. Permission to use material from these articles
is gratefully acknowledged. Data for the tables in chapters 5, 6, 7, and 8
appeared in somewhat different form in Myrna M. Weissman et al., "The
Social Role Performance of Depressed Women: Comparisons with a Normal
Group," *American Journal of Orthopsychiatry* 41, no. 3 (April 1971),
copyright 1971, The American Orthopsychiatric Association, Inc. Chapter 7
contains material from Ruth C. Bullock et al., "The Weeping Wife: Marital
Relations of Depressed Women," *Journal of Marriage and the Family,* August
1972, and from Eugene S. Paykel and Myrna M. Weissman, "Marital and
Sexual Dysfunction in Depressed Women," *Medical Aspects of Human
Sexuality,* June 1972. Portions of chapter 8 appeared in Myrna M. Weissman,
Eugene S. Paykel, and Gerald L. Klerman, "The Depressed Woman as
Mother," *Social Psychiatry* 7 (1972), copyright 1972, Springer-Verlag, and in
Myrna M. Weissman and Risé Siegel, "The Depressed Woman and Her
Rebellious Adolescent," *Social Casework,* November 1972. An unrevised
form of chapter 9 appeared in Eugene S. Paykel et al., "Dimensions of Social
Adjustment in Depressed Women," *Journal of Nervous and Mental Disease*
152 (1971). Material in chapter 10 appeared in Myrna M. Weissman,
Gerald L. Klerman, and Eugene S. Paykel, "Clinical Evaluation of Hostility
in Depression," *The American Journal of Psychiatry* 128, no. 3 (September
1971), copyright 1971, The American Psychiatric Association. Material in
chapter 11 appeared in Eugene S. Paykel and Myrna M. Weissman, "Social
Adjustment and Depression: A Longitudinal Study," *Archives of General
Psychiatry* 28 (May 1973). Portions of chapter 13 appeared in Myrna M.
Weissman, "Casework and Pharmacotherapy in Treatment of Depression,"
Social Casework, January 1972.

To our own families

Contents

Foreword

The appearance of this report by Weissman and Paykel of their comprehensive study of forty depressed women is timely and noteworthy. In recent decades there has been a noticeable increase of scientific interest and public concern with the affective disorders, particularly depression, or "melancholia" as it was called in previous eras. Scientific interest was initiated within the mental health professions out of their awareness of the increasing number of patients, especially young adults, coming to treatment because of behaviors and complaints related to suicidal wishes, sadness, and other depressive manifestations. Public concern in the United States was mobilized following the dramatic revelation that Senator Thomas Eagleton, the 1972 Democratic vice-presidential candidate, had been hospitalized three times for episodes of depression. The public is becoming more aware of the complex nature of depressive disorders and the extent to which they strike persons in all walks of life, at all ages, and from all social strata.

The middle part of the twentieth century became known as the "Age of Anxiety"; the latter portion of this century may become known as an "Age of Melancholy." Western society has passed through similar ages of melancholy, as evidenced in the seventeenth-century wave of melancholy in England, described by Thomas Burton in his famous *Anatomy of Melancholy*, and also in the ennui and weltschmerz characteristic of the romantic movement in the first part of the nineteenth century. A new age of melancholy may be upon us as Western society confronts the gap between the widespread hopes for economic and social progress promised by the marvels of technology and the realities of the earth's limited resources, the dangers of uncontrolled population growth, and the failures of political movements to produce social justice. Depressions seem to arise not when things are at their worst but when there is a discrepancy between one's aspirations and the likelihood that reality will fulfill these wishes and hopes, whether for oneself, one's family, or the larger social group with which one identifies.

Seen in this historical perspective, the research described by Weissman and Paykel will be of significance for many audiences: public officials and citizens involved in the development of public policy related to health and social services; researchers and investigators in psychiatry, mental health, and the social and behavioral sciences; and mental health practitioners, particularly psychiatrists, psychologists, social workers, nurses, and psychotherapists involved in the care and treatment of patients.

Public Policy

At first glance, it would appear unlikely that a report of clinical research on forty depressed women would have much consequence for public policy. However, as the reader becomes aware of the concurrent trends, described by the authors, which document the widespread prevalence of depressions in the general population and the extent to which depressions impair individuals during their most productive life-periods—young adulthood and maturity—he or she will realize that public policy requires increasing attention to the depressive disorders. The nation needs assurance that proper resources are being made available for research into the causes, nature, and treatment of depressions. Perhaps more relevant to public policies, as the nation debates the desirability of various national health insurance programs and other reforms in the health care delivery

system, is the anxiety that the guidelines for coverage be sufficiently broad to cover the costs of treatment of emotional and
psychiatric disorders. If not, significant numbers of the population afflicted with the various manifestations of depression will
be denied the available effective treatments and the consequent
capacity to experience greater personal satisfaction, a rapid
return to social and economic productivity, and an alleviation
of distress for family, friends, and neighbors.

Current formulation of national health policy is predominantly
focused on those disorders which have high mortality rates—
cancer, heart disease, stroke. At the same time, there is equal
need for priority for research and treatment into those disorders
which do not have high immediate mortality rates, but do, nevertheless, impair the satisfaction of individuals and their capacity
to fulfill their social roles as parents, family members, or as
members of the labor force. While depressions predominantly
affect morbidity, that is, symptoms and functioning, we should
not forget that there is also a significant mortality rate. Suicide
rates have not gone down appreciably nationwide, and all the
research evidence indicates that the highest risk group for suicide are those individuals with recurrent and severe depressions.
In fact, long-term follow-up studies of individuals with severe
depressions reveal that as high as 15 percent die of self-inflicted
causes.

Research Implications

For investigators in the fields of mental health and behavioral
science, this research highlights a number of significant features
in methodology: first, the use of a control group comprised of
normal subjects; and second, the application of quantitative
social science techniques for the assessment of social adjustment.

Much psychiatric research has justifiably been criticized for
the failure to employ control groups. All too often, inferences
are made from small numbers of mentally ill patients, and the
conclusions derived are generalized to the population at large.
This tendency in clinical research flies in the face of the established tenets of experimental science. Only recently, however,

have researchers in clinical psychiatry accepted the value and feasibility of such control groups. Thus, this study is noteworthy in that the nuclear sample of forty depressed women is compared to forty normal women matched for age, social class, and marital status.

Contrary to often expressed common wisdom in mental health, Weissman and Paykel readily found "normal" people whose lives are characterized by personal satisfaction, limited personal distress or symptomatology, and apparent success in fulfilling their roles as breadwinners, parents, spouses, and neighbors. All too often, psychiatric researchers have "discovered" psychopathology everywhere and proclaimed the universality of neurosis. While the lives of these forty "normal" women may be far from any preconceived ideal of complete psychological maturity and social adjustment, the data indicate the existence of a large reservoir of individuals with reasonably adequate social performance and significant levels of satisfaction and adaptation to the immediate demands of familial life, given standards of the culture and social setting to which they belong.

The second methodologic feature of note is their use of quantitative and systematic approaches to the assessment of social adjustment. The authors draw upon previous research by Frank, Barrabee, Finesinger, Katz, and Gurland to develop both a systematic and quantified scale for assessing social adjustment, a scale sensitive to the different roles that the women played— mother, spouse, neighbor, family member. They identify dimensions of social adjustment which cut across specific roles, dimensions such as performance, interpersonal communication, friction and hostility, and personal satisfaction. As will be discussed below, this methodologic advance is a practical application of a very important theoretical approach pioneered by American psychiatry, namely, the application of social science to psychiatric phenomena based upon the theoretical approaches first formulated by Adolph Meyer and Harry S. Sullivan.

Future research on the nature of depression will have to acknowledge these standards employed by Weissman and Paykel; no longer will it be possible for investigators to comment upon the social-psychological life of depressed women without the guarantee of evidence from the appropriately matched control group and without the use of quantitative techniques for the assessment of personal experience comparable in validity, reliability, and sophistication to the techniques reported upon in this volume.

Implications for Clinical Care

For the clinicians involved in the day-to-day treatment of patients with depression, for psychiatrists, psychologists, nurses, social workers, and psychotherapists, the findings of this study will be of immediate value. Whereas other reports of the social life of mental patients have tended to polarize biological approaches against psychological approaches, Weissman and Paykel do not hesitate to make use of drug therapy to ameliorate the symptoms of the acute depressive episode. At the same time, they focus on the social adjustment and life experience of depressed women and bring to the attention of clinicians, whether biologically or psychotherapeutically trained, the importance of systematic inquiry into the family experiences and social life of the patient, not only during the acute episode but, perhaps more significantly, in the months following the acute episode.

Conventional psychiatric teaching has emphasized the inherent tendency of depressions to resolve rapidly with apparent minimal residual impairment. While this may be true in regard to intellectual impairment, too often clinicians have not gone beyond the superficial manifestations of behavior in the clinical interview to inquire systematically as to impairments in the patient's relations with spouse, children, parents, neighbors, and work associates. Clinicians are even less likely to obtain firsthand observations from home visits or informants. When such data are collected and systematically recorded, as in the Weissman-Paykel study, the picture emerges of the depressed women's protracted impairment in social adjustment. These women are severely impaired in their capacity to express emotion and to effect communication, vital roles in the personality development of young children and in the integration of family life, both in the nuclear family and in the extended family. As American society moves increasingly away from the emotional supports provided by the extended family, the nuclear family becomes more and more the central vehicle for socialization and affective integration. Given this historical situation, the impairment of the mother's capacity for affective integration has widespread implications for the children, spouse, and relatives.

Conclusion

These findings and their implications for public policy, research methodology, and clinical practice are best understood in the context of the intellectual richness of current psychiatric theory and practice.

This work is another manifestation of the fulfillment and fruition of the uniquely American school of psychiatry, the interpersonalist and social psychiatric school. As Havens recently described in his perceptive study of psychiatric thought, the social psychiatric school represents one of the discrete schools of modern psychiatry.* Along with the objective-descriptive school rooted in nineteenth-century biology, the psychoanalytic school, and the existentialist school, social psychiatric approaches have rapidly established themselves in the twentieth century as a major theoretical approach to the mind.

Of interest is the American source of this theoretical contribution. All the other schools of psychiatry emerged in Western Europe. The first proponent of the importance of personal experience and social relations was Adolph Meyer. Meyer was born and educated in Switzerland, but his ideas and professional development reached maturity in the United States, where he was associated with many of the leaders of pragmatism, the uniquely American school of philosophy. As a teacher and clinician, Meyer's impact was initially greatest in the Baltimore-Washington area, where many of his students influenced the development of psychiatry as a clinical specialty in institutional programs and in national policy.

The most important theorist of the Meyerian school was Harry Stack Sullivan, who coined the term "interpersonal" and drew

* Havens, L. L., *Approaches to the Mind* (Boston: Little, Brown, and Company, 1973).

attention to the extent to which psychiatric phenomena are determined by the patient's "here and now" interpersonal field —the give-and-take transactions between the patient and those in his immediate social milieu. Sullivan studied the psychiatric ward as an interpersonal field, but in subsequent studies his approach was expanded by social epidemiologists and other researchers to include the family, the neighborhood, and even the urban community. Consequently, a widespread alliance has developed between researchers in clinical psychiatry and investigators in sociology, anthropology, and psychology.

After a period of great growth around the time of World War II, there seemed to follow a lag, with the interpersonal school not moving beyond theoretical exposition or case description. Lately, however, there has been the growth of quantitative techniques and the use of experimental design, while studies of social epidemiology, of the social psychology of mental illness, and of family dynamics have gained greater critical depth and a new sophistication in methodology.

The studies by Weissman and Paykel embody the best of this approach. The very idea of looking at the family and social life of depressed women in comparison to nondepressed controls could only originate in those trained from a point of view that regards social and personal experience as important for the understanding of mental illness as are genetics, biochemistry, or neurophysiology, fields identified as important by nineteenth-century continental psychiatry.

The interpersonal field and the individual's adjustment to it are partial determinants of the patient's illness. At the same time, once the illness has developed, it exerts a powerful influence in itself on the patient's capacity to perform her social obligations and on the reactive responses of those around her to her symptoms, complaints, impairments, and frustrations. This social approach shares with psychoanalysis a conviction that personal experience and its meaning are major determinants of illness and the patient's response to change. It differs from psychoanalysis in that, while psychoanalysis emphasizes the unconscious determinants of behavior and early childhood personality development, the interpersonalist approach emphasizes the immediate social transactions in which the individual participates. A social or interpersonal approach does not necessarily deny the importance of unconscious mental processes or of childhood experience but holds that they reach their capacity to determine behavior through their ability to influence the patient's definition of her situation in the here and now. In this way there is a union between the interpersonal approach in psychiatry and the symbolic interactionist school of social psychology rooted in the ideas of George Herbert Mead, Charles Cooley, W. I. Thomas, and, recently, E. Goffman.

While this approach has been written about theoretically and applied to narrative and anecdotal case descriptions, it has too seldom been united with techniques of quantitative, experimental design where appropriate control groups are studied with techniques such as rating scales and systematic interviews capable of rigorous validation. The research reported upon by Weissman and Paykel unites the best of quantitative and qualitative approaches to illuminate issues of far-ranging clinical and social importance.

GERALD L. KLERMAN, M.D.

Preface

There is little doubt that depression is a topical subject. It has been referred to as the epidemic of the 70s, is seen reaching into the younger age group, and is reflected in an increase in suicide attempts. There has been considerable public interest in the topic. Information on the symptoms, causes, and treatment has recently appeared in many United States magazines and newspapers.

This book was begun well before the popularity of the subject. It deals with an aspect of depression—social adjustment—which has received little study. In it we describe the social and family life of women when they are acutely depressed and when they recover. To gain a frame of reference we compare these women with their psychiatrically normal neighbors. The findings we report are based primarily on detailed rating assessments, representing a standard approach in psychiatric research at the present time. To extend these descriptions and give them practical meaning, we supplement the numerical findings with clinical descriptions. In all instances we select the cases to exemplify the research findings. We have disguised all case material and possible identifying data in our genuine concern to protect the confidentiality of the patients and "normals" and their families.

Many readers will rightly question our omission of men. They may wonder why we act as if depression were the exclusive domain of women. The substantial suicide rate among men offers sufficient evidence that such is not the case. However, as we discuss in chapter 1, custom and, in many instances, economics divert men away from seeking help. This is true for most illnesses, and is no less so for psychiatric ones. For that reason men are seen less frequently in psychiatric outpatient clinics and consequently were less available for our study.

The reader may be vexed to find that our methodology is not presented until chapter 4 and that our findings do not begin until chapter 5. The introductory chapters have different purposes.

Chapter 1 reviews the current state of knowledge about depression. We discuss what is commonly believed about, although not necessarily agreed upon, etiology, treatment, prognosis, together with some current issues. This review is meant to set the stage for those readers less familiar with clinical depression. Recent changes in psychiatric services and the issues they raise lead to the research questions of our study, which are presented at the end of chapter 1.

Chapters 2 and 3 review material related more specifically to the study. In chapter 2 the elusive concept of social adjustment is defined, and techniques for its measurement are discussed. In chapter 3 we review the studies on social adjustment and depression. Most of these have been theoretical or hypothesis-generating and are dependent upon clinical descriptions rather than more sophisticated rating methodology. Chapter 4 begins the study proper with a description of the methodology and the characteristics of the subjects. From that point on we present and discuss our findings.

MMW
ESP

Acknowledgments

The study of depressed women and their normal neighbors grew out of a larger collaborative study of the maintenance treatment of depressed women conducted at the Connecticut Mental Health Center-Yale University School of Medicine and Boston State Hospital-Tufts University School of Medicine. It would never have been undertaken without the maintenance treatment study which provided the resources, the questions, and the methodology. It is difficult to define accurately the sources of one's ideas and points of view, and, for this reason, we want to express our deep appreciation to all who were involved in the collaboration and thereby contributed directly and indirectly to this volume.

In particular, we are indebted to Dr. Gerald L. Klerman, who initiated the Yale study, assembled and inspired its research group, first suggested that we compare the patients to normals, and later urged us to publish our findings; to Dr. Alberto DiMascio, who initiated and directed the Boston Study and generously offered his ideas and his encouragement; and to Brigitte Prusoff, M.P.H., who advised at all points on the statistical procedures, capably supervised the data staff, and assisted us with ideas and solutions.

Clinical care and assessment of patients were ably provided by Drs. Abram Chipman, David Haskell, Clive Tonks, and the late Mason de la Vergne, and by social workers Ruth Bullock, M.S.W., Eva Deykin, M.S., Effie Geanakoplos, M.S.W., Barbara Hanson, M.S., and Shirley Jacobson, M.S. Social adjustment assessments were provided by Jean Fasman, Susan Papparella, Catherine Roby, Risé Siegel and Margaret Zwilling, and data analysis by Janis Tanner and Risé Siegel, assisted by Brooke Craven.

Special thanks are given to Joan Smolka for manuscript typing and organization and to Jerilyn Martin in recognition of her team spirit whenever additional help was needed. Sallye Fink and Karen Fox provided editorial review.

We thank Dr. Jerome Myers for advising us on the selection of the normal sample and Dr. Barry Gurland for allowing us to adapt the Structured and Scaled Interview to Assess Maladjustment (SSIAM) before it was published. The term "normal neighbors" was derived from the studies of Drs. Shirley S. Angrist, Mark Lefton, Simon Dinitz, and Benjamin Pasamanick.

We extend thanks to Dr. Morton Reiser, chairman of the department of Psychiatry of Yale University, and to Dr. Boris Astrachan, director of The Connecticut Mental Health Center, for creating a stimulating atmosphere and giving us freedom to do this work. We are grateful for the support provided by the Psychopharmacology Research Branch of the National Institute of Mental Health, Department of Health, Education and Welfare, through Grants MH 13738, MH 15650, and MH 17728.

Finally, our appreciation is extended to all study participants, the women, their husbands and families, who, with willingness and hope, provided the information for this research.

I.
REVIEW AND OVERVIEW

1
Perspective on the Research

The Nature of Depression

Depression covers a spectrum of moods and behavior that ranges from the disappointment and sadness of normal life to the bizarre, suicidal acts of severe melancholia.[1] There are at least three or four meanings to the term—a mood, a symptom, a syndrome, and, some would maintain, a disease or group of diseases. Depression, as a normal mood, is a universal phenomenon which is familiar to us all and from which no one escapes. It is characteristically evoked by loss of close interpersonal relationships and blows to self-esteem. Its universality suggests that it performs important protective functions that have rendered its survival useful in evolutionary terms.

Depression as symptom, or abnormal mood, is also common. The borderline between the normal and the pathological is here, as often in psychiatry, indistinct (Katz 1970). Depression of mood that is unduly persistent, pervasive in nature, or in-

1. This chapter will review selected aspects of depression in order to set our study in sufficient context to make it comprehensible to the general reader who is not a clinician. This review is not intended to be exhaustive, and those seeking more general information are referred to a number of recent monographs, particularly those of Beck (1967) and Mendels (1970).

3

appropriate to circumstances is generally considered pathological. The symptom of depression is again a common one, experienced by most psychiatric patients, including many whom
the psychiatrist would not regard as primarily suffering from
depression but in whom the depression is incidental to another
disturbance.

Beyond the symptom we can distinguish a more specific and
limited psychiatric meaning, that of the syndrome. The term
syndrome is borrowed from medicine and refers to a cluster of
symptoms and functional disturbances that usually have a common mechanism but a variety of causes. This is clinical depression as the psychiatrist usually thinks of it and as we will be
concerned with it.

The last meaning of the term depression is as disease or group
of diseases. This medical labelling is more controversial. A disease in the medical sense is distinguished not only by a group
of symptoms but by a specific cause, a functional disturbance,
a predictable course, and specific treatment. Attempts have
been made to isolate within clinical depression two or more
types, classified by such labels as neurotic, psychotic, reactive,
endogenous. These are of considerable research interest, and,
since they impinge on the present study, will be discussed later.
However, their practical application in guiding treatment is still
limited.

Symptoms of Depression

The symptoms making up the depressive syndrome span a wide
range. They have been studied in detail by Cassidy (1957) and
Beck (1967), among others. The most common and central disturbance is that of the depressive mood. This is not necessarily
described by the patient as "depression" but as feeling sad,
blue, down in the dumps, unhappy, unable to enjoy life. Crying
commonly occurs. On the other hand, some depressed persons
do not cry, and describe themselves as "beyond tears." The
mood disturbance of the depressed patient resembles that of
normal unhappiness multiplied in intensity and pervasiveness.
Another mood that often accompanies depression is anxiety—
a sense of fear and intense worry. Both depression and anxiety

may show diurnal variation, that is, a pattern of change whereby certain times of the day, such as morning or evening, are consistently worse or better.

There are many additional disturbances which accompany the central mood disturbance. The most characteristic are disturbances of thinking, often summarized as helplessness, hopelessness, and worthlessness. The last two are the most prominent. Feelings of worthlessness are common. They range from a vague sense of lowered self-esteem and denigration of accomplishments to intense feelings of failure. Feelings of guilt and self-blame for real or imagined failings often accompany the sense of worthlessness. For example, a fifty-year-old woman may become consumed with guilt because of a premarital affair which occurred thirty years before. A young mother may feel that her relatives are criticizing her care of her infant and be frightened that she will unintentionally harm the child by her own ineptness.

Feelings of hopelessness may range from concern over realistic future problems to the sense that the future is entirely grim, all is lost, or even that one faces nothing but eternal damnation. Closely allied with these feelings may be thoughts of suicide, ranging from the feeling that life is not worth living, to wishing one were dead, to thoughts of taking one's life, to unsuccessful or successful suicide attempts. Clinical depression is the major, although not the only, cause of suicide. A devoted young woman, certain that she is a failure as a wife and mother, may consume a bottle of sleeping pills so that the family can be free of her.

Helplessness takes different forms. Feelings of being helpless, useless, and unable to function are common, and actual activities may be quite impaired. There may be withdrawal of interests, poor concentration, neglect of personal grooming, difficulty in completing work or housework; at the most extreme, there may be complete incapacity even to care for oneself.

Psychomotor changes, alterations in the speed and amount of psychological and motor functions, are common disturbances. Many depressives show a slowing in the speed of thoughts, speech, and movement which, in the rare extreme case, may extend to virtual immobility and absence of speech. The opposite state of overactivity or agitation is not uncommon and is usually associated with an unpleasant sense of tension. The overactivity varies from a minor degree of restlessness—inability to sit still without crossing and uncrossing the legs, moving arms, lighting cigarettes—to ceaseless pacing up and down. With modern treatment such severe states are fortunately rare.

Sleep disturbances occur singly or in combination in different patients. They include difficulty getting to sleep on retiring; disturbed and intermittent sleep with troubled dreams and waking very early in the morning. Occasionally patients sleep excessively rather than too little. Appetite disturbance is common and may be in either direction. The common problem is loss of appetite, often with considerable weight loss. Sometimes, instead, appetite is increased. This occurs more commonly in women; many women recognize an increase in their appetite as a concomitant of normal depression and premenstrual tension. Menstrual disturbances may occur, particularly failure of menstruation. Sexual function is impaired, particularly by lack of interest in sex, impotence, or frigidity. Constipation may occur, and is a particular source of concern to some depressives. Physiologic autonomic accompaniments of anxiety such as dry mouth, palpitations, rapid breathing, butterfly sensations in the stomach, frequent urination may be present. These may be regarded by the patient as signs of serious physical illness. Indeed, undue hypochondriacal preoccupation with bodily functions is as common as their actual disturbance. Headaches, lack of energy, heaviness in limbs, various pains may worry the patient and be interpreted as due to illness. A middle-aged woman who has nursed her father through a terminal illness with strength and patience, may believe she has cancer and become certain she is going to die. A completely negative physical examination offers no reassurance, as she feels the truth is being kept from her.

Although there are a large variety of manifestations which may accompany depression, not all depressed patients show these features. Severe cases are easily recognizable by the presence of persistent sadness, crying, feelings of worthlessness, guilt, helplessness, and hopelessness, suicidal wishes and psychomotor retardation or agitation. More diagnostic acumen may be required where presentation is with other associated symptoms such as anxiety and tension, loss of interest and impaired capacity to perform in work and other activities, insomnia, constipation, hypochondriacal complaints, or atypical pain.

Causes

The causes of clinical depression are complex. They include stressful life events, genetic predisposition, vulnerability to certain stresses based on personality and other factors, and probably biologic and neuropharmacologic abnormalities. Depression in any single patient probably results from a convergence of causes.

The most obvious of these causes is that of life stress. A variety of stressful events tend to precede depression. Of course, such events happen to all of us all the time. However, comparison of events reported by depressed patients at the time of onset of the depression with those reported in similar time periods by control subjects leaves little doubt that depressives have experienced more stress (Paykel, in press). The kinds of events reported by depressed patients span a wide range. The evidence suggests that almost any kind of life event, depending on its special circumstances and the stresses associated with it, may lead to depression. Certain kinds of events tend to be involved. These include separations and losses (both physical and interpersonal), arguments and difficulties with loved ones, blows to the self-esteem, and other events categorized as undesirable. Separation from close persons is the most common event reported. In a recent study by our research group (Paykel et al. 1969), 25 percent of depressives reported such an event in the six months prior to the onset of depression, as opposed to 5 percent of the general population in a comparable time period. These events also play a central role in classical Freudian psychodynamic formulations of depression (see chap. 3).

It would be tempting to regard life events as the primary, if not the only, cause of depression, if the situation were not obviously more complicated. Some depressions arise in the absence of any obvious psychological precipitant. In a New Haven survey these made up about 15–20 percent (Paykel et al. 1971). For others the precipitating stress is an event which many other persons, and perhaps the patient also, have experienced at another time without depression following it. Even the grief following the death of a spouse, one of the most serious of losses, is in most cases resolved without depression of such severity and persistence as to necessitate psychiatric help (Clayton 1971). We have to view a number of causes as involved in the development of depression at one particular time in one particular individual. As well as the event, there must be an equally important contribution in the person's susceptibility to the event.

One such additional element of susceptibility is genetic in origin. It has long been apparent that there is a tendency for depression to be inherited. The exact mode of genetic inheritance is uncertain; a Mendelian dominant with incomplete penetrance has been suggested by some (Slater 1936), multifactorial inheritance by others (Odegaard 1963). Probably there are several types of inheritance, operating in different cases. Winokur and colleagues (Winokur 1970) have distinguished several different types of inheritance. According to them, bipolar manic-depressive disease may be inherited by two genes, one of which is sex-linked. They have distinguished two further types of depression without mania in terms of genetic inheritance. In one type, characterized by early onset, depression tends to occur in female relatives, alcoholism in males; in the second type, with late onset, depression occurs in both sexes (Gershon 1972).

Another related possibility is that persons of certain personality, itself genetic in origin or related to early experience, may be vulnerable to certain particular stresses, or to stress in general. For instance, there is evidence, although it is not completely clear-cut, to suggest that persons who experience loss of a parent in childhood are more vulnerable to depression in adult life (Heincke 1970). It would not be surprising if childhood loss sensitized the individual to adult loss.

In recent years biological phenomena have received increasing study as concomitants and potential causes of depression. A wide variety of biological changes have been shown in depressed patients, including changes in body sodium (Coppen and Shaw 1963) and calcium (Flach 1964), glucose metabolism

(Mueller et al. 1969) and adrenal cortical hormones (Sachar 1970). Currently, the greatest interest focuses on brain neuropharmacology and on evidence suggesting that depression may result from a relative or absolute diminution of available norepinephrine at central nervous system synapses in certain regions of the brain (Schildkraut 1965).

The discovery of neuropharmacological abnormalities is not surprising, nor does it preclude psychological causes. We think and feel with our brains, and all psychological events must be presumed to have neurophysiological and neuropharmacological substrates. The neuropharmacological mechanisms which have been investigated might form final common pathways for both psychological and biological causes. Some depressions might be due primarily to neuropharmacological dysfunctions, resulting in reduced norepinephrine; others might be due to events whose psychological effect would presumably have parallel neurophysiological phenomena resulting in reduced release of norepinephrine. In other cases both effects might apply, the life event tipping the balance more easily into depression because activity of the norepinephrine-producing system was already reduced.

Another set of potential biological causes are hormonal. There has been much interest in the relation of depression to female sex hormones. However, in spite of evidence suggesting that occurrence of depression may be linked to the menstrual cycle, research has not succeeded in relating depression to any specific hormone, and the situation remains unresolved.

One suggestive piece of evidence lies in the observation that clinical depression may occur more commonly in females than males. Published surveys show sex ratios of between 2:1 and 3:1. The reasons are probably complex and not necessarily hormonal. Other suggestive evidence comes from the cyclical changes in hormones with the menstrual cycle. Minor feelings of depression are a common part of the syndrome of premenstrual tension. Moreover, they are a common occurrence in the first few days after childbirth, when major hormonal changes take place. There is also an increased incidence of serious clinical depression in the postpartum period. In none of these cases has a responsible hormone been clearly identified. Lastly, depression has been related to the menopause. Recent research, however, throws doubt on whether there is any increase in the occurrence of depressions around the time of the menopause (Rosenthal 1968, Winokur 1973). Those depressions which do occur at that time may be more related to such psychological causes as the departure of children from the home (Deykin et al. 1966) than to any hormonal changes.

Classification

Because of diversity of symptoms and of apparent contributing causes, numerous attempts have been made to define subtypes of depression with specific features of symptomatology or causation. One such, Winokur's suggestion that there may be at least two genetic types, has already been mentioned.

One classification, which has been referred to as dualistic, divides depressive subtypes into endogenous and reactive, or psychotic and neurotic (Klerman 1971). The two terminologies are not identical in meaning, although they overlap in connotations and have been used interchangeably. "Reactive" and "endogenous" refer to causation. Reactive depressions are those occurring in response to external stress; endogenous (from within) depressions are those occurring in the absence of obvious precipitants. "Psychotic" and "neurotic" refer to clinical picture and are utilized for other psychiatric disorders as well. Psychotic disorders are more severe ones in which contact with reality is lost, while neurotic disorders are milder, and contact is retained. Psychotic depressions are those more severe episodes often accompanied by delusions and other evidence of loss of reality. The link between these two formulations is that endogenous (unprecipitated) depressions often tend to be psychotic in clinical picture, while reactive depressions tend to show neurotic pictures. Endogenous depressions also tend to occur in nonvulnerable, stable, obsessional personalities.

In recent years a number of studies have applied statistical techniques to classification and have confirmed the existence of a broad distinction between these two kinds of depression (Mendels and Cochrane 1968). However, the separation between them appears weak. Although typical cases do occur, most depressions appear to be intermediate, showing features of both types.

This simplistic classification into two types does little justice to the range of disorders seen. Other types of depression have also been described. Most clear-cut is manic-depressive illness, that is, depression in patients who also have a history of episodes of mania, with elation and overactivity, and often a history of cyclic episodes of depression and mania. Such bipolar depressions have assumed special importance in view of evidence of their genetic specificity (Winokur 1973) and their special responsiveness to the drug lithium. They also tend to be unprecipitated and probably can be regarded as one specific subgroup of endogenous depressions. They are, however, relatively uncommon.

Robins and his associates have recently proposed a classification—primary and secondary affective disorder—based on chronology and the presence of associated psychopathology (Robins and Guze 1972). In this classification, primary affective disorder refers to a disorder in a patient who has no other psychiatric disturbance or whose only previous disorders were mania or depression. Secondary affective disorder occurs in patients who either currently or in the past exhibited other disders such as hysteria, anxiety, alcoholism, and so on (Feighner 1971). This classification avoids the issue of severity of illness or the presence of life stress and attempts to separate patients clearly suffering from depressive symptoms from those with symptoms secondary to other disorders.

A variety of other types have also been proposed, although none is entirely satisfactory. Certainly, however, depressed patients span such a range of persons and clinical manifestations that attempts to divide them further are worthwhile. The hope underlying such efforts is that there may be specific groups responding to different but specific treatments.

Prognosis

The prognosis for the acute depressive episode is generally good. Beck reviewed a number of studies from the era prior to antidepressants and concluded that complete symptomatic recovery occurred in 70–95 percent of cases. The median duration of the attack was approximately six months among inpatients and three months among outpatients. It is hard to make comparisons with more recent studies, in view of the changes in the definition of depression previously described, compounded by different inclusion and outcome criteria, and by the fact that treatments vary. In one representative sample of depressives (Paykel et al. in press), followed up for ten months after presentation at a variety of treatment facilities, all but 25 percent had achieved a substantial remission at some point, and most of the remainder had shown improvement. Relapse, although often limited in severity, had, however, already occurred in 16 percent. The median length of time from treatment until remission was two months. Endogenous depressives were found to have a considerably better prognosis than neurotic depressives, which was consistent with other evidence that they respond better to tricyclic antidepressants and E.C.T. In keeping with modern trends most of this sample were neurotic depressives.

The remission need not be complete, however, particularly since in many depressed patients the episode develops on a background of minor neurotic symptomatology. Although Kraepelin originally delineated manic-depressive psychosis from schizophrenia partly by complete recovery from episodes, as opposed to the gradually deteriorating course of schizophrenia, the partial nature of recovery in some depressives has long been recognized (Lewis 1936). In the study referred to above, about 70 percent of the patients had no or only borderline symptoms after ten months; however, 20 percent had symptoms of mild intensity and 10 percent symptoms of moderate intensity (Paykel et al., in press). Long-term studies are needed to calculate the full risk of relapse or recurrence (Klerman and Barrett 1973). Beck, on the basis of his review, suggested that about 47–79 percent of patients will have a recurrence at some time and felt the latter figure was probably more accurate. Moreover, there is a real risk of ultimate death by suicide. A recent review of suicide following primary affective disorder (Robins and Guze 1972) suggested that about 15 percent of depressives will ultimately take their lives. These studies underline the need for effective maintenance treatments.

Treatment

The most prominent development in the treatment of depression in the last fifteen years has been the introduction of a range of effective antidepressant medications (Kline 1969). The main class of drugs used is that of the tricyclic antidepressants, particularly imipramine and amitriptyline. Monoamine oxidase inhibitors, such as phenelzine and tranylcypromine, are nowadays used much less extensively. Their efficacy is less clear (Cole 1964) and their side effects are potentially fatal. Recently a third class of drugs, represented by a single substance, lithium, usually as its carbonate, has been found effective in the treatment of mania (Schou 1970). Its efficacy in depression and in manic depressive disorder is currently under study (Klerman and Paykel 1970).

The superiority of the tricyclic antidepressants over placebo is undoubted, and has been shown by well-executed, controlled trials (Klerman and Cole 1965). However, their efficacy is limited. There is fortunately a high spontaneous remission rate in depression, and many apparently drug-induced remissions are probably spontaneous: the amount of added gain due to the drugs, while definite, is probably limited. Moreover, drug-induced remission is slow, usually taking two to four weeks. Thus the antidepressant medications do not provide a definitive therapy for depression. Among somatic treatments, electro-shock (E.C.T.) still has an important and useful, although limited, place in severe depressions resistant to medications. Hospitalization is still an important measure in more severe or resistant cases, providing adequate care and protection against suicidal risks and a temporary respite against environmental pressures.

The antidepressant medications have by no means replaced psychotherapy. Indeed one important function of the drugs may be to sufficiently alleviate the depression to render the patient accessible to psychotherapy, since the severely depressed patient is liable to produce in therapeutic interviews a ceaseless round of self-recriminations which merely further lower his self-image. As recovery develops, psychotherapy becomes an important means of preventing recurrence and of facilitating social adaption.

In practice, some form of psychological intervention is usually combined with antidepressant medication, although either treatment may be used independently. There are a wide range of psychological treatments which differ in aim, intensity, duration, the individuals involved, and the professional training of the therapist. These treatments include both individual and group therapy, family or marital therapy, behavior therapies, social casework, and psychoanalysis. Detailed treatments vary widely, even with a single modality, and will not be described here. Generally, psychological treatments have two aims. The first is to hasten the patient's recovery from the depressive episode by providing emotional support and reassurance, opportunity for ventilation, and by dealing with the consequences of the illness and preventing further impairments. The second focuses on the maladaptive patterns or early antecedents that predisposed the patient to difficulties, and involves a more basic restructuring to avoid further episodes.

One problem regarding the psychological treatments is that their use has not yet been subject to the same rigorous evaluation in controlled trials as has the use of medication. This problem has been highlighted recently as debate has recurred about the adequacy of medication as a sole treatment. Many clinicians see medication as a quick, simple, and inexpensive way of reducing the symptoms of depression. These clinicians tend to feel that reduction of symptoms will automatically improve most social impairment. On the other hand, there are clinicians who question the use of medication in the treatment of depression. These clinicians feel that the depressed patient's impaired social and interpersonal functioning may not be modified by medication, but that his anxiety may be diluted by the medication so that the patient is diverted from improving the underlying and predisposing personality problems (Bonime 1962). There are others who question the use of medication to solve what they consider to be basically human or social problems.

Although these questions appear primarily to involve the efficacy of medication alone, on closer scrutiny they imply something about the efficacy of psychotherapy as an alternative treatment. For proper resolution, controlled trials of drug-psychotherapy combinations are required, and such studies are under way in several centers.

Current Issues

Popular interest in depression has raised several issues about its prevalence and about the age and sex distribution of those suffering it. In particular it has been asked whether it is becoming more common, is extending its incidence into younger age-groups, and why most depressives are women.

To first consider prevalence, there is little doubt that depression is a common disorder. It is difficult to determine exactly how common since many depressed patients do not reach psychiatric treatment but are treated by their family physicians. Probably many others receive no treatment. There is some consensus that the prevalence of manic depressive disorder is low, about 1 in 1,000 (Silverman 1968). There is no agreement about the prevalence of neurotic depression except that it is much higher. Studies in general populations have indicated that as many as 23 percent of the population (Srole et al. 1962) may show feelings of depression that in most cases are not sufficiently intense to require treatment and most likely correspond to depression as pathological or normal mood rather than as clinical symptoms. There is good evidence that there has been an increase in the diagnosis of depression in psychiatric outpatients; it is unclear whether this reflects an epidemic, as described by Schwab (1970), of the tendency to fit a diagnosis to a disorder for which there is available treatment.

Although the question of prevalence is unresolved, there has been a clearly documented change in the clinical picture of depressed patients seeking help (Rosenthal 1968). Once believed to be a severe disorder of middle age and most commonly treated in hospital, today depression is commonly seen in younger people, is milder in severity, and is more often treated outside the hospital. Furthermore, the depressed patient is likely to show a clinical picture which is neurotic rather than psychotic (Paykel et al. 1970). Some of these trends probably reflect greater willingness to seek treatment earlier and the availability of effective treatment. Others may reflect real changes in characteristics.

With respect to age, psychiatrists are certainly now seeing more young patients with depression. In a survey in New Haven the mean age of a representative sample of depressed patients in treatment was thirty-five years, a good deal younger than might be expected of a complaint of middle and later life. Many of these patients were in their twenties. Part of the increase undoubtedly reflects the great increase in the young adult general population resulting from the postwar baby boom. Moreover younger patients, reared under different conditions, might be more tolerant of psychiatry and more prepared to come for treatment.

One piece of evidence that suggests a real rather than an artificial increase in depression in the young is the current incidence of unsuccessful suicide attempts. One U.S. study found a remarkable increase in the number of suicide attempts in an urban community in the last fifteen years, an increase which could not be explained by population or service changes (Weissman et al. 1973a). The majority of the attempters were found to be under thirty years of age, and a subsample of these young attempters were as a group at least moderately depressed (Weissman et al. 1973b). Similar trends have been noted in Great Britain, Australia, and Israel. However, rates for successful suicide in the young have not clearly risen (Seiden 1969).

There has been a tendency to broaden the concept of depression when discussing its occurrence in youth, which may confuse the prevalence figures. Included as symptoms of depression in adolescents have been deviant behavior, drug abuse, and general maladjustment (Gallemore and Wilson 1972). It is questionable whether all these behaviors can be classified as depression, although there are parallels between the symptoms of depression and the feelings of alienation, powerlessness, and cultural anomie expressed by some young persons involved in deviancy (Klerman 1972).

The predominance of depression in women has led investigators to postulate a sex-linked mode of inheritance (Gershon 1971) and to seek hormonal causes. It is interesting to note exceptions to this picture of female predominance. Galen (A.D. 131–201) observed that depression was more common in men but more serious when it did occur in women (Jackson 1972). There are alternative explanations for the predominance of female depressives which suggest that the differences may be less than they appear. The higher rate of female admissions for depression could be due to the general tendency for men to seek medical treatment less frequently than women either out of custom or out of need to support their families. It might also reflect the tendency in our culture for tearfulness and helplessness to be regarded as feminine manifestations that cannot be acknowledged by males. Furthermore, the higher rate of alcoholism among men may be an attempt to mitigate symptoms of depression and an alternative to seeking psychiatric treatment. Rather than data based on hospital admissions, community studies of untreated cases are required to determine if the sex differential is real.

The apparent increase of depression, especially in young people, and its preponderance in females have prompted speculations about the role of social conditions and the rapid pace and pressures of an accelerating outside world. Schwab has pointed out historical parallels in suggesting that depression reached epidemic proportions in late Elizabethan and early seventeenth-century England, when political and social conditions characterized by the lack of a cohesive value system or shared sentiments culminated in civil war (Schwab 1970).[2] If life stress, especially negative events and separations, is associated with the development of depression, American society, with its psychological, social, and geographical mobility, should be fertile ground for depression. Nearly one-fifth of all Americans relocate annually. This figure indicates that adaption to separation from familiar friends and family is required of a sizeable portion of persons (Weissman and Paykel 1972). The disadvantaged and changing role of women has been suggested in recent years as a cause for the predominance of depression in women (see chapter 5 for further discussion of this issue). There are a num-

2. For history of depression in different societies, see: Ilza Veith, "Elizabethans on Melancholia," *JAMA* 212: 127–31, April 1970; or Venkoba Rao, "History of Depression—Some Aspects," *Indian Journal of History of Medicine* 14: 46–56, 1969; or Aubrey Lewis, "Melancholia: A Historical Review," *The Journal of Mental Science* 80: 1–42, January 1934.

ber of other similar examples. The effects of such social influences and of their changes over time are difficult to demonstrate conclusively. Their relative contributions to the incidence of depression are still unclear.

Historical Changes in Psychiatric Care

There have been remarkable changes in psychiatric practice since the 1950s. These changes were brought about by the introduction of effective psychotropic drugs, more humane public attitudes toward mental illness, the increasing availability of alternatives to hospitalization, and the awareness that social factors play a role in the etiology and the treatment of psychiatric disorders.

The development of effective psychotropic drugs made it possible to rapidly reduce the symptoms of many psychiatric disorders. Introduced at a time when discharge rates from mental institutions were already beginning to increase, these drugs accelerated the new trend. Drug therapies, combined with new approaches in psychological therapies, such as crisis intervention, partial hospitalization, and family therapies, made it possible for most disordered persons to be spared the debilitating effects of hospitalization and to remain at home. Those patients who required hospitalization spent only a short time there. Extensive services were developed outside the hospital to ensure treatment within the community. These services were aimed at providing prompt treatment that would prevent further disorder and, consequently, would avoid the need for hospitalization. In 1963 in the United States, authorization was given for the construction and staffing of community mental health centers. Private-office psychiatric treatment had always been available to the select few who were able to pay its cost. The mental health center became a community alternative for the majority. Psychiatric practice, which at the turn of the century had been mainly with the floridly psychotic in asylums, by the 1970s was focused on strenuous efforts to avoid hospitalizations of any length and towards the treatment of more mildly disturbed individuals who remained at home.

Social Adjustment—An Index of Disturbance

This changing emphasis in treatment both mandated and was a consequence of an increased awareness that mental disorders occur in a social system or, to put it more simply, that the patient's family life, friendships, and work can contribute to the disorder and must be taken into account in treatment. Institutional care, especially if it was of long duration, involved only the patient; psychiatry in the community involved both the patient and the family.

The traditional approach of the psychiatrist, as medical doctor, to the patient's abnormalities had been the symptoms of psychopathology—the abnormalities of thought, feeling, and perception experienced by the patient. In the community this has had to be supplemented by an expansion into the social world of the patient and involves the addition of a new index of disturbance, that of social adjustment. Social adjustment includes judgments about the patient's adequacy as a spouse, friend, worker, parent, family member, member of the community, and life satisfactions.

The first studies of social adjustment in psychiatric patients were those of schizophrenics discharged from a mental hospital. This was to be expected, as the majority of hospitalized patients were schizophrenics who had been much improved by the new drugs and could now be discharged. The morbidity of schizophrenia was severe, and there was considerable concern that discharge might have serious consequences, as clinical experience began to show that ability to remain in the community was only a minimal measure of successful treatment. Despite remission of symptoms, patients were often restricted in their social activities, family responsibilities, and interpersonal relations.

Outpatient treatment was found to present problems. The outpatient was not in the position to give up family responsibilities, and impaired social functioning might not be tolerated at home. The emphasis on outpatient psychiatric treatment and the availability of pharmacotherapy for rapid symptomatic relief revolutionized psychiatric care, but it also created new dilemmas. Early studies of the posthospital adjustment of seriously disturbed patients, mostly schizophrenics, documented these problems.[3]

The community adjustment of the depressive has been of less pressing concern for several reasons. Depression had a much higher spontaneous remission rate than schizophrenia prior to the introduction of modern therapies, and there were relatively few depressives among the chronic hospital population that returned to the community with the introduction of pharmacotherapy. It was classically taught that the recovery of depressives was complete, as contrasted to that of schizophrenics, who show a deteriorating course and function marginally between episodes. Moreover, the social impairments of depressives are less gross and the assessment of these impairments requires more subtle measures. However, studies of depression are clearly important because of the greater frequency of the disorder and because its common occurrence in mothers during reproductive years could have a serious impact on family life.

The Program and Questions

Growing out of the frequency of depression in outpatient psychiatric clinics and the many unanswered questions about its long-term treatment, a collaborative study was begun in 1968 in New Haven, Connecticut, and Boston, Massachusetts (Klerman et al. 1973a). The aim of this collaboration was to find maintenance treatments for depression which would enhance

3. An excellent review of studies on posthospital adaptation of psychiatric patients can be found in Shirley Angrist, Mark Lefton, Simon Dinitz, and Benjamin Pasamanich, *Women after Treatment* (Appleton-Century Crofts, New York, 1968). Angrist, when reviewing these studies, concluded that the patient's rehospitalization was dependent on degree of symptoms, while level of performance was most closely associated with the makeup of the setting into which the patient was discharged. The study by Angrist of schizophrenic women discharged from hospital is particularly of interest because it was one of the few studies to use a normal group as a comparison. Angrist found a high level of impaired functioning in these patients, even though they managed to remain at home. This study cautioned against the negative consequences on the family of housing a very sick person. Another list of similar studies on posthospital adjustment of psychiatric patients can be found in Jerome Myers and Lee L. Bean, *A Decade Later: A Follow-up of Social Class and Mental Illness* (Wiley, New York, 1968).

the patient's functioning in the community, facilitate social adaptations, and prevent recurrence and relapse.

In planning the maintenance study, we felt the need from the start to examine social adjustment in a substudy of depressed patients and normals, since many of our research questions in the larger maintenance study concerned the patient's functioning rather than symptoms. On reviewing the literature, we discovered many clinical descriptions but a remarkable dearth of controlled studies of social adaptation in depression.

This substudy was prompted by the lack of data on the social adjustment of depressed patients. The existence of a group of patients for whom was being gathered a considerable amount of clinical information provided a ready opportunity. We decided to study the social adjustment of forty sequentially chosen depressed women admitted to the maintenance treatment study in New Haven. The New Haven study was selected for logistic reasons since both authors were situated there. We had every reason to believe that these forty patients were representative of the total sample of depressed patients in both clinics.

The study we planned was both longitudinal and comparative. It was longitudinal in that we intended to follow the course of these forty depressed patients over a period of twenty months. This would enable us to study patterns and changes in the patients' social and family life during the acute depressive episode, recovery, and, in some cases, relapse.

The study was also comparative. There was a clear need for norms, and we planned to use as controls women in the community who were similar in style of life as reflected in age, religion, neighborhood of residence, physical health, race, and social class, but who differed from the patients in that they had no psychiatric disturbance and had never received any psychiatric treatment. These control subjects would give us a base line of expectations against which to compare our patients, a base line which might deter us from falsely labelling behavior as abnormal or as a consequence of the depression.

We hoped in this way to gain insights into unresolved questions about the adaptations of the depressives. The study examined the natural history of depression in terms of the social and interpersonal functioning of depressed persons during the acute illness and recovery. Specifically, it asked several questions. What social dysfunctions occur during an acute depressive episode and in what ways does the functioning of the depressed woman differ from that of her healthy neighbor? What is the course of the social dysfunctions during recovery? Which aspects of dysfunction subside and which endure? Which might require, and be amenable to, therapeutic intervention? To what extent are these social dysfunctions consequences of symptomatic illness and to what extent are they reflections of enduring character traits which may predispose to the development and recurrence of depression and destine the family to complicated interpersonal relationships?

The intent of this research was to uncover information on the social morbidity of depression. Its primary significance lay in the provision of descriptive information in a neglected area. We were interested in the consequences of the depression to the individual, the family, and the community both in magnitude and time. Beyond this, we hoped it might provide clues to the development process of the illness, to treatment, and to prevention of recurrence.

2
Social Adjustment and Its Measurement

This chapter is intended for those who have an interest in methodology or are about to embark on studies of social adjustment. We will review the concept of social adjustment, techniques for clinical measurement in psychiatry, and previous attempts to measure adjustment. This material represents a relatively new thrust of psychiatric research, arising from the broadening of traditional indices of psychopathology as discussed in chapter 1.

The Nature and Components of Social Adjustment

Social adjustment is broadly defined as the interplay between the individual and the social environment. Specific ways of behaving, referred to as roles, are commonly accepted as appropriate, and the individual is expected to conform in his role performance to these loose norms. These roles span the range of everyday activities including work, extra-familial leisure, extended family, spouse and children.

In general terms, social adjustment concerns the individual's ability to function in roles. We include in social adjustment performance of tasks, involvement with other persons, and satisfactions in these specific roles, but we exclude internal thinking and nontask behavior usually referred to, when abnormal, as symptoms. In conceptualizing social adjustment we differentiated roles, as suggested by Parson and Bales (1955) into: *instrumental roles*—those concerned predominantly with the person's adaptation in the larger society and relations to external goal objects; *expressive roles*—those concerned predominantly with the maintenance of affectional relations among members of the family group. While social roles usually contain both instrumental and expressive components, most tend to be weighted in one direction. The predominantly instrumental roles are work and economic status, whereas the primarily expressive ones involve interpersonal relations such as marital or parental role, membership in the extended family, social participation in the wider community. The separation of instrumental from expressive roles allowed us to look at behavior which might be independent. A person might improve in one kind of role and become more impaired in another, for example, being successful at work and yet maladjusted as a parent.

We are also concerned with various kinds of behaviors within roles and with those that cut across roles. A major distinction, to which attention does not appear to have been clearly drawn in the literature, is between behaviors involving performance at tasks and those referring more specifically to patterns of interpersonal relationships. Among the former are such issues as frequency of attendance and adequacy of performance at work, carrying out of the manifest tasks of housework, or physical care of children. These give us a picture of gross adequacy of function. The second important aspect of behavior is that reflected in patterns of interpersonal relationships that involve all the role areas, such as overt friction, dependency, dominance, communication. These are more complex areas which may mirror enduring personality characteristics and in which society's expectations are less clear.

Social function primarily involves behavior in the person's usual social milieu. Therefore, it is an important dimension for psychiatric outpatients but less immediately relevant to the hospitalized patient. The hospitalized patient operates within a set of expectations quite different from the usual ones and the demands made upon him reflect an expectation of impaired performance. No adequate judgment can be made of work performance, for example, from the limited roles expected of patients in the hospital ward. It would be more accurate to say that the hospitalized patient does not function in his work role (often because he cannot). Again, while there are relationships aplenty for the hospitalized patient, they occur within a different set of standards than those which occur at home. In the hospital the patient has assumed a sick role that is a deviant one. While regression and dependency implied in the sick role may be functional during an illness, in that they allow the patient to withdraw temporarily from crises, they are highly dysfunctional for the recovery. One of the objectives of modern community psychiatry is indeed aimed at reducing the debilitating effects of the institutionalism that can occur after a prolonged assumption of the sick role. Given this particular orientation, we will turn to the issues involved in the measurements of these constructs.

Rating Scales and Clinical Measurements

One major method for evaluating behavior in psychiatric research involves the use of rating scales. The history, rationale, and use of rating scales is a sufficiently broad topic to warrant an independent study and has been ably reviewed by a few authors. The reader might best refer to them for comprehensiveness (Lyerly and Abbott; GAP Report, 1966; Torgeson 1958; Bonjean et al. 1967; Waskow).

A rating scale, as defined by Lyerly and Abbott, is a defined dimension along which judgments are placed. Such a scale may take various forms. It may, for instance, be a set of ordered categories with numbers attached or a series of adjectives arranged in a sequence corresponding to an increasing or decreasing amount of severity; it may require discrete yes-no judgments to a series of items from which a quantitative score is obtained. There is confusion over the term "scale," which may also refer to numerical indices from several closely related scores combined into a single score, as well as to an entire instrument composed of such composite scales. Since the latter usage is common, we will accept it.

The main, although not the only, principle behind such scales has been that of applying precision and quantification to clinical phenomena. While they have been used in psychology for more than half a century, their evolution in psychiatry has been slower (Klerman 1971). Although a number of scales were in use before World War II, the great expansion in their use and sophistication in psychiatry since the 1950s has been spurred on by the need to evaluate new psychopharmacologic agents. The availability of computers to undertake complicated statistical manipulations has made these methods feasible, and there are now many rating instruments.

Raters may be psychiatrists, psychologists, nurses, trained research interviewers, relatives, or the patients themselves. The information to make ratings may be obtained through the administration of a structured or unstructured interview with an informant, case records, or the subject's paper and pencil responses to a series of questions (self-report inventories). The material rated in these clinical instruments may involve any portion of a wide range of behaviors, including symptoms and abnormal behavior expressed at interview, feelings and mood states, abnormal behavior in the ward or in the home, and social adjustment in the community. The most common format of a modern rating instrument is a booklet with detailed instructions and a section for responses in the form of numerical or categorical variables. These responses are precoded for transfer to punch cards and computer analysis.

The use of quantified rating scales provides a number of advantages (Lyerly and Abbott). They provide a guide to a systematic assessment of behavior and insure that important areas are not missed. They facilitate communication between professionals by establishing precise semantic definitions and numerical frames of reference. They provide useful ways of documenting change (GAP Report). Most important, they greatly facilitate the carrying out of research by providing data which is accurate, dependable, and suitable for statistical manipulation.

There are certain requirements that a scale must fulfill in order to perform these functions adequately. One is reliability; that is, the scale should be relatively free of measurement error. Another is validity; it should measure what it purports to measure. A third requirement, related to validity, is the scale's sensitivity to patient change and its ability to distinguish between treatments. The assessment of reliability and validity sometimes presents problems, and the strategies involved in behavioral assessments have been widely reviewed in the psychological literature.

Clinicians often object that rating scales involve simplification and loss of information. The complex and unique circumstances of the individual are reduced to a rating which may only weakly reflect the true situation. This criticism contains some truth. However, the loss of information is usually more than made up for by the elimination of bias and the ability to apply statistical techniques for data manipulation and formal hypothesis-testing. Nevertheless, the human flavor of the situation may be lost and impossible to reconstruct. For these reasons, in reporting results we will also rely on nonqualitative clinical descriptive information about the social relationships of our subjects.

Rating Scales for Social Adjustment

Since the impetus for the development of rating scales has come from the investigation of psychopharmacology, assessments of clinical symptoms have been foremost and highly developed. A moderate number of reliable and valid interview and self-report symptom scales (Hamilton 1960; Lorr 1962; Overall 1962; Frank 1961; Raskin 1967), and nursing assessment scales (Burdock 1960; Honigfeld 1965; French 1970) have been devised. Social adjustment measures have, until recently, received the least attention although some well-constructed and validated scales have been developed. This review is not intended to be exhaustive, but will describe some of the social adjustment measures which are particularly relevant to this book.

One of the earliest scales, which set the stage for numbers of later developments, was that of Miles, Barrabee, and Finesinger (1951) (the Normative Social Adjustment Scale). These authors distinguished the need to assess social adjustment separately from symptoms and devised five-point scales to measure patients' interpersonal relationships, occupational, marital, and sexual adjustment. Although these scales were highly global in nature, compared with the specificity of subsequent instruments, modifications of them were found useful in recent studies of psychotherapy and behavior therapy in phobic patients (Gelder et al. 1967).

Another pioneering development was that of Parloff, Kelman, and Frank (1954) (the Social Ineffectiveness Scale). In the context of a study of psychotherapy, these authors also pointed out the need to assess symptoms and social functioning separately. They devised a scale in which attention was paid to assessing detailed patterns of behavior in a variety of roles; the subsequent use of the scale in a number of psychotherapy studies has been documented (Frank 1961).

In a further development, Mandel (1959) (the Mandel Social Adjustment Scale) described a scale which operationalized concepts similar to those contained in the scale of Miles et al. and included as a valuable methodological addition detailed anchor points for rating. Among other scales adopting similar formats was one by Shader and Binstock (1966).

Others have taken somewhat different departures. Ruesch has regarded social disability as resulting from a combination of impairment and its inability to be tolerated in a social situation (Ruesch and Brodsky 1968) and has described a scale for the assessment of social impairment (Social Disability Scale). Linn (1969) has chosen to focus a social adjustment assessment on systems rather than roles. This scale, because of its orientation away from roles, has been used successfully in studies of the aged where major role-function (such as work or marriage) may be absent.

Spitzer and Endicott have devised a variety of useful scales that are detailed, highly developed, and in wide use (Psychiatric Status Schedule; Psychiatric Evaluation Form). The scales combine separate symptom and social performance items so that a complete assessment can be obtained in one interview (Spitzer et al. 1970; Endicott and Spitzer 1972a, 1972b).

Katz and Lyerly (1963) (Katz Adjustment Scale) have employed a technique of rating by relatives, instead of by the patient, as a way of lessening error found with professional or self-reports. This scale has been widely used in mental health research, including community field studies (Hogarty and Katz 1971).

In England, Cooper et al. (1970) have developed an instrument which requires that a key relative (usually spouse or parent) participate in the interview with the patient. Several specialized scales have also been developed in recent years to assess specific aspects of social function. For instance, Kreitman et al. and Burgess and Cottrell have devised scales for assessments of marital interactions. Hogarty (1972) has developed a method of assessing the patient's readiness for hospital discharge. Brown and Rutter have developed measures of family life and relationships, based on separate interviews with psychiatric patients and their spouses, followed by a conjoint interview (Brown and Rutter 1966; Rutter and Brown 1966).

A number of excellent studies of the posthospital adjustment of schizophrenic patients (Angrist et al. 1968; Pasamanich et al. 1967; Freeman and Simons 1963) have incorporated assessments of the subject's adjustment at work and in social relations. In general, because of the nature of their samples, they have not focused on more subtle aspects of interpersonal relations.

A recent step beyond the Social Ineffectiveness Scale, and originating from the same research group, is the Structured and Scaled Interview to Assess Maladjustment (SSIAM) devised by Gurland et al. (1972). This comprehensive instrument contains sixty rating items, each with detailed anchor points. The items derive from five role areas—work, social and leisure life, family of origin, marriage, sex, with a sixth section for overall assessments. In each area detailed patterns of behavior and feeling are rated on four kinds of scales that can be used as systems of scoring—behavior, friction, distress, and inferential. This promising instrument is being incorporated in a number of research applications at the time of writing, and further work should be of great interest. The rating instrument used in the present study was derived by modifications of an earlier version of the SSIAM.

A particular feature of the SSIAM and the Social Ineffectiveness Scale is the incorporation of subtle aspects of behavior in interpersonal relationships, such as dependency, reticence in communication, rebelliousness. These areas are poorly represented in many scales that concentrate on concrete measures of purely task-oriented behavior, such as attendance at work. The gross deficits of work impairment, which may characterize chronic schizophrenics or depressives at the height of illness, may have little relevance to the recovered depressive whose patterns of interpersonal relationships might nevertheless be quite aberrant. Moreover, it is these subtle disturbances of interpersonal relationships that are often seen as the prime targets of psychotherapy. Indeed, the whole area of social adjustment is of particular importance in studying the effectiveness of psychological treatments (Fiske et al. 1970; Fox et al. 1968; Parloff et al. 1954; Strupp and Bergin 1969).

Factor Analysis of Social Adjustment Measures

One useful statistical manipulation often applied to rating instruments is that of factor analysis. This technique may serve two purposes. Primarily it can serve to identify empirically derived clusters of items that tend to behave as groups. These groups of items can be combined into single scales or subscales leading essentially to a reduction in variables that explain observed relationships. Such grouped items or factors may be more sensitive to changes since the items are homogeneous in the way they behave. Second, factors can be more easily understood, or used to formulate and test hypotheses. Factor analyses may provide a kind of elaborate face validity. The statistical techniques involve extraction of a number of hypothetical dimensions from a matrix of intercorrelations, so that these hypothetical dimensions may "explain" the observed relationships between variables. These factors are not absolute. They depend a good deal on technique, interpretation, and experimenter selection.

Factor analysis has only recently been applied to social adjustment (Linn 1969; Gurland 1972; Katz 1963; Spitzer and Endicott 1970). In this respect, scale development for social function has lagged behind symptoms for which many factor analyses have been reported (Goldberg et al. 1963; Lipman et al. 1969, Lorr et al. 1962; Overall et al. 1962; Raskin et al. 1967). Some authors have implicitly treated social maladjustment as a unitary concept by summing all items in the scale to derive a total score. Most others have used the familiar concepts of role performance. While helpful, this system of organizing behavior ignores the possibility of consistent patterns of behavior across several roles.

In summary, there is still need for refinement of these concepts and for consensus among researchers using these scales. This chapter has been intended to review briefly the progress made. The application of quantitative techniques in the evaluation of patients has a rather young tradition in psychiatry. The present study of depressed women originated in this tradition.

3
Social Adjustment in Depression

In this chapter we will review previous studies of social adjustment in depression with regard to four major areas for research study. First, what do previous studies reveal about the kinds of social impairment that patients experience during an acute depressive episode? Second, what happens to these impairments as the acute episode subsides? Do the social disturbances remit, and if so, how quickly and completely? Third, what are the patterns of any residual impairments? Finally, do previous studies indicate the origins of the social malfunctions found? Are they secondary consequences of depressive symptoms, or reflections of long-standing patterns of maladaption predisposing to depression—or are they both?

Our first conclusion from this review can serve as an introduction. There are no previous systematic studies of social adjustment in depression. There have been related studies containing explicit or implicit statements about adjustment in depression that provide information related to these major questions.

There are several sources of information. The most direct but least common is the specific study of social impairments in patients during and after a depressive episode. Although there has not been a comprehensive study, there have been several studies which have dealt with delineated aspects of social impairment.

A second and more common type of information source comes from follow-up studies of depressed patients. These studies describe partially or completely recovered patients. Unfortunately, these studies often lack data about patients during the acute depressive episode.

A third source of information is to be found in the psychoanalytic literature. Psychoanalytic authors have often described patients during an acute depression, focusing especially on personality disturbances that seem closely related to social maladaptions. Depending mainly on astute clinical observations of small numbers of patients rather than on formal study, these case reports provide a fascinating body of hypotheses. There have also been empirical studies of personalities of depressed patients that imply specific patterns of social relations and provide a fourth source of information.

Studies of Social Adjustment during Acute Depression

Most studies of social impairment during an acute depressive episode lack controls and depend heavily on impressionistic observations. One relatively comprehensive study of depression employing controls was that of Cassidy et al. (1957). These authors compared one hundred hospitalized manic-depressive patients with fifty medically sick controls of comparable age and background in an attempt to gain quantitative base-line information on manic-depressive disease. As expected, they found highly significant differences between the groups on most symptoms. The manic-depressives also showed many social impairments, which were regarded as consequences of the depressive illness rather than its cause. The impairments included alcoholism, job loss, marital discord, business failures, lawsuits, and automobile accidents. While the authors did not find any single personality typical of the manic-depressive, this study suggests that widespread social disturbances may accompany depression.

Impairment in work has long been recognized as a concomitant of depression and is frequently included in symptom rating scales used to assess depressive symptoms. However, attendance at work is usually assessed rather than effectiveness, adequacy, and satisfaction. In an intensive study of symptoms reported in 1934, Aubrey Lewis made the astute observation that reported feelings of incapacity and inadequacy at work were greater than the patient's actual performance decrement. He also discussed the relationship of work impairment to such factors as psychomotor retardation and anxiety over tasks.

Diminution in sexual interests and activity is another widely recognized concomitant of depression (Beck 1967; Woodruff et al. 1967). Once again, its detailed components have received less study.

The association of depressive symptoms with conflictual relations between the depressed woman and her children has received attention. Unlike the work and sexual impairments, which have usually been regarded as consequences of depression, the disturbed parent-child relationship has usually been viewed as a cause. Deykin and her colleagues (1966) observed an association between the development of clinical depression and the termination of child-rearing, which they called the "empty nest." They reported that conflict between the depressed woman and her adult children was frequent, although not always overt, and the underlying problem concerned the patient's dissatisfaction over the amount of emotional interaction she received from her children. The reestablishment of a healthier parent-child relationship was regarded as important in the patient's improvement.

Jacobson and Klerman (1966) also explored conflicts between depressed women and their grown children and showed that improvement in the patient's clinical state was associated with increasing agreement between the patient and her family as to role expectations. Although both these studies were based on small samples and are best regarded as pilot studies, they suggest specific kinds of hypersensitivity and ambivalence that may be found in acutely depressed patients. Bart (1967), in a large study of hospitalized, middle-aged depressed women, also focused on the relationship between the woman and her children and noted that women who were overinvolved in their children's lives were prone to depression when the children left home.

Hostility in depression has been empirically studied and incorporated into theoretical formulations. The latter will be described in the review of the psychoanalysts. In regard to the empirical studies, Friedman (1970) assessed verbal hostility in hospitalized depressed patients during the height of illness and the recovery. He compared these ratings with those from volunteer community controls and found that acutely ill depressives showed more resentment but less evidence of verbal hostility than normals, and that the hostility decreased even further with recovery. This study suggested that overt expression of hostility was not essential to recovery, an observation that was also made by Klerman and Gershon (1970), who failed to note any correlation between clinical improvement from depression and outward expression of hostility.

Other studies have suggested that the expression of hostility in depression varies with personality type. Gershon et al. (1968) found evidence of different patterns of hostility in depressed patients. The obsessional patients showed diminished outward hostility, which increased with recovery. On the other hand, patients with hysterical personalities showed increased overt hostility, which subsided with their recovery.

Follow-up Studies

The general findings of follow-up studies were reviewed in chapter 1. Here we will concentrate on what they tell us about social morbidity. Kraepelin, in his earliest delineations of manic-depressive disease, contrasted the complete clinical remission which developed between episodes with the gradual and progressive social deterioration which occurred in schizophrenia (Kraepelin 1913). Most authors agree with this general contrast. Lundquist (1945) based recovery on a rough estimate of the patient's ability to resume his work and ordinary mode of life. He estimated that in these terms about 80 percent of the depressives recovered completely from the first attack, with a range of 92 percent for those under thirty years of age, to 75 percent for those in the thirty-to-forty age-group. This study, which used work performance as outcome criterion, indicates that even prior to the development of modern treatments most depressives resumed functioning after an episode. Nevertheless, not all did, and it was not clear how much of this was due to residuum of illness and how much due to preexisting disturbance perhaps reflecting personality disorders.

Hordern et al. (1964) found that depressed women who were about to respond to amitriptyline could be differentiated, as early as one week after the start of treatment, by their tendency to show improvement on ratings of work and interests. This observation was confirmed by Kessell and Holt (1965) who followed up the same patients for up to eighteen months, and showed an association between presence of symptoms and poor work performance.

The improvement in work performance, although rapid, may not be complete. Honigfeld and Lasky (1962) carried out a follow-up study which was particularly interesting since it attempted to use control data based on retrospective assessments of base-line performance of each patient prior to illness. Subjects were ninety-seven depressed male patients from thirty-four Veterans Administration Hospitals who had been included in a drug treatment study. Follow-up evaluations were made at twenty weeks and one year. The authors found a return within twenty weeks to base-line levels of adjustment in overall mental health, family adjustment, and quality of interpersonal adjustment. These levels were maintained one year later with a slight improvement in the patient's overall functioning. There was, however, a striking tendency for discharged patients to experience vocational impairment. These findings may not be typical since the study was carried out at a time of economic recession (1960–62), when mounting unemployment was a national U.S. problem. The depressed subjects were male veterans, a special group for whom issues of service-connected disability may sometimes impede recovery.

Burke et al. (1967) were specifically concerned with the social functioning of depressed women. They evaluated the post-hospital adjustment of fifty-five depressed women six months after discharge. Social adjustment included adequacy of role performance, social activities, and self-care. Fifty-five percent of the patients were found to have moderate to excellent adjustment, 22 percent fair adjustment, and 23 percent poor adjustment. Case material illustrated that patients considered to have an excellent outcome were able to resume household duties, take part in social and community activities, and visit friends. Married patients tended to achieve a better adjustment than those patients without a husband. Patients achieving excellent adjustment tended to respond to return of depressive symptoms with renewed activity, while those with poor adjustment coped by withdrawing from activity. Overall, the authors concluded that the probability of an exhospitalized depressed woman functioning at a high level in the community was greatly improved if she was married, showed good social interactions, demonstrated few depressive symptoms, and was under fifty years of age.

Chwast and Lurie (1966) followed fifty-eight depressed former inpatients, who underwent a resocialization program for six to eight months after discharge, in order to determine the extent to which the resocialization program would reduce social estrangement. Patients were assessed before and after the socialization program on a scale which examined the patient's peer relations, quality of participation, and satisfaction. These indices showed improvement over the course of the resocialization program. Absence of an untreated group in the study leaves the contribution of the therapeutic program in doubt. However, both the Burke and the Chwast studies suggest that the patients' social recovery follows their symptomatic recovery.

Winokur et al. (1969), studying a group of severely ill hospitalized patients with carefully defined bipolar manic-depressive disease, obtained less favorable findings. Patients were followed eighteen and thirty-six months after the index episode. The authors found that only 14 percent of patients were well in every way after an average follow-up of twenty-four months, and 11 percent were chronically ill. Patients at follow-up were often described as chronically disabled. Some had stopped working steadily or were not working at all, even though they had been working at a previous time. Many had decreased their social circle due to an inability to meet people; others drank excessively, had chronic marital problems, or were considered too dependent by the family. Patients who had only a partial symptomatic remission or were chronically ill were significantly more impaired in most social areas than were those who had total remission. However, a substantial number of the completely remitted patients also had social impairments. The authors concluded that manic-depressive disease disturbs the interpersonal and social fabric of the patient's life and the family's.

Psychoanalytic Observations

Although the frame of reference and the accompanying terminology of the psychoanalysts are not primarily social, the malfunctions described are easily translatable into terms of social function. The primary psychoanalytic emphasis is on the psychodynamic mechanisms underlying the depressive state. This involves both a description of the state of depression and of the preexisting character traits predisposing to depression and liable to persist after symptomatic recovery. Although both may be relevant to social function, it is predisposing character traits manifested before the episode and enduring after recovery which contain the clearest social implications.

For detailed expositions of psychoanalytic theory the reader is referred to more authoritative sources, including the originals, and Gaylin's compilation (1968). Abraham was the first of the psychoanalytic writers to develop a theory of depression. He described the depression-prone person as dependent, sensitive to loss of love, and having basic defects in self-esteem. Before the depression develops, the patient is energetic in his pursuits. This undirected and forced sublimation is used to ward off internal conflict. The sublimation ceases as the depression develops, ability to carry on work ceases, and close interpersonal relationships are fraught with difficulties. With the symptomatic recovery the work is resumed overzealously. These same themes can be found in most subsequent psychoanalytic writings.

Freud, in 1917, developed his concepts of depression from the theories of Abraham. Like Abraham, he commented on the ambivalence of the depression-prone person towards love objects and his hypersensitivity to situations of being slighted or disappointed. Further, the acutely depressed person was described as disinterested in the outside world, with a lost capacity to love and inhibited in activities. The vulnerability to depression was related to an early loss. A more recent real or imagined loss led to a recapitulation of this earlier situation, with unresolved feelings of resentment towards the loved person that were unacceptable to the patient and became directed instead towards the patient himself. The depression allowed the patient to avoid expressing his hostility openly. During the illness the conscientious traits disappeared, work was impaired, and interpersonal difficulties with intimate associates increased.

Sandor Rado emphasized the dependency found in depressives. "They cling to their objects like leeches" (Gaylin 1968, p. 74). However, like Freud and Abraham, he commented on the unexpressed hostility of depressives to the loved ones.

Otto Fenichel, too, emphasized the dependency of those persons predisposed to depression: "They passively need to feel loved" (Gaylin 1968, p. 109). In discussing the conflict with aggressive tendencies in the depressive, he noted that "while they have a tendency to react to frustration with violence . . . then oral dependence impels them to try to get what they need by ingratiation and submission."

Bibring laid particular emphasis on loss of self-esteem in depression. He used a different framework of ego psychology, but his observations about the behavior of depressives were consistent with those of the previous writers mentioned. He described depression as a way of reacting to frustration whenever the individual finds itself in a state of (real or imaginary) helplessness against overwhelming odds. Like the other psychoanalytic writers, he commented on the predisposition to depression of dependent personalities and those people unable to live up to their aspirations. He also noted an inhibition of work and goal-directed behavior during the acute illness. Bibring, however, went further in describing the particular impairments of work. He likened the inhibition of work to boredom and noted that goals were maintained in depression as well as in boredom but with an ability to reach them that was either inadequate or prohibited.

Mabel Blake Cohen and her colleagues gave one of the fullest descriptions of the depressive's character in a study based on intensive psychoanalysis of twelve manic-depressive patients. This study focused on the patients' families and their role in the development of the disorder. These authors postulated that the depressive comes from a family in which there is concern about social approval and striving for prestige. The patient becomes selected out to achieve the prestige for the family. There is intense competition in the family and little concern for interpersonal relations. In later life, presumably to counteract this envy, the patient develops a pattern of underselling himself. When well, the adult depressive may appear at ease with others. However, there is little intimacy in these relations, communication is poor, and social performance is stereotyped. The depressive continues to undersell himself, and the process paralyzes the use of his own endowments. He begins to hate himself because he senses the fraudulence of his behavior. Impairment in verbal communication was described fully by Cohen, as well as by Spiegel, and was seen as a major therapeutic problem. This process of underselling and the inability to express wishes directly is similar to the ingratiating behavior and resentment of depressives described by Fenichel.

This brief summary does not do justice to psychoanalytic theory but is intended to highlight the theories that might describe the patient's social function. There are really several different patterns implied by different authors. These include sensitivity to situations of loss; obsessionality and conscientiousness; dependency and submissiveness; difficulties with hostility; defective communication in interpersonal relationships.

The first of these, sensitivity to loss, does not have clear implications for social function. It does have important implications for studies of precipitating events, since it suggests that one particular kind of event, loss of a loved one, should predominate (Paykel in press).

The second pattern concerns conscientiousness and obsessionality. Writers such as Abraham and Cohen have variously described depression-prone subjects as energetic, conscientious, rebellious, competitive, striving for prestige, obsessional, vulnerable to blows to self-esteem. This is a consistent theme with clear implications for social function. The depression-prone individual might be expected to place particular importance on the work role with emphasis on good performance and the achievement of success.

A further major pattern described is that related to dependency and the oral character. This has been well summarized and its evolution described in a recent review of the depressive personality by Chodoff (1972). Many authors, including Abraham, Freud, Fenichel, and most prominently Rado, have emphasized the dependency of the depression-prone person which might be expected to form a consistent pattern in social and interpersonal relationships.

A further major theme concerns hostility. Here the social implications, although of major importance, are less clear-cut. The clearest implications are for acute depression, which is considered closely related to a hostility that is directed internally onto the self. This is assumed by many to be associated with a decrease of externally directed hostility, although theory would not appear to require it to be. After recovery, it is less clear what patterns might be expected and how they would be manifest in social relationships. Certainly we might expect some difficulty in handling hostility in relationships: possibly, persistent patterns of ambivalence or inhibited overt hostility.

The last major theme concerns communication. The implication is that depressives are unable to express needs, wishes, and feelings openly and directly. This pattern has been described as quite marked during the acute episode. The pattern of defective communication is seen as a major therapeutic issue by Spiegel (1960). The recovery pattern of depressed patients has been less clearly described, although implicit in Cohen's work is the notion of continued impairment in direct communication. Instead, indirect communication in the form of ingratiating behavior is presumably substituted.

Empirical Studies of Personality

Numerous studies not employing the psychoanalytic framework have attempted to demonstrate that depressives have characteristic personalities. These studies span many decades.[1] Unfortunately, many of these studies share a serious deficiency with the psychoanalytic studies: they lack suitable control groups

1. For recent reviews of the depressive personality, the reader is referred to Chodoff et al. (1972), and Metcalfe (1968).

which would indicate whether the phenomena described are specific to depressives. Also, as in psychoanalytic studies, they often depend on clinical information and lack adequate rating techniques. Further, empirical techniques for measuring personality are not well developed, and available techniques, such as self-reports, observer ratings, projective and other tests, all have disadvantages (Vernon 1964).

One of the earliest studies to employ control groups was that of Bowman (1934). He presented case comparisons of depressives, schizophrenics, general paretics, and normals to determine personality differences. In comparisons of depressives and normals he drew a number of scattered conclusions about depressives which did not easily suggest any recognizable specific personality type.

Several more recent studies have been concerned with the concept of the neurotic constitution, originally delineated by Slater in 1943. Slater studied 2,000 neurotic soldiers, among whom were 348 with depression. He suggested a constellation of features predicting ultimate illness. These features included clinically abnormal personality, neurosis in childhood, a poor work record, and a family history of neurosis.

More recent studies adopting a similar concept have made use of a specific self-report rating scale, the Maudsley Personality Inventory (Eysenck 1959). Kendell and DiScipio (1968) found recovered depressives to show higher than normal scores on neuroticism on this instrument. However, Coppen and Metcalfe (1965) found that, overall, recovered depressives did not score differently than normals on this scale. When individual items making up the scale were examined, the depressives did show evidence of a worrying, tense attitude to life, combined with denial of fantasy and imagination, and a rigid, limited habit-bound personality (Metcalfe 1968; Julian et al. 1969).

An ingenious study was reported by Burns and Offord (1972). These authors set out to test the hypothesis that depressives have premorbid personalities strikingly oriented towards achievement. As a tool they used school records of twenty depressed women, thirty-five of their siblings, and forty-nine matched controls. The findings of the study were essentially negative. The depressives showed no more evidence of good school achievement or upward social mobility than their siblings or their classmates.

The previous studies concerned unselected groups of depressives. A number of studies have, instead, examined personality characteristics of subtypes of depressed patients, comparing them with other depressive types or nondepressive control groups.

One such group is that of manic-depressives. Manic-depressives, as described by Kraepelin, Bleuler, and Kretschmer, show personalities which are cyclothymic in the sense of being prone to cyclical mood swings, sometimes with persistent mild depression or elation. There have been few studies which have attempted to operationalize this personality concept and measure it in depressives and control groups. In recent years some studies (Perris 1969; Coppen 1966) have compared bipolar manic-depressives with unipolar depressives (depressives who have never had a manic episode). In these studies manic depressives have tended to show normal or syntonic personalities in contrast to somewhat neurotic personalities shown by unipolar depressives.

Another series of studies of manic-depressives derived from the psychoanalytic theories of Mabel Blake Cohen et al. (1954). Gibson (1957) sought to test these, using a questionnaire based on social work interview and hospital records to study twenty-seven manic-depressives and seventeen schizophrenic controls, together with Cohen's original twelve manic-depressives. Manic-depressives were found, in confirmation of Cohen, to come from families in which there was marked striving for prestige with the patient as the instrument of this need; the family showed marked concern for social achievement and the childhood background was characterized by envy and competitiveness. Reliability of this data was, however, questionable.

Becker and associates carried out a systematic series of studies into these aspects. In an initial study (Becker 1960), remitted manic-depressives were compared with nonpsychiatric controls. Manic-depressives scored significantly higher on measures of value achievement, authoritarian trends, and conventional attitudes, but not on direct self-ratings of achievement motivation or on performance output. A second study (Spielberger et al.

1963) produced somewhat similar results. In another study (Becker et al. 1963) similar findings were found in neurotic depressives and schizophrenics, but not normals, suggesting that these background characteristics may underlie psychiatric illness in general rather than manic-depressive illness. However, Woodruff et al. (1970) found that male manic-depressives and their brothers achieved more education and higher occupational status than unipolar depressives and their siblings, which would tend to support the original concept.

Another series of studies sought to ascribe specific personalities to involutional depressives. W. B. Titley in 1936 compared involutional melancholics with manic-depressives and normals. Samples were small, comprising ten persons in each group. He concluded that involutional melancholics had a common pattern of premorbid traits which included "a narrow range of interests, poor facility of adjustment to social trends, inability to maintain friendships, intolerance and uniformly poor adult sexual adjustment . . . profound reticence . . . meticulosity in regard to person and work." This pattern was in contrast to normals and manic-depressives, who resembled each other in being more outgoing and less rigidly obsessional. Palmer and Sherman (1938) reached similar conclusions on the basis of a comparison between fifty involutionals and fifty manic-depressives, but without presenting any statistical calculation of their data. More recent work has cast serious doubt on the existence of a group of involutional melancholics showing any specific features either of symptoms or of personality (Tait et al. 1957; Rosenthal 1968; Kendell 1968).

Another series of studies has compared the personalities of endogenous and neurotic depressives. In clinical descriptions, personalities of endogenous depressives have tended to be described as stable and obsessive, those of neurotic depressives as neurotic, inadequate, or vulnerable (Klerman 1971). By and large, research studies have confirmed these impressions. Neurotic depressives were found to score higher than endogenous depressives for neuroticism on the Maudsley Personality Inventory by Garside et al. (1970), Kendell and DiScipio (1968), and Paykel et al. (1971). They were rated as inadequate by Kiloh and Garside (1963), Carney et al. (1965), and Mendels and Cochrane

(1968). Rosenthal and Gudeman (1967) and Mendels and Cochrane (1968) also found them to be less obsessional, although Kiloh and Garside (1963) did not. Kiloh and Garside (1963), Rosenthal and Klerman (1964), and Mendels and Cochrane (1968) also found them to show more evidence of hysterical personality, although Rosenthal and Gudeman (1967) and Kay et al. (1969) did not. Most of these studies employed only internal comparisons between the two depressive types, so that it is not possible to say how either group compared to normal in personality.

When depressives are looked at as a whole, relatively little in the way of specific personality features can be established, although there is some general tendency toward features loosely regarded as neurotic. When specific groups of depressives are examined, it is a fairly consistent finding that neurotic depressives show strongly a tendency to break down under stress. Endogenous unipolar depressives tend to show normal personalities. Although the findings are not clear-cut, there is suggestive evidence that manic-depressives may be characterized by achievement and a need for it of the kind described in the psychoanalytic studies of Cohen et al. Other patterns described by psychoanalysts, such as dependency and defective communication, have received little attention in empirical studies. One problem with some of the earlier studies, as with psychoanalytic reports, is the separation of effects of illness from personality. At the height of illness habitual personality patterns may be largely obscured. The more recent studies take care to postpone evaluation of personality until after recovery.

Conclusions

This review of studies suggests that remarkably little has been firmly established as to the nature and course of social impairment in depression. Studies of the acute depressive episode in general suggest that there is considerable social impairment at its height. There is some consensus that work performance is especially implicated and that sexual performance is also impaired. A few studies show a close temporal association between depressive symptoms and interpersonal difficulties, although whether these are viewed as precipitants or concomitants of depression varies with the theoretical orientation of the worker. In all these aspects, studies have neither been sufficiently detailed nor adequately comprehensive as to the potential range of maladjustments.

Follow-up studies suggest there is considerable improvement in social function with the remission of symptoms. Some of the studies would suggest that improved work performance is an early concomitant of symptomatic remission, although the elegant study of Honigfeld suggests the contrary. The degree and completeness of the social remission is uncertain. A few studies suggest that the improvement in social function may stop considerably short of complete restoration of normal adjustment, with a residuum of diminished work performance and friendships, disturbed interpersonal relations, and marital breakdown.

Hostility, which occupies a central position in some psychoanalytic theories, has come in for special study. The studies available suggest a mixed picture for the acute state: in some patients hostility may be reduced, but in others it may be increased. Certainly, inhibited overt hostility is not an invariable concomitant of depression, nor is its increase an invariable concomitant of recovery.

The psychoanalytic literature suggests that there are enduring personality characteristics in depression-prone individuals. These difficulties include dependency on others, lack of assertiveness, ambivalence in close relations, obsessiveness and a need for achievement in work, and difficulties in communication. These traits are described as being exaggerated during the illness, except for work and social interactions, which diminish sharply.

Direct empirical studies of the depressive personality do not suggest consistently any uniform pattern of the depressed personality other than perhaps a general tendency to neuroticism, which might be reflected in a tendency to maladjustment, without any specific pattern. Among depressive subtypes, neurotic depressives appear to show this neurotic personality pattern markedly. Endogenous depressives are reported as showing relatively normal personality which might be reflected in normal social adjustment after recovery. In addition to cyclothymic personalities, manic-depressives in some studies appear to show a pattern of achievement orientation, consistent with that described by psychoanalysts, which might be reflected in good work performance.

The direct literature on social function in depression is too sparse to permit conclusions as to the causes and origins of the maladjustment. Two opposing views permeate the literature. One is that the disturbances are secondary consequences of the symptomatic illness. This view has been stated most clearly and explicitly by Winokur et al. (1969). The authors described the social and interpersonal changes which immediately followed the episode "as epiphenomena, i.e. the result of having a psychological illness and hospitalization" (p. 102). In this view, the social consequences should largely remit with symptomatic recovery. The second and opposing view is typified by the psychoanalysts. In the psychoanalytic view, the interpersonal difficulties are the reflections of enduring personality difficulties which predispose to the depressive episode and are closely related to its central mechanisms. In this view, the basic disturbances would be expected to persist after symptomatic recovery. There is also a third possibility, related to some extent to the second. The social malfunctions, such as they are, may reflect causes of the depression which are situational rather than personality-related. The literature on the "empty nest" is largely oriented to this possibility. However, causative chains may well be complex. Thus, Winokur et al., although regarding the social dysfunction as a secondary consequence of illness, concluded that "the relationship between persistent symptomatology and continued social dysfunction is not so clear as to cause and effect. Very likely there is a reciprocal relationship in which those symptoms that persist cause psychosocial disturbance which, in turn, alters the symptoms that are experienced by the patient" (p. 102).

These conclusions aim at the heart of the questions regarding social adjustment in depression. Our own study of social adjustment was designed to investigate similar issues in greater detail.

4
Design and Methods
of the Study

In this chapter we will present the research design and procedures of our study. We will describe the subjects and their selection, the method used to assess social adjustment, the timing of the assessments, and the treatments intervening between them.

There were two groups of subjects for the study: forty depressed women and a comparison group of forty normal women who were their neighbors. All subjects were female, between the ages of twenty-five and sixty, living in the greater New Haven, Connecticut, metropolitan area.

The Depressed Patients

The forty depressed women were patients under psychiatric treatment. The prime criterion for inclusion for treatment was presence of clinical depression of at least two weeks duration, and sufficiently severe to be rated at least 7 on a scale ranging from 3 to 15, obtained by combining separate 1–5 assessments of verbal report, observable behavior, and secondary symptoms of depression (Raskin 1970). Verbal reports of depression included such phenomena as: feeling blue, helpless, hopeless, worthless; a loss of interest, wishing one were dead, and crying spells. Depressed behavior at interview included: looking sad, crying easily, speaking softly; psychomotor retardation or agitation. Secondary symptoms of depression included: insomnia, anorexia, difficulty concentrating, constipation. Patients in whom the depression appeared secondary to another predominant syndrome were excluded. These other syndromes included: anxiety reactions, phobic state, obsessional neuroses, and schizophrenia. Personality disorder was not a ground for exclusion. Excluding criteria for schizophrenia were specified in detail; they covered prominent psychotic symptoms corresponding to a narrower European or English diagnosis of schizophrenia (Gurland et al. 1972) rather than the wider definition of schizophrenia sometimes employed in the United States. Disturbances of social behavior or interpersonal relations were not grounds for exclusion. Other positive grounds for exclusion included alcoholism, drug addiction, organic brain syndrome, mental deficiency, pregnancy; serious physical disease rendering the patient unsuitable for drug treatment, such as liver disease, cardiovascular disease, epilepsy, cerebrovascular disease, hypertension; ongoing psychotherapy in another clinic; and treatment with a tricyclic antidepressant in the past six months with failure of response. Subjects included were thus presenting at the clinic during an acute depressive episode which had not received definitive treatment.

These depressed subjects were forty consecutive patients admitted to the New Haven clinic and were part of a larger study of treatment of depression, carried out in two centers (Connecticut Mental Health Center at Yale University School of Medicine in New Haven and Boston State Hospital in Dorchester, Massachusetts, affiliated with Tufts University School of Medicine). The two-center study primarily concerned maintenance therapy of recovering depressed women with medication and psychotherapy. Selection was a two-stage procedure. Patients were referred from a variety of sources, and initial ratings were carried out by one of several research psychiatrists. Patients who met the clinical criteria for inclusion specified above were then treated for four to six weeks with amitriptyline in a flexible dosage of 100–200 mg. This treatment was entirely outpatient for thirty-five of the forty subjects, the remaining five having been hospitalized briefly (less than four weeks). Those who showed 50 percent improvement at the end of four weeks' treatment (or six weeks in cases of doubt), when rated on the same 3–15 scale used for initial rating, were included in the maintenance therapy study, and thus became eligible for our study of social adjustment.

Exclusion and Refusal Rate of Depressed Patients

Fifty-seven depressed women met the initial inclusion criteria for the study and were admitted for treatment with amitriptyline of the acute symptoms of depression. Of these fifty-seven women, forty (70.2 percent) entered the maintenance study and became the cohort for the study of social adjustment. The remaining seventeen women did not enter maintenance treatment for the following reasons: nine (15.8 percent) did not sufficiently respond to the particular antidepressant in the four-to-six-week period of acute treatment; two (3.5 percent) responded to the antidepressant with a reduction of most symptoms in a few days so that original diagnosis was questionable; two (3.5 percent) terminated due to drug side effects; and four (7.0 percent) were noncooperators in terms of missing appointments or taking inadequate amounts of medication. The nine patients who did not respond to medication and the two who had side effects might have entered the study if an alternative antidepressant could have been used in the study design. The majority of patients coming to the clinic showed the minimal response to medication necessary to enter the study and were representative of most depressed patients coming for outpatient treatment. There were no important sociodemographic or clinical differences between patients entering the study and those who did not.

The Normal Controls

The forty normal controls (normals) were selected from the general population and resided in streets adjacent to those where the patients lived. The aim in their selection was to obtain a group of subjects, comparable on sociodemographic and other variables, but lacking in psychiatric illness, in order to compare their social function with that of the depressives and to delineate those abnormalities characterizing the latter.

Selection criteria were therefore constructed to obtain a comparable group. The normals, like the depressives, had to be between the ages of twenty-five and sixty and were similarly excluded on grounds of medical illness. However, the normals were excluded on the grounds of psychiatric illness as well. Criteria for exclusion were as follows.

Medical illness. Evidence of any current or past medical disease that would exclude the subject, if a patient, from receiving a long-term course of maintenance medication, that is, any serious current disease, current pregnancy, current or previous severe liver disease, cardiovascular disease, epilepsy, cerebral vascular disease and hypertension.

Psychiatric symptoms. Evidence of marked and overt psychiatric symptomatology either currently or in the last five years, for example, depression, extreme anxiety, psychotic disorder. Symptoms were determined at a screening interview. They were not, however, inferred from the existence of social maladjustment. Subjects who had received psychiatric treatment in the last five years were automatically held to fit this exclusion criterion. Treatment was defined as contact made on more than one occasion with psychiatrists, social workers, psychologists, or any member of a treatment team of any mental health facility. This did not include welfare workers, but included family doctors if, for example, a lengthy course of tranquilizers was prescribed.

Sociodemographic variables. Subjects were initially selected by a procedure which will be described and which appeared likely to insure sociodemographic comparability between patients and normals. Characteristics were monitored carefully with regard to age, race, marital status, religion, and social class. When some imbalances started to develop, further restricting criteria were incorporated for the later normals.

Although we will refer to the controls for convenience as "normals," they do not exactly fit either of the two usual definitions of normality. They were not completely representative of the general population, in that psychiatric and medical illness were excluded; thus they did not fit the "statistical" norm based on the average characteristics of the general population. Neither, however, could they be regarded as corresponding to the "ideal" norm of perfect function—there was no exclusion of subjects on grounds that their social function itself was poor.

The procedure for selecting the normal sample was as follows. The depressed patient's street was located on a map, and the next parallel street was selected for sampling. The number of the patient's house was located in the city directory on this parallel street and the occupant of that house became the normal subject. Where this proved to be a small business or shop, the closest available house was approached. If there was no parallel street, the nearest perpendicular street was taken. In cases where the house selected had no resident who fitted the criteria, the house ten numbers away in the listings of the city directory was approached. This procedure was followed until a suitable person was found, or the end of the street reached. In the latter case, the next parallel street was tried or, where there was no parallel street, the nearest perpendicular street.

After a house had been located, the initial contact was made by letter, the resident's name and street number being taken from the city directory. A letter was sent to the female member of the house briefly explaining the survey (see Appendix for letter). A fee of $10 was offered to all participants. A research assistant telephoned one to two weeks later to ascertain suitability and willingness to cooperate. Considerable effort was made to contact people by telephone, but after numerous unsuccessful attempts a second letter was sent asking them to telephone if they would like to take part. Subjects who did not have a telephone were contacted by letter. The absence of a telephone was not a ground for exclusion. In the cases where the person had moved and left no forwarding address, the next eligible person was contacted as described above.

Once a subject had been selected, a research assistant conducted a brief screening interview. If the subject fitted the criteria, the main assessment interview was carried out. If not, the next eligible person was contacted.

Exclusion and Refusal Rate: Normal Controls

One hundred sixty-nine subjects were sent initial letters to determine their eligibility for the normal sample. Of this total, twenty-nine (17 percent) had moved and could not be located; thirty-eight (22 percent) refused to be seen for a screening interview; sixty-two (37 percent) were excluded by the interviewer because they did not meet the study criteria. Of these sixty-two excluded subjects, thirty-nine did not meet the age and social class criteria, one did not speak English, sixteen had excluding medical conditions, four had been under psychiatric treatment, and two manifested obvious untreated psychiatric symptoms. The remaining forty subjects of the original 169 met all the criteria and constituted the normal sample for this study.

Even after the criteria have been defined, there is always a question of representative sampling of the population studied. One way to examine this issue is by rate of refusal. In this regard it should be noted that the largest number of subjects were excluded by the study criteria. The actual subject refusal rate, 22 percent, was moderately low, and some of those who refused may have been found ineligible on other grounds such as medical or psychiatric, if interviewed. Of course, we do not know anything about the 17 percent of subjects who had moved and could not be located. The 17 percent annual relocation rate is consistent with expectation in the United States (U.S. Bureau of Census 1971).

General Characteristics of Subjects

Depressed patients and normals were closely comparable on sociodemographic characteristics (table 4.1). Taken as a whole, the subjects showed a wide range of ages—from twenty-five to fifty-eight—but were predominantly middle-aged (mean age—forty-two years). The proportion of Negroes is consistent with their representation in the population from which the sample was drawn. More than 50 percent were Catholic, mainly of Italian extraction, reflecting the largest ethnic group in metro-

TABLE 4.1   SOCIODEMOGRAPHIC CHARACTERISTICS

		Depressed Patients		Normals		Significance of Difference*
		N	%	N	%	
Age	25–34	14	35.0	9	22.5	
	35–44	9	22.5	13	32.5	N.S.
	45–60	17	42.5	18	45.0	
Race	White	36	90.0	35	87.5	N.S.
	Negro	4	10.0	5	12.5	
Religion	Catholic	22	55.0	22	55.0	
	Protestant	13	32.5	16	40.0	N.S.
	Jewish	2	5.0	1	2.5	
	Other	3	7.5	1	2.5	
Social Class†	1 & 2	4	10.0	6	15.0	
	3	7	17.5	11	27.5	N.S.
	4	19	47.5	15	37.5	
	5	10	25.0	8	20.0	
Marital Status	Married	28	70.0	34	85.0	
	Divorced, separated, widowed	9	22.5	3	7.5	N.S.
	Single	3	7.5	3	7.5	
Work Role	Works outside the home	11	27.5	16	40.0	N.S.
	Housewife	29	72.5	24	60.0	

* Using chi square test.
† Based on A. Hollingshead, "Two Factor Index of Social Position" (© Yale University, 1957).

politan New Haven.[1] The majority were from the middle to lower social classes (Social Class 3, 4, 5 on the Hollingshead Two-Factor Index). Subjects were all women, mostly married and with children. The majority were housewives, although a substantial minority of one-third were holding at least half-time jobs outside the home.

Clinical characteristics were examined on the forty depressed patients. The depressive episodes were relatively acute, 48 per-

1. See J. K. Myers and L. L. Bean, *A Decade Later: A Follow-up of Social Class and Mental Illness* (Wiley, New York, 1968), pp. 36–57, for a description of the ethnic and social composition of New Haven, Connecticut.

cent being three months or less in duration, and only 17 percent longer than a year. However, 70 percent of patients had had at least one previous depressive episode and 25 percent had made a suicide attempt prior to the present episode. In diagnosis, thirty-one patients (78 percent) were regarded as neurotic depressives, five patients (12 percent) as psychotic depressives, two patients (5 percent) as involutional melancholics, and two patients (5 percent) were bipolar depressives as defined by having had a previous manic episode.

Assessment of Social Adjustment: The Social Adjustment Scale (SAS)

Social adjustment was assessed by research assistant raters using the Social Adjustment Scale (SAS), a rating scale developed primarily for this study. The scale was intended to be both a descriptive instrument and an outcome measure in the larger study of maintenance treatment.

The scale was not original in conception, but built on the work of several scales, including those of Klerman and Deykin and Mandel (1959). Most heavily, however, it was derived from the Structured and Scaled Interview for Maladjustment (SSIAM) devised by Gurland et al. (1972) (see chap. 2). This comprehensive instrument is one of the few in the literature which assesses detailed patterns of interpersonal relationships. In its basic design and much of its content, the SAS was derived from the Gurland scale. The extensive modifications, which included elimination of some items, addition of others, and considerable rewording, were aimed at developing an item pool appropriate to middle-aged women.

The process of modifying the scale took six months. After the initial item pool had been developed, a series of pilot studies were carried out in which a variety of psychiatric patients, including depressives, were interviewed. After development of the final instrument and training of interviewers, a reliability study was carried out.

The interview format and separate precoded scoring form for the fully developed Social Adjustment Scale are incorporated in the Appendix. The scale contained forty-eight rating items. The items and the hypothesized groupings which guided their inclusion are set out in table 4.2. Items could be grouped in two independent ways.

Role areas. The major division was into six role areas: work (in main work-role as either worker, housewife, or student), social and leisure, extended family, marital (as spouse), parental, and marital family unit. An overall judgment of performance in each role and overall performance was made by the interviewer. This judgment was a relatively unstructured and intuitive synthesis of all available information on the subject. The grouping by role areas reflects the system commonly used in summing items in social adjustment scales.

Qualitative categories. Within each functional role, items fell into up to five qualitative categories, reflecting the principles guiding construction of the scale, and a possible alternative theoretical system for scoring it. Not all categories were equally represented in all roles, depending on appropriateness. The major division was into three main categories of behavior, feelings and satisfactions, and overall evaluations, in which the bases for rating differed. In the behavior category, an attempt was made to rate actual behavior rather than the subject's perception of its adequacy. For satisfactions and feelings the subject's perceptions and feelings alone were used.

Within the category of behavior, three further subcategories were defined. The first subcategory, performance, measured concrete and easily quantified behaviors concerning instrumental role performance. The second and third subcategories reflected finer aspects of interpersonal relations, which were derived primarily from Gurland's SSIAM. One of these, labelled interpersonal behaviors, included a number of different specific maladaptive behaviors in interpersonal relations. In some roles the boundary between this subcategory and that of performance was loose. The other subcategory, friction, measured the frequency of one specific type of behavior, overt arguments, across other various role areas.

Each item was rated according to defined anchor points. Most of the items were on five-point scales in which the first point reflected excellent status (the ideal norm), the second point mild impairment approximating to our expectation of an aver-

TABLE 4.2 SOCIAL ADJUSTMENT SCALE (SAS), ITEM CONTENT AND ORGANIZATION

Qualitative Categories	Work	Social and Leisure	Extended Family	Marital as Spouse	Parental	Marital Family Unit	Additional Item
				Role Areas			
Behavior		Diminished contact with friends					
Performance	Time lost Impaired performance	Diminished social interactions Impaired leisure activities Diminished dating		Diminished intercourse Sexual problems	Lack of involvement Impaired communication	Economic inadequacy of family unit	
Interpersonal Behaviors		Reticence Hypersensitive behavior	Reticence Withdrawal Family attachment Rebellion	Reticence Domineering behavior Dependency Submissiveness			
Friction	Friction	Friction	Friction	Friction	Friction		
Feelings and Satisfactions	Distress Disinterest Feelings of inadequacy	Social discomfort Loneliness Boredom Disinterest in dating	Guilt Worry Resentment	Lack of affection Disinterest in sex	Lack of affection	Guilt Worry Resentment	
Overall Evaluations	Overall work performance	Overall social and leisure performance	Overall evaluation of role in extended family	Overall evaluation as spouse	Overall evaluation as parent		Overall evaluation of all roles

age rating for the general population (the statistical norm), and the remaining three points degrees of definitely impaired function. Exceptions were the overall evaluations, which were on seven-point scales.

The scale was set out in the form of a semistructured interview administered to the patient and taking between forty-five minutes and an hour and a half. The order of items was predetermined, as was the initial question for each item. For all items the time period rated was the two months immediately prior to interview.

Scoring systems will be discussed further in chapter 9. In addition to the scores for individual items, three provisional summated scoring systems based on theory were incorporated in the scale design. The first was by role area, the second by qualitative category irrespective of role area. The third system consisted of a single summary score derived by summing all items in the scale except the overall evaluations. An additional system was derived by factor analysis.

Administration and Timing of Ratings

Social adjustment interviews were administered by one of two research assistant raters. Both were experienced interviewers. One had a bachelor's degree in psychology and previous experience in psychological research, the other a bachelor's degree in sociology and professional training and experience in social work. Prior to the study, the interviewers underwent extensive training in use of the scale.

The depressives were interviewed in the research clinic where they were being treated. The normals were interviewed in their homes. The interviewer initially explained the purpose of the interview, the areas to be covered, established the two-month time interval to be used in rating, and questioned the subject about any significant changes in functioning during this two-month period when rating scores would need to be averaged. The questions from the interview format were then introduced in sequence, and after each the patient was encouraged to talk freely. Whenever necessary, questions were pursued further to make possible an exact assignment to a scale point. If the subject offered additional or conflicting information during the course of the interview, ratings of items were altered accordingly, as soon as the discrepancies had been clarified with the subject. Upon completion of the interview the rater immediately made overall evaluations of each area rated. All ratings were made on a separate precoded form suitable for key punching. Analyses were carried out by computer from punched cards.

Timing and sequence of interviews differed in the two groups. The normals were assessed only once—immediately after selection, a short time after the initial interviews of depressed women. Since the normals were randomly selected from the general population, following up their social adjustment was unlikely to be productive. Although individual subjects might change substantially, there was no reason to expect the mean normal base line of the group as a whole to change.

The depressed women were interviewed and rated on six separate occasions over twenty months, during the acute depressive episode, the recovery, and at follow-up. The initial interview for patients occurred at entrance to the maintenance study. This followed four to six weeks of initial treatment with amitriptyline. Since the time period rated was the last two months, this covered the height of symptomatic illness and early recovery. Subsequent interviews took place after two, four, eight, fourteen, and twenty months.

Subsequent to initial interview all patients were treated in the larger maintenance therapy study, during which time they received either individual weekly psychotherapy or low-contact monthly interviews, combined with either amitriptyline, placebo, or no pill. Maintenance treatment continued for eight months after inclusion in the study, when it was terminated. Repeated ratings coincided with two months and four months of maintenance treatment, its termination, and six- and twelve-month follow-ups after termination of the eight-month treatment. For the most part in this study we will report all the subjects as a single group, rather than being concerned with treatment differences, since a larger sample would be required to examine these differences.

Reliability Study

If the results of a rating procedure are to be useful, it is important that they be as free as possible from measurement error. A separate reliability study of the Social Adjustment Scale was therefore undertaken by the two raters prior to the beginning of the study, on an additional sample of eighteen depressed women. With both raters present in the room, one conducted the interview (the raters alternated as interviewers with each patient), and both made ratings on the basis of this interview, without communicating the ratings to each other.

Two indices of agreement were used: the proportion of ratings showing agreement, and the Pearson correlation between raters (see Appendix, table B.1). With respect to raw agreement, since the scales (except for the overall evaluation) were on five-point ranges, a maximum of a one-point disagreement would be permissible. Complete agreement would be even more desirable, but is rare in clinical ratings. Agreement was best for the concrete rating items in the work role, worst for social and leisure activities. Overall, agreement with respect to all items was adequate. Complete agreement was shown on 67 percent of the items, and another 29 percent were one point apart. Only 3.9 percent of the ratings differed by more than one point. Pearson correlations ranged from a low of .33 for friction at work (which was based on a low range of values so that a correlation coefficient was not entirely appropriate) to a high of .97 for economic inadequacy. Only one other rating gave a correlation below .60; most were above .70. The mean correlation over all items was .83, indicating that the ratings were of acceptable reliability.

Additional Data

The information collected by the ratings in the Social Adjustment Scale was supplemented by clinical narrative reports and additional rating assessments. Following the interview, the rater submitted brief narrative summaries for both the patients and normals. The summaries described the subject's current family situation and supplemented the numerical ratings.

Additional information concerning the patients was obtained during the course of treatment. It is important to note that this came from sources other than the raters who assessed social adjustment at interview, and was not available to the raters. Ratings on patients and normals were comparable. At first interview this comparability was complete. By the later interviews with patients, it is possible that the fact that the rater had seen them before enabled an easier communication of information. Otherwise, comparability remained. The additional narrative information we will present was largely derived by psychiatrists and social workers who were treating the patients and were uninvolved in the social adjustment ratings. While enabling us to expand greatly on the patterns of maladjustment, this information does not destroy the comparability of social adjustment ratings of patients and normals. Narratives were recorded at psychiatric interview and at follow-up. For those patients treated with weekly psychotherapy by social workers, detailed notes were recorded following all therapeutic interviews. In most instances family members were also interviewed by the social workers and psychiatrists. The perceptions of problems by the families as well as direct clinical observations of family members were recorded. This information was particularly important in the descriptions of the marital problems in chapter 7 and the patients' children in chapter 8. All records were read after completion of the rating study, and relevant details were extracted.

Additional assessments were made by raters other than those who assessed social adjustment, using such quantified rating scales as the following.

1. Psychiatric symptoms. Ratings were made by the psychiatrists using two rating scales, the Brief Psychiatric Rating Scale (BPRS) (Overall and Gorham 1962) and the Clinical Interview for Depression (Paykel et al. 1970) which was a modification of the Hamilton Rating Scale for Depression (Hamilton 1960). These ratings were made weekly during acute preliminary treatment, monthly during maintenance treatment, and at fourteen-month and twenty-month follow-up.

2. Self-reports. Patient self-reports of symptoms and mood were obtained on two instruments: the Inventory of Psychic and Somatic Complaints (IPSC) and the Mood Scales, both described

by Raskin et al. (1969). These were completed at the commencement of preliminary treatment, and subsequently at the same time as social adjustment ratings.

3. Detailed social and psychiatric histories were recorded on a precoded form at the commencement of preliminary treatment. In addition, patients completed a self-report questionnaire for neuroticism and extraversion, the Maudsley Personality Inventory (Eysenck 1959).

4. Additional information included recorded details of the quantity, type, and content of therapeutic interviews completed by the therapists on standardized rating forms (Weissman et al. 1971).

The main source of information for this study was a structured interview with the patient by a trained rater, supplemented by psychiatrists' rating assessments, psychiatrists' and social workers' clinical interviews with the patient, and direct observations of families. Since there is debate about who is an appropriate informant in such studies, these issues are discussed further in Part IV.

II.
THE ACUTE
ILLNESS

In Part II we will describe in detail the dysfunctions shown by these acutely depressed women when compared with their normal neighbors. Our first strategy was to compare patients and normals on the forty-eight individual ratings of the social adjustment scale. To give a preliminary overview, we found widespread and major differences between the groups, extending over all roles. Patients differed from normals on forty of the forty-eight items. These items extended across all roles, and included the overall evaluations of each role. In all instances the depressed patients were the most impaired. There was a general trend for normals to show only minimal impairment, with average scores indicating good adjustment, or minor maladjustment with limited difficulties. By contrast, average scores for the depressed women showed moderate to marked maladjustment with relatively persistent, pervasive, and severe difficulties. Having established these findings on the rating scale, we then turned to the case material for additional information.

The most convenient framework for examining the narrative material and comparing it with the research ratings was within each role, such as work, marital relationships, and parenthood. Therefore, we first explored the dysfunctions in a role framework. Chapter 5 describes problems in work; chapter 6 describes social activities, relationships with friends, and with extended family; chapter 7, marital and sexual relations; chapter 8, relationships with children. We then looked for ways of summarizing the patients' main disturbances, and we looked for dimensions of maladjustment extending across roles. For example, a patient may be having difficulty with her family and friends because she is unable to talk openly to them. In that case her impaired communication would be an important dimension of her adjustment that cut across her roles as mother, wife, and so on. Through the statistical technique of factor analysis we did find an alternative framework. In chapter 9 we will show that these dimensions provide another way of looking at the social dysfunctions shown by these women. In chapter 10 we will step inside one of these dimensions of special interest and examine hostility in depression.

5
Work in Depression

Satisfying work has been described as a basic human need which establishes individual identity and self-respect and lends order to human life. Work is considered crucial to the psychiatric patient's community tenure (Pasamanich et al. 1967; Angrist et al. 1968; Myers and Bean 1964; Freeman and Simons 1963) and is included in most standard psychiatric assessments. In this chapter we will examine the work performance of depressed women, either in or outside the home, and will explore the relationship between work, role conflict, and depression.

In general, a man works outside the home and usually provides the essential financial support for the family. His inability to work would certainly result in family hardships and setbacks. The concept of work in the marketplace does not apply to a housewife who is primarily a homemaker. It may not even apply to a housewife working outside the home, if she is not the family's main financial support. The work role most often assumed by married women involves work in the home. If the married woman is employed outside the home, she is usually expected to see to it that the home chores are carried out (although these expectations are currently changing). Inability to carry out household chores may not have the immediate dramatic effect on the family's status that loss of the main income would, but it can have serious impact on family harmony, force realignment of roles, and create resentment in the family members who must assume this work. The family resentment may be especially felt by outpatients whose sick status has not been legitimatized by hospitalization. Family members may misinterpret the patient's diminished performance as willfullness or laziness and may not be able to see that it is part of a symptomatic disorder.

Work has also become a controversial issue for women. Women, it is pointed out, are overwhelmed by their multiple roles and overworked, especially with regard to monotonous household tasks. Yet they are underutilized in the marketplace for jobs that are interesting and satisfying. The current conflicts and changes in woman's role have an impact on all women.

Work differs somewhat from other areas of social adjustment in that the work problems of depressives have received considerable comment, as reviewed in chapter 3. Diminished work is believed by the clinical writers to be a characteristic of the acute depressive episode. The psychoanalytic writers suggest that withdrawal from work during the height of illness is in sharp contrast to the depressives' premorbid or recovery adjustments which are described as obsessional, competitive, hard-working, conscientious, and reliable (Freud 1950; Gaylin 1968; Cohen 1954; Gibson 1958).[1] This premorbid and recovered adjustment is also said to be quite different from that of the schizophrenic who, even between episodes, may function marginally. If the depressive is indeed a good worker, this characteristic may contribute to high family expectation.

Assessments

Economic independence of the family unit was assessed for all women. To explore the work role, we divided both the patients and the normals into two groups, those who were predominantly housewives and those who were employed outside the

1. See C. J. Burns and D. R. Offord, "Achievement correlates of depressive illness," *J. Nerv. Ment. Dis.* 154: 344–51, 1972, for a discussion of occupational and educational achievement in manic-depressive illness.

home. These are by no means mutually exclusive roles, but the balance between them greatly affects the expectations in each. Each group was assessed only on the predominant role. House-wives were defined as those who did not work outside the home, or did so less than half-time. They were asked about their ability to carry out household tasks—cooking, cleaning, and so on. Women who worked outside the home were asked about their specific occupation.

Financial Problems

Since the exact income of a family, within certain limits, may not be a true measure of its economic viability, we assessed financial problems by inquiring if the family finances had been adequate in the previous two months to cope with the demands on them, or if it had become necessary to take out loans or depend on outside aid.

We found that the depressed women had significantly more financial problems than the normal women, but that neither group was having serious problems (table 5.1). On the whole, the depressed women had minor financial problems, and the normal women reported that their income was adequate for their needs. Since husbands were the main breadwinners in this study, impairment of the wives' earning capacity was seldom of major impact. Only a very few subjects were receiving public assistance. The direct costs of treatment in the last month did not contribute to economic problems, since treatment in the research clinic was free. It is possible, however, that costs of treatment received from other sources earlier may have contributed.

Housewives

Twenty-nine (73 percent) of the depressed women and twenty-four (60 percent) of the forty normals were housewives. In rating the work role of a housewife, each woman was assessed as follows: the number of days she did her work, her ability to perform certain tasks such as preparing meals, doing the housekeeping and shopping; her distress, interest, and feelings of adequacy about her work; the amount of friction she encountered

TABLE 5.1. SOCIAL ADJUSTMENT IN WORK ROLE

Role	Variables*	Depressed Patients			Normals			Significance of Difference
		N	Mean	S.D.	N	Mean	S.D.	
Housewife:	Time lost	29	2.76	1.60	24	1.17	0.48	<.001
	Impaired performance	29	2.93	1.36	24	1.17	0.48	<.001
	Friction	29	1.45	0.78	24	1.00	0.00	<.01
	Distress	29	3.21	0.90	24	1.79	0.66	<.001
	Disinterest	29	3.48	0.91	24	1.79	0.72	<.001
	Feelings of inadequacy	29	2.90	1.08	24	1.17	0.48	<.001
	Overall evaluation†	29	4.10	1.37	24	1.50	0.66	<.001
Employed Outside Home:	Time lost	11	2.27	1.35	16	1.47	0.83	NS
	Impairment	11	1.82	0.98	16	1.13	0.35	<.05
	Friction	11	1.73	0.91	16	1.27	0.46	NS
	Distress	11	3.18	0.87	16	1.27	0.46	<.001
	Disinterest	11	2.73	1.27	16	1.47	0.83	<.01
	Feelings of inadequacy	11	2.00	1.27	16	1.13	0.35	<.05
	Overall evaluation†	11	3.18	0.87	16	1.40	0.51	<.001
Economic Status:	Economic inadequacy	40	1.70	1.07	40	1.15	0.53	<.01

* Higher scores indicate greater impairment.
† Scale range 1–7. Range for remaining variables is 1–5.

with neighbors, shopkeepers, tradesmen, and other people related to her housework who were not close friends; and an overall evaluation.

Consistent and striking differences in performance of household tasks were found between depressed and normal housewives (table 5.1). The depressed women were often completely unable for days or weeks to carry out their usual household tasks; when they did carry out those tasks, the adequacy with which they were done was severely impaired. Spouse and children were often required to help out. Friction in the housewife role was assessed only with respect to such persons as milkmen, delivery boys, shopkeepers, since friction with spouse and children was assessed elsewhere. Even in this somewhat artificial context the patients reported some friction. It was completely absent for the normals. The depressed women felt considerable distress while doing their housework, were only minimally interested in what they were doing, and usually felt inadequate in their performance.

By contrast, the normal women performed their household tasks consistently and effectively, with interest and without undue friction, subjective discomfort, or feelings of inadequacy. Overall, the depressed women were rated as moderately to severely impaired, and the normals as having minor or no difficulties.

Clinical descriptions supported this picture. The housework during the acute depression was a radical departure from the usual performance. Family expectations were high, and families reacted with bewilderment and anger when mother took to bed and expressed disinterest in what needed to be done—a common occurrence during the worst days of her depression. Worry shifted to other family members, usually the spouse, who was often unaccustomed to carrying these responsibilities. The simplest chores became a burden. One woman could not decide what to prepare for meals and required her husband to make all the decisions for her.

E.P. was a 48-year-old woman and the mother of 6 children now mostly grown. She had reared the children, helped her husband in their business and took great pride in her homemaking skills, especially her cooking. When feeling well she made her own noodles and baked the bread. Now depressed, she could barely get the morning coffee and had no interest in the house. The day before her first appointment she had stayed in bed all day. Her husband came home early and did the cooking and the children did the laundry.

Patients resented husbands and children who ignored their incapacities and would not help out. Staying in bed was described by one woman as "going on strike," the only way her family would believe that she was ill and would help themselves.

Women Employed Outside the Home

The women who worked outside the home were asked similar questions about attendance, impairment, friction, distress, disinterest, and adequacy in their performance on the job. As many as eleven (27 percent) of the forty depressed women continued to attend outside jobs during the acute episode. This was noteworthy considering that most of these women were not the sole support of the family and were doing the household chores as well. Looking into the recent past, an additional seven depressed patients had given up outside jobs in association with the development of symptoms. A total, therefore, of eighteen of the forty women had been working immediately prior to illness, and eleven (61 percent) out of eighteen retained their jobs during the depressive episode. A few of the housewives who were not assessed as workers maintained minimal part-time jobs in addition to their housework. For example, one woman worked in a diner about twelve hours a week. The normals, too, often worked—sixteen (40 percent) of the forty were working at the time of assessment.[2]

The frequency with which both groups held jobs outside the home reflects an increasing trend in the United States, one especially evident in women whose children are past infancy. The depressives did not appear to deviate from the trend. Although work performance was impaired in the depressives, it was not absent. Even the women who could legitimately stay at home continued working during the acute episode, although at reduced efficiency.

The number of workers in both the depressives and the normals was small, and caution is necessary in interpreting these results. However, some interesting patterns were found. Work attendance and friction did not differ significantly for depressives and normals, although the depressives were slightly more impaired (table 5.1). In both cases there was reasonably good attendance and little overt friction. There were significant abnormalities, but not large ones, in the depressed women's impairment and feelings of adequacy at work. The depressed women were, however, substantially more distressed at work and moderately disinterested in what they were doing.

An interesting difference emerged between those depressed women who were primarily housewives and those who worked

2. There was no significant difference between depressives and normals in the number working.

outside the home. The latter appeared to be less impaired at work. We can make the comparison more directly by comparing ratings on the two groups of depressives. If this is done, in table 5.1 we find all the ratings except that for friction are lower (less impaired) in depressed workers outside the home than in housewives. This comparison can only be tentative as we cannot be sure the ratings are strictly parallel in the two groups. However, if they were not comparable, we would expect a similar trend to appear in the normals. In fact, it does not. Thus it would appear that the difference is a real one. In line with this trend, the overall evaluation of the employed depressives (3.18) was almost a full point lower than that for housewives (4.10), while for normals the two evaluations were almost identical (1.40 and 1.50).[3]

There are at least two possible and probably contributing factors for this finding. First, the ability to hold a job outside the home may be indicative of milder illness. Patients who are more severely disturbed—either in their depressive symptoms or in their social functioning—are more likely to have ceased working and hence to be nominally housewives, in terms of the criteria of this study. Although it would be surprising if this factor did not operate to some extent, its effect does not appear to have been major. Ratings of symptoms had been made by psychiatrists on the depressed patients, quite independently of the social adjustment assessments. When depressed housewives and workers were compared on degree of depression and overall severity of illness, no significant differences were found. An alternative explanation is that there is something protective in the work situation which enables function in this context to be preserved. Probably this lies in the differing quality of the two situations. In particular, housework chores cannot be readily detached from the expressive roles of housewife and mother. As we will show in later chapters, these roles were considerably impaired during the depressive episode. The woman who is in conflict with her family may be less inclined to do housework

3. Statistical comparisons between the depressed housewives and depressed employed workers indicated that the differences in effectiveness of performance, interest, and feelings of adequacy in work were significant, with housewives being more impaired. There did not appear to be any carryover of these effects to other roles during the acute episode.

for them. Thus, work outside the home is less emotionally colored by interpersonal relations, whereas the performance of housework is more readily affected by feelings about the nuclear family. We will discuss the protective aspect of work in a later section on role conflict.[4]

Work Prior to the Depressive Episode

The findings so far concern work patterns during the acute illness. In chapter 11 we will examine the patient's performance through to the recovery. However, the recovery period still shows the persisting consequences of recent illness. Therefore, retrospective information about the period prior to the depression is of interest, especially when the findings are related to the psychoanalytic hypothesis that the depression-prone character, when well, is obsessional and ambitious.

We have already presented one piece of evidence about work performance. Eleven of forty depressed women were working during the acute episode. An additional seven had stopped work because of symptoms, to make a total of eighteen working just prior to the episode (none had started work because of depression). This compares with sixteen of forty normals working at the time of interview. The difference is trivial. Thus there is no evidence that more of the depressed women were impelled by obsessionality or ambition to work in outside employment.

Taking a job is a somewhat oblique index of a tendency to hard work. What about performance in specific jobs? We had some evidence with respect to housework. Compulsiveness covers a variety of degrees. In its most gross forms, it might describe a patient who washed her hands many times a day while cooking. Such gross pathology was not apparent in these patients. More relevant in this context would be minor tendencies to obsessionality. A number of depressed women were noted to be perfectionistic house cleaners, meticulous and "house

4. See A. R. Martin, "Idle hands and giddy minds," *Amer. J. Psychoanal.,* 29: 147–56, 1969, for case descriptions of the protective effects of work in depression; or P. R. Singer, A. G. Burstein, and M. V. Robinson, "The psychotherapy of work," *Comprehensive Psychiatry* 12: 165–69, March 1971, on the therapeutic role of work.

proud." A few women appeared to value the tidiness of their house over personal comfort. Cookies were not allowed in the TV room; floors were washed frequently. However, a number of the normal women were similarly described. Both depressed and normal women had in their ranks sloppy housekeepers who hated to make beds and who let the dishes pile up unwashed.

We must be cautious in coming to firm conclusions, as our information was retrospective and standards of housekeeping are culture-laden. Nevertheless, in gross terms these depressives could not be described as having unduly compulsive premorbid adjustment, nor were they clearly inadequate. They were within the normal range. This information would not support the view that obsessionality characterizes those women who ultimately become depressed.

Role Conflict and Work

The conflict inherent in the changing role of women has recently been a subject of popular and professional concern, and no discussion of work and women would be complete without comment on it. As one advertisement has stated, "I am mother, wife, laundress, chauffeur, teacher and mistress, I am a woman. . . ." Ambiguity in roles creates dissatisfactions, raises unfulfilled expectations, and produces considerable strain on the woman's attitude towards her work at home or outside. Because our study was not designed specifically to investigate these conflicts, we will describe only the more commonly expressed ones.

Depression sometimes was associated with an aimlessness and futility characterizing the woman's dissatisfaction with her current housewife role and an inability to find alternatives that were satisfying. While these conflicts could emerge at any stage, they seemed to occur more frequently around periods of transition, particularly when the woman no longer needed to be fully occupied with the care of her children and had considerable time on her hands (Deykin et al. 1966; Briggs et al. 1965). At this point she was faced with the problem of how to make the next thirty years of her life meaningful. With decreasing family size, increasing longevity, and increased self-expectation, the time over which the married woman undertakes other roles in addition to being a mother is becoming longer.[5] It is thus likely that many more women will be faced with this problem in the future and that clinicians treating depression will see women who are having difficulty making these transitions.

As one patient put it:

Somehow housework alone and dusting things a few times seemed pointless, now that the children needed me less and were away from home so often with their friends. Days at home were dull, the weekends especially were "nothing" days—just my husband and I puttering with odd jobs.

At forty-eight years of age she felt as if there was nothing to look forward to. Her life was finished. She described with enthusiasm her job as a laboratory assistant before her marriage, but it had been so long since she had worked that she lacked confidence to return to the job.

We have already described the finding that patients working outside the home tended to show less impairment in the work role than did housewives. We have mentioned that one of the reasons may be the inability to separate housework from family relationships. In one sense, this is tantamount to saying that one of the protective functions of work outside the home is that it allowed the woman to escape the otherwise omnipresent demands of the family. Of course, work also does more than that. It provides a new set of relationships and satisfactions. Many patients explicitly sought jobs for these reasons and derived considerable benefit from them. This was particularly evident during the months after the acute illness, as recovery and restoration of function occurred. A satisfying job during this period could be therapeutic.

While working at an interesting job might contribute significantly to a woman's self-respect, a job for which she was either under- or overqualified, or one that was overwhelming, multiplied her chores and contributed to futility. The search for alter-

5. For a timely discussion of changing family patterns and transition of women's roles within and outside the family, see A. S. Rossi, "Family Development in a changing world," *Amer. J. Psychiat.* 128: 1057–66, March 1972; or "Special Section on the Women's Movement," *Amer. J. Orthopsychiat.* 41: 708–87, October 1971.

natives to housework presented a number of problems. Women with few qualifications found that the outside job did not broaden horizons but only deepened calluses. The children still required meals and the house still needed cleaning. If no assistance was offered to her at home, she eventually felt overworked and resentful. In a number of families there was acceptance of working women but not adjustment of role behavior. This phenomenon was well described by Leland Axelson, who found that many husbands supported philosophically the idea of the working wife but that this did not lessen the friction which arose as a result of her working (Axelson 1963).

O.P. was 25 years old and the mother of three children. Without a high school diploma her job opportunities were limited but she felt that she had to get out of the house. The children's noise, the chaos, and her own feelings of hopelessness led her to take a job as a waitress. After 8 hours of waiting on tables she came home to cleaning her house, preparing meals. On weekends she had to catch up with the chores left during the week. She felt even more inadequate as she got further behind and was exhausted.

While the more recent writers on the "women's movement" predict that decreased differential between the roles of men and women is inevitable, this view was not easily accepted by the families we are describing. Coming primarily from traditional backgrounds where the woman took care of her house and children, surrounded by relatives living nearby, the families had no model of the working woman. Practical questions arose, such as who should help her with the housework and whether her husband should get her entire pay check. Many of our women felt conflict about work and felt caught between the pressures of a new climate of opinion and those of a traditional upbringing.[6]

Younger women with small children who missed the stimulation of the work world and disliked being home with the

6. Several papers on educated married women point out similar conflicts between traditional upbringings and the desire for more independent recognition outside the home. See M. M. Weissman et al., "The Faculty Wife: Her Academic Interests and Qualifications," *American Association of University Professors Bulletin*, 287–92, September 1972; and Weissman et al., "The Educated Housewife: Mild Depression and the Search for Work" *American Journal of Orthopsychiatry* 43: 565–73, 1973; C. Pincus et al., "The Educated Woman in Transition," to be published, 1973.

children found that working presented not only all the psychological difficulties we have described but the additional practical ones of finding adequate child-care.

As the women were followed through recovery, their conflict in the work role was reflected in considerable shifting between the roles of worker and housewife, that is, workers gave up jobs and housewives became employed. Twenty-seven out of the forty depressed women remained in their original status as either housewives or workers during the eight months—twenty as housewives and seven as workers. An additional thirteen shifted between being full-time housewives and taking on outside jobs. We compared those who kept their original role with those who changed work roles and found significant differences in initial social adjustment. Those with changing work roles were initially the most disinterested in their work, felt the most inadequate, and were generally more impaired.

In summary, the evidence strongly shows that the depressed housewife is seriously impaired in carrying out her work at home. This impairment has an impact on the family, which has high expectations and is forced to assume, often with reluctance, the unattended chores. The story for women who work outside the home is different. Outside work is protective and is continued despite symptoms and distress. Looking at this another way, the woman who continues an outside job despite complaints of symptoms can still need treatment for depression.

6
Social Activities, Friends, and Relatives

Friendships, participation in social groups, recreation, and relationships with close relatives are normal human activities. Although the context may be heavily determined by one's background, the person who totally withdraws from such activities is considered abnormal. While depression is antithetical to a vivacious social life, we would still expect that the depressed patient, especially the outpatient, might participate in social groups and maintain contact with friends or relatives.

Friends, relatives, and recreation become more important as psychiatric treatment is undertaken in the community, since the patient outside the cloistered shelter of the hospital has many unplanned hours to occupy each day. How this time is spent may influence the course of the disorder. The patient who remains withdrawn and isolated from people, and who does not have interesting hobbies or supportive friends and relatives, may have a guarded prognosis.[1]

Social and leisure activities with friends, and relationships

1. Some behavior therapists use pleasant leisure activities as positive reinforcements to reduce depressive symptoms. See Peter M. Lewinsohn and Julian Libet, "Pleasant Events, Activity Schedule and Depressions," *J. Abnorm. Psychol.* 79: 291–95, 1972.

with extended family will be discussed together in this chapter because of certain similarities. They are predominantly expressive roles in that they concern interpersonal relationships. However, the interpersonal relationships are of a less intimate kind and are outside the immediate family group, which for most of our subjects was the marital family. Besides a theoretical similarity, there were similarities in the actual findings for these two roles when they were examined separately.

Assessment of these areas poses problems because of their variation with socioeconomic and cultural groups. Since, however, the normals were chosen because of their similarity to patients in class and culture, we could examine the impact of depression without major contamination by varying life styles.

Social Activities and Friendships

Social activities were measured by the individual's actual participation in, interest in, and enjoyment of activities, and by relations with persons other than close relatives. We assessed the number of contacts with friends, either by telephone or in person; the amount of participation in such activities as entertaining, visiting, going to movies, club or church meetings, sports events, political activities; gardening; the use of spare time for hobbies. Interpersonal relations with friends were measured by the amount of overt friction and arguments, the ability to talk openly with friends, and the degree of hypersensitivity in social situations. Lack of enjoyment of social activities was assessed by the person's discomfort in social situations, feelings of loneliness, desire for more companionship, and the amount of boredom during free time.

Two additional items concerning heterosexual dating referred only to persons who were currently unmarried. Ratings assessed, first, the actual amount of dating and, second, the subjective interest in dating regardless of the amount.

The general pattern was for the depressives to be more socially impaired than the normals (table 6.1). However, the differences were a good deal less marked than were those found for work in the previous chapter. Scores for patients on the five-point ratings tended to be in the 2's and 3's for social and leisure

TABLE 6.1 SOCIAL ADJUSTMENT IN SOCIAL AND LEISURE ACTIVITIES

Variables*	Depressed Patients			Normals			Significance of Difference
	N	Mean	S.D.	N	Mean	S.D.	
Diminished Contact with Friends	40	3.35	1.03	40	2.55	1.13	<.01
Diminished Social Interactions	40	3.35	1.35	40	2.38	1.41	<.01
Impaired Leisure Activities	40	3.45	1.11	40	2.40	1.24	<.001
Friction	39	1.49	0.79	40	1.13	0.34	<.01
Reticence	39	2.36	1.44	40	2.25	1.43	N.S.
Hypersensitive Behavior	39	2.23	1.09	40	1.50	0.82	<.01
Social Discomfort	39	2.44	0.97	40	1.38	0.54	<.001
Loneliness	40	1.93	1.19	40	1.40	0.55	<.05
Boredom	40	2.68	1.25	40	1.48	0.72	<.001
Diminished Dating (Unmarried Subjects)	7	2.29	1.89	5	3.80	1.30	N.S.
Disinterest in Dating (Unmarried Subjects)	7	2.89	1.45	5	2.40	1.52	N.S.
Overall Evaluation†	40	4.10	1.15	40	2.41	1.04	<.001

* Higher Scores indicate greater impairment.
† Scale range is 1–7. Range for remaining variables is 1–5.

activities, much as they had been for work. However, several scores for normals were also above 2, indicating minor to moderate maladjustment. This pattern for the normals was quite different from the one they showed at work, in which they tended to show little, if any, impairment. Patient-normal differences were less marked here because the normals also departed from ideal adjustment, which was regarded as including very active involvement with the outside community.

Depressives showed a pattern of limited outside involvements, subjective dissatisfaction and discomfort, with friction in those relationships which occurred. They tended to be in contact with one or two friends during a two-month period. They went out socially once or twice a month and had few or sporadic spare-time interests. Relations with friends which did occur were impaired. The depressives reported friction which was relatively mild but was associated with hypersensitivity and anger, and might take hours or even days to overcome. They were frequently distressed, ill at ease, and tense in the company of friends, yet felt lonely, isolated, and bored in their leisure time.

The normal women were also limited in their contacts with friends, reporting contacts with about four friends within the two-month period, few social interactions (going out about once every two weeks) and few spare-time activities. They had leisure interests but spent little time at them. Although the normals' social participation was mildly impaired, it was less so than that of the depressed women. The normal women had little friction with their friends, were rarely hypersensitive, usually enjoyed social company, felt no discomfort with their friends, and did not feel lonely or bored. They were, however, reticent in discussing their feelings; patterns for normal and depressed women were closely similar in this respect.

Few subjects in either group were unmarried, so that assessments regarding dating were too few to establish any trends.[2] The two groups did not show any prominent differences.

Narrative data confirmed the trends found by the ratings, without suggesting any major additions. The depressed women were not participating gregariously in social life, but neither were they totally isolated and reclusive. Participation, though limited, was present and characterized by discomfort, uneasiness, and sensitivity in social situations and with friends. These discomforts might not be apparent to the casual observer, yet they were a considerable problem to the patient. The depression appeared to interfere in the patient's ability to involve herself fully in activities, so that recreation did not divert her from her discomfort.

For the normals the pattern was one of relatively limited social participation also but without the friction, discomfort, or dissatisfaction found in the depressives. Active and frequent participation outside the home, many friendships, wide interests and hobbies were not aspired to by these women. These trends appeared to be lifelong and part of the accepted pattern of the culture in which our women lived.

---

2. Several of the older subjects were not asked the questions on dating.

The Extended Family

It is commonly accepted that the mental health of individuals cannot readily be dissociated from their relationships with their families. At the very best, the family can be the source of a strength that mitigates the effects of the illness. The family can also be a strain, and, at worst, a prime cause of the patient's disturbance.

The family is a complex concept. Most of us have two families. The first is the family of origin, which includes our parents and in which we and our siblings are the children. The second is the marital family in which we are the parents and have a spouse and children. For the married adult the family of origin becomes the extended family, with parents, siblings, and other more distant relatives. Thus with marriage, or prior attainment of adulthood, there is a change in the immediate interpersonal milieu of the patient. Although the family of origin is the important family for the young, for married persons the spouse and children are usually more important. Family studies suggest that the understanding of functional disturbances cannot afford to stop at the boundaries of the marital family, since the extended family also can form part of the pathological drama (Spiegel and Bell 1959; Bell 1962; Bell and Vogel 1960; Ackerman 1958; Lidz 1963; Post 1962).[3] There is increasing evidence that a high incidence of social problems such as alcoholism and gambling, together with a variety of emotional problems, can be expected in the blood relatives of patients with some forms of affective disorder (Winokur 1970; Gershon et al. 1971; Post 1962). Whether the mechanism is by genetic inheritance or social interaction, family relationships are important.

Several purposes might be served by evaluating the relationship between the acutely depressed patient and the extended family. We might learn to what extent the family is a resource during the course of treatment, to what extent the patient needs

---

3. A large literature, discussed from a variety of vantages, exists on the psychological role of extended families in psychiatric disturbances. For a review see J. Spiegel and N. Bell, "The Family of the Psychiatric Patient," in *American Handbook of Psychiatry*, vol. 1, ed. S. Arieti (Basic Books, New York, 1959), pp. 114–50.

to be protected from the family's injurious interventions, and lastly, how much the individual family members themselves might be vulnerable to breakdown. However, we did not gather systematic data on family history of illness and cannot discuss this last issue.

The limits of the extended family for this study included all close relatives who were not part of the marital family; that is, parents, in-laws, aunts and uncles, siblings. Adult children who were living away from home were also regarded as extended family. Although the inclusion of these children here might be open to debate, we felt that relations between adult patients and children living away from home more closely resembled relations with other adult extended family than with younger children, for whom the patient has active responsibilities for nurture and supervision and with whom she is in intimate, day-to-day relations in the household.

In assessing the extended family role we were mainly interested in the quality of relationships: how well the person was getting along with the various members; her ability to discuss her problems with them; her withdrawal from them or her undue dependence on them for advice, money, or help; the presence of rebelliousness or defiance towards them; her feelings of guilt, resentment, and undue worry about them.

Although the depressives tended to have relations that were more impaired than those of the normals, here, too, as with social activities, the differences were not striking, and were only significant for five of the nine variables (table 6.2). However, the pattern was different from that of social and leisure activities. In social activities some impairment relative to the ideal was found in both groups. With the extended family, neither the depressed nor normal women were very impaired. Relationships in this area were not greatly affected by depression.

For both patients and normals extended family relationships were moderately harmonious, and dependency for assistance and advice in times of need was relatively low. Neither group of women behaved rebelliously toward or worried unreasonably about their extended families. There was one especially notable absence of impairment. The depressives were not unduly dependent on their extended families. Dependency is one abnor-

TABLE 6.2. SOCIAL ADJUSTMENT WITH THE EXTENDED FAMILY

Variables*	Depressed Patients			Normals			Significance of Difference
	N	Mean	S.D.	N	Mean	S.D.	
Friction	35	1.63	0.97	39	1.33	0.53	N.S.
Reticence	39	3.46	1.47	40	2.68	1.27	.05
Withdrawal	37	1.73	0.96	40	1.13	0.34	.001
Dependency	38	1.61	0.79	40	1.45	0.71	N.S.
Rebellion	38	1.16	0.50	40	1.03	0.16	N.S.
Guilt	39	1.56	0.79	40	1.18	0.39	.05
Worry	39	1.51	0.82	40	1.65	0.74	N.S.
Resentment	39	2.23	1.31	40	1.38	0.63	.001
Overall Evaluation†	39	3.41	1.19	39	2.23	0.78	.001

* Higher Scores indicate greater impairment.
† Scale range is 1–7. Range for remaining variables is 1–5.

mality frequently ascribed to depressives (see chap. 3), but it was not apparent in relationships with extended family.

The depressed women's relations with their families were not characterized by overt conflict but by marked disengagement and withdrawal. One facet of this withdrawal was in communication, which was diminished and characterized by reticence. In spite of this withdrawal, the depressed woman was resentful towards her extended family and guilty.

Following the birth of her third child, Mrs. D. became insecure about her ability to manage the children. She felt her relations watched her with disapproval. Her sensitivity to their criticism, real or imagined, became grossly exaggerated as she became more depressed, and she resented their interference. She began to avoid seeing them and made excuses to avoid spending Sunday dinner with them. Her disengagement was perplexing to them as she never discussed what was troubling her, and on the surface remained friendly.

It should be noted that the normal women were also somewhat reticent with their extended families and communicated with them in a relatively distant and restricted way, although not as markedly as the patients.

As might be expected, acute depression dampened the spirit for social encounters. Surprisingly, however, its effect on extended family relationships was limited. Close relatives were not ideal comforts to the patients, as relations with them were disengaged and somewhat withdrawn. On the other hand, the extended family relations were not particularly disharmonious and did not seem to contribute to overt conflicts. While there were exceptions, these findings do not support the notion that blanket involvement of the extended family in the patient's treatment is of critical importance. A look at the more intimate family—husbands and children—in the next chapters will show a different situation.

Normality and Cultural Groups

Since social participation and relationship with relatives, perhaps more than any other areas, may depend on how and where one was reared, a word is in order about the social and ethnic backgrounds of the subjects, both patients and normals.[4] It is likely that background rather than psychopathology accounts for the relatively low level of social interaction among the normal women and contributes to the patterns of interactions with families.

The majority of our subjects were working class, Roman Catholic, and Italian. These women, coming from the predominant group in New Haven, overlapped in ethnic background and social class with the "urban villagers" of Gans (1962) or the blue-collar workers of Kimarovsky (1957). They did not share the values of college-educated, middle-class women, which include active participation outside the family in charitable and political activities, or in developing intellectual interests and hobbies. Other than to visit their families, they did not often go out socially, nor did they wish to. Here, as in their attitude to work, they were primarily oriented to families. They assimilated comfortably the values derived from an older generation, in a different way than might be found in their college-educated equivalents in the same community.

4. See Jerome K. Myers and Bertram H. Roberts, *Family and Class Dynamics in Mental Illness* (Wiley, New York, 1959), pp. 172–98; or Jerome Myers and Lee L. Bean, *A Decade Later: A Follow-up of Social Class and Mental Illness* (Wiley, New York, 1968), pp. 175–97, for a discussion of the limited social participation of certain social classes. Myers's studies are of particular relevance since his subjects were derived from the same community as ours. There is undoubtedly an overlap in ethnic background between the subjects in these two studies.

Their family activities were, however, close knit, to a degree not entirely reflected in our assessments. There were ties to parents and in-laws. These relatives often lived nearby and maintained continuing involvement in their grown child's family. Contact with the extended family was frequent, but our findings show that in fact much of it was superficial. They often met daily over coffee, and shared practical problems but were reticent in discussing deeper feelings. Contrary to some views of normality, limited social contacts and active involvement with extended family in the normals did not detract from satisfactions in their marriage, or harmony in the mother-child relations, nor did these women experience divided loyalties between their nuclear and extended families, as would be expected in middle-class families.

Given this family pattern, mental health professionals working with these groups should weigh the consequences of any therapeutic attempt to encourage more community participation or distance from the extended family. Participation in such middle-class modes of social behavior is at variance with the norms of the individual's referent group, and the treatment may be experienced by the individual and family as disruptive rather than helpful. This same pattern may not be evident among younger persons or among socially mobile individuals for whom independence from their extended family, geographical mobility, new social values, and assertiveness in relations to parents may become desired. The discrepancies between the values of depressed persons of working- or lower middle-class background and the values of younger middle-class professionals may be a source of misunderstanding.

7
Marital and Sexual Relations

In this chapter we will describe one of the most central areas of social functioning—marriage and sexual relations. In recent years the importance of the marriage in the genesis of psychiatric disorder on the one hand and as a focus for its consequences of the disorder on the other has been widely discussed (Anthony 1970; Lidz 1957, 1966; Sampson 1964). A good deal of literature has described the disturbed marital interactions of neurotic patients in general (Eisenstein 1956; Kreitman 1969, 1970; Nelson 1970). Only sparse information is available on the specific characteristics of marital relationships in depressed patients. In regard to sexual relations, diminished sexual potency and impotence are well-documented phenomena in depressed males; sexual dysfunction in depressed women has been less adequately studied.

Assessments

The role of spouse includes both instrumental activities such as care of the home and the expressive aspects of the wife's relationship with her husband. The instrumental portion of the housewife role has already been evaluated in the work role (chap. 5). Our discussion of marital adjustment, therefore, predominantly concerns the interpersonal relationship. Within this relationship we assessed sexual adjustment separately from other aspects of marital relations as the two do not necessarily parallel each other.

Three ratings concerned sexual adjustment. Under the rating of diminished sexual intercourse we assessed actual frequency of intercourse; under sexual problems, impaired qualities of the sexual relationship including absence of orgasm and dyspareunia (pain on intercourse). Under disinterest in sex we were concerned with a subjective state—the amount of interest felt in sexual intercourse regardless of its frequency. These ratings were made only for married subjects. The heterosexual adjustment of single subjects was assessed by the ratings on dating and interest in the opposite sex described in the last chapter, since the norms and expectations regarding sexual intercourse for the single are less clearly defined and more variable than for the married.

Eight other items concerned the marital relationship. Five of these concerned actual behavior rather than subjective feelings in the marriage. "Friction," as in other roles, rated frequency of overt arguments. "Reticence" rated communication and the degree to which it was free and open. "Domineering behavior" rated decision-making in the home and the degree to which it was controlled by the wife; "submissiveness" was the opposite pole of the same dimension. "Dependency" concerned emotional and physical (but not financial) dependency on the husband.

Three specific items involved subjective feelings—the amount of affection, guilt, and resentment felt towards the husband. At the end of the assessment of marital and sexual adjustment an overall evaluation of the marital relationship was made by the interviewer.

In addition to these ratings, the narrative histories, including psychotherapy records, contained a wealth of material concerning the marriages. Taken together the material indicated dysfunctions that were more specific than the rather diffuse and limited maladjustments found in social and leisure activities and relationships with extended family (chap. 6).

Comparisons with Normals

Findings for depressed women and normals are shown in table 7.1. The majority in both groups were married—twenty-eight (70 percent) of the forty patients, thirty-four (85 percent) of the forty normals. As already shown in chapter 4, this difference in marital status was not significant. Of the remaining subjects, not dealt with in this chapter, nine depressives and three normals had previously been married and were widowed, divorced, or separated. Thus, only three depressives and three normals had never married. This is a very different situation to that found for schizophrenics who, because of the effects of the illness, with its younger age of onset and the preexisting schizoid personality, commonly have never married (Angrist 1968; Stevens 1969; Turner 1970).

The depressed women showed widespread impairments involving almost every aspect of their marital and sexual relationship, and highly significant differences were found between the depressed and normal women. Depressed women were more reticent in discussing their personal feelings and problems with their spouses, more submissive and dependent, felt less affection towards spouses, more guilt and resentment, and experienced more friction and arguments with spouses. In sexual relations, the depressed women had a slightly lower frequency of intercourse than normals, considerably more problems during intercourse, and very little interest in sexual relations. In contrast, the normal women reported smooth, open, independent, assertive, and affectionate relations with their spouses, few sexual problems, and an interest in sexual relations.

The normals were rated near the unimpaired end of the scale, while the depressed patients were moderately impaired. There was only one exception to this general pattern. On a rating of "domineering behavior" the married patients were not significantly different from normals and there was a trend, although not significant, for them to show even less domineering behavior than the normals.

These impairments, which will be described in detail, fell into five broad areas: problems with interpersonal communication,

TABLE 7.1 SOCIAL ADJUSTMENT IN MARITAL ROLE

Marital Area Assessed	Variables*	Depressed Patients N = 28		Normals N = 34		Significance of Difference
		Mean	S.D.	Mean	S.D.	
Communication	Reticence	2.74	1.26	1.77	0.92	<.001
Submissiveness and Dependency	Domineering behavior	1.30	0.61	1.44	0.89	NS
	Submissiveness	2.33	1.24	1.65	0.77	<.01
	Dependency	2.48	0.98	1.94	0.78	<.05
Sexual Relations	Diminished sexual intercourse	3.00	1.21	2.32	1.30	<.05
	Sexual problems	1.83	0.92	1.27	0.52	<.01
	Disinterest in sex	2.65	0.80	1.56	0.75	<.001
Feelings towards Spouse	Lack of affection	2.30	1.14	1.65	0.69	<.01
	Guilt	2.90	1.21	1.35	0.54	<.001
	Resentment	1.83	1.00	1.38	0.55	<.05
Interpersonal Friction	Friction	2.30	1.10	1.77	0.61	<.05
Overall Evaluation†		3.70	1.17	2.52	0.83	<.001

* Higher scores indicate greater impairment.
† Scale range is 1–7. Range for remaining variables is 1–5.

submissiveness and dependency, feelings toward spouse, overt interpersonal friction, and sexual relations.

Communication

The normals usually described full and easy communication, reporting that they and their spouses could discuss most things openly and with humor. They exhibited pride in the level of understanding between themselves and their husbands and were not embarrassed by discussing personal feelings in the interview. The depressed women, by contrast, had moderate disability in communication with their spouses. They rarely discussed problems with their spouses even when depressed. Moreover, for most of the depressed women during the interview itself, discussion of personal matters such as sexual relationships was embarrassing.

The blocked communication seen in depression contributed heavily to a steadily increasing level of tension in the home. If the husband reacted to the tense atmosphere, the depressed patient's response was usually tears, further withdrawal, and little relief from the tension. Her comments, when she did attempt to communicate, were typically short-phrased, abrupt remarks that served more to cloud than to clarify the situation.

L.Z. was a 42-year-old, attractive woman married almost twenty years. Her husband had characteristically attempted to fight off his own depression through the use of alcohol, and over the years had withdrawn more and more into himself. Although their sexual adjustment had never been fully satisfactory, they continued regular relations up until three years before the interview, when relations ceased entirely. The patient never discussed her feelings of rejection and assumed her husband must be having an affair. She retaliated by becoming involved with another man, which made her feel guilty. During the course of her treatment, as she recovered, she began to discuss with her husband her feelings of rejection and learned that his impotence was probably due to drinking. He had not been involved with other women, but had been unable to discuss his problem with his wife.

In some marriages the patient's symptoms unwittingly became a form of control; in the next case the husband feared upsetting his wife, as she might break into tears or make a suicide attempt.

P.N. was a 38-year-old married woman with two children. She had a history of previous depressive episodes and always considered herself anxious and shy. This presentation of herself allowed her considerable latitude with her family, who comforted and protected her. She became depressed when her husband planned a family vacation, long desired by him; as she began to prepare for it, she voiced feelings of guilt and inadequacy at not being up to the task. She could not verbalize what concerned her specifically about the vacation. The family was afraid to leave her alone and her teenage son would miss social activities or her husband would come home from work early to stay with her. The vacation was not taken and they were unwilling to bring up the subject for fear of producing an exacerbation of symptoms. Her husband, who was very disappointed about not taking the vacation, felt somewhat resentful but did not say so directly.

Submissiveness and Dependency

There was no significant difference between patients and normals in regard to domineering behavior. Neither group was domineering. The rating for "submissiveness" examined the opposite pole of the behavior. The normals were generally not submissive. They described a candid relationship with their husbands in which they would defend an opinion that differed from the husbands', giving in quietly only on minor issues.

The depressed women were submissive and unable to assert themselves. They consistently reported an inability to say "no," a phenomenon discussed by Horney (1937), which sometimes appeared to be a lifelong pattern.

B.L. was a 42-year-old housewife with four children. She took a temporary part-time job with her husband's encouragement to help supplement his low earnings, as the children needed clothes for the new school year. Her husband then stayed out of work in direct proportion to the amount of money the patient earned, so that her efforts to improve their financial state were futile. However, she gave her husband whatever money he requested. Although she felt he was unreasonable and was furious at him, she never overtly complained. As she became increasingly depressed, she gave up her job and, finally, her household responsibilities, and stayed in bed.

Interviewers also assessed dependency in the respondent. This variable was defined to include the degree to which the depressed woman depended on her husband for emotional support and to assume household tasks which she was unable to perform, such as feeding the children, doing the laundry, deciding on family activities.

While the normals were reasonably independent, the depressed patients were moderately dependent on their husbands, not only in making simple decisions but in caring for the children and arranging daily activities. When confronted with a task, the depressed patient often felt impelled to seek help before attempting to undertake it herself. This dependency took on a demanding quality which was often a source of irritation and confusion to the husband, who fluctuated between being overprotective and doubting her need for help.

B.P., a 34-year-old housewife, called her husband daily at work for reassurance, talking about her depressed feelings, her inadequacies, and her inability to carry out household chores. Most of the time he tried to reassure her of her competence, but also would take over the responsibilities she rejected. Sometimes he would become quite irritated and demand that she "grow up" and act her age.

During the illness, the depressed woman was especially dependent on her husband with regard to the children. If she had small children she often required considerable help with their physical care. Teenage children sometimes exploited their mother's helplessness by becoming aggressive and rebellious. If the husband adopted an active role with the children, this could help to reduce the disorganization. In a few cases the husband and teenage children formed an alliance against the mother. The consequent deviant behavior of the teenagers increased and was disastrous to the entire family.

Feelings towards Spouse

The subjects' feelings towards their spouses were rated with respect to affection, guilt, and resentment. Normals reported consistent feelings of affection for their spouses, few misgivings about their own adequacy as wives, and little or no resentment towards the spouses. The depressed women were moderately ambivalent in their feelings of affection, felt considerable guilt and a sense of failure in their marriages, and were moderately resentful towards their spouses. The depressed woman often viewed with disappointment the failure of the husband to measure up to her expectations of what comprised "a good husband."

A.S. was a 28-year-old mother of three small children, married nine years. Her husband, a minor executive, was described as dependable, hard-working, and considerate. The marriage had been stable and mutually satisfying. Six months after the birth of her third child she became depressed. She was anergic, feared being alone, worried about dying, and became quite dependent on her husband, demanding much of his time and attention to combat her fears. At the height of her illness, it was necessary for him to assume all the child care.

She had lost all sexual interest, a contrast to their usual good sexual relationship, and felt that she no longer loved her husband. She was extremely guilty about her emotional rejection of him, especially as she saw him trying to comfort her and working overtime to manage the children and his work. She felt guilty about disappointing him, not only as a sexual partner, but as the household manager. At the same time, she resented that he had assumed so much of her responsibilities, saw him as intruding upon her household domain, and preferred not to have him near her.

Interpersonal Friction

The depressed patients reported frequent tension and overt friction, which ranged from nagging, sarcasm, and arguments to physical violence, in contrast to the normals' relatively smooth marital relationships.

M.E. was a 52-year-old woman, married for twenty years. There was a history of extramarital relationships in both partners. The two oldest children were continually baiting and manipulating their parents into tense situations. They were either the catalyst or subject of almost every argument. Mrs. E. described her relationship with her husband as characterized by manipulation, "needling," and provocation that on several occasions erupted into physical violence. As her depression lifted, she and her husband actually began discussing real differences between themselves on various issues, instead of the usual insinuations and sarcasm. "After twenty years of holding things inside, I am finally able now to let others know what I feel," she said.

In general, the marital relation was a significant barometer of clinical status. Increased friction in the marriage frequently signaled a clinical relapse. We saw a few dramatic suicide attempts in the context of an acute marital disruption.

L.W. was a 25-year-old mother of three small children. She blamed her depression on her husband's poor treatment of her, especially his lack of support in disciplining the children. Her husband and his cousin, whom she deeply resented, were visiting together one evening. She felt her husband was indifferent to her frustrations with the children that evening, and she had to do something to get his attention. When the two men decided to go to a movie together, she was enraged. She grabbed a bottle of pills and stuffed them all in her mouth.

The maladjustment of the depressed woman in other areas also impinged upon the marriage. The diminished gratifications with friends, in work, or leisure put more pressure on the marriage and more demands on the spouse for comfort. While some spouses were able to respond to their wives' increased needs and became quite paternal and supportive, many spouses resented the demands. Even the most tolerant spouse eventually reached his limit and reacted against the increased demands.

Sexual Relations

Although the patients were sexually more impaired than the normals, the findings hinted at an interesting distinction in the pattern of impairment. As shown in table 7.1, the most striking difference between patients and normals was with respect to the patients' feelings about sex rather than actual behavior; patients reported marked disinterest in sex, but differences between patients and normals in the actual frequency of sexual intercourse were less striking.

The depressed women did continue sexual relations, although at a diminished frequency. The normals had sexual relations with their spouses about once a week and the depressed patients about once every two weeks. There was, however, a considerable difference in the quality of the sexual relations. The normals reported few sexual problems, found sex enjoyable, and often initiated intercourse. The depressed women had difficulty achieving orgasm, reported dyspareunia, and rarely, if ever, initiated sexual relations.

Emerging from the ratings and case material is a pattern of a woman with a considerable distaste for sexual intercourse that she is unable to communicate to her husband. Partly as a result of feelings of guilt, she apparently continues to comply with her husband's initiation of intercourse, but with little enjoyment and usually without ability to achieve orgasm.

L.O. was an extreme example of this pattern. A 26-year-old woman, married for 4 years, she had had no sexual education or preparation for marriage or childbirth and had selected her husband because of availability rather than feelings of affection or respect. While depressed, intercourse was repulsive to the point of nausea. She submitted because this was her duty, and had relations with comparative regularity. She found the experience repugnant and never achieved orgasm.

The pattern of submission and resentment which characterized the general marital relations of the depressed women was particularly evident in sexual relations. Sexual relations were maintained during the acute depression, although with a frequency diminished to about half that of normals. As was found in the depressed woman's other activities, there was a discrepancy between feelings and behavior. Although she continued to have sexual relations, her feelings of interest and enjoyment were markedly impaired. The continuation of sexual relations in an effort to please her husband did not contribute to marital intimacy. She usually felt more resentment towards her spouse after relations since he did not understand how she was feeling. This estrangement would be quite marked if an orgasm had been feigned.

The depressed woman's reticence made it impossible for her to discuss sexual matters directly because of her embarrassment. A sophisticated, emancipated facade sometimes belied a rather naive understanding of sexual matters and inhibition in discussing them. This, together with the fact that the most obvious indicator—frequency of intercourse—does not fully reflect dysfunction, means that a good deal of sensitive interviewing may be required to fully ascertain sexual adjustment in the ordinary clinical treatment situation.

S.T. was a 29-year-old wife of a lawyer and mother of three small children, born in rapid succession and all unplanned. She was intelligent, highly articulate, involved in a number of civic organizations. In recent times she had become interested in the women's liberation movement. Despite her apparent sophistication, her verbal facility, and her protests about women being sex objects, she was sexually very inhibited. She was too embarrassed to request contraceptive advice from her doctor and, as she was fearful of becoming pregnant, she refused sexual relationships. She could not discuss sexual matters with her husband, either, and this contributed to further disinterest in him.

Guilt and Adultery

Guilt is an almost universal concomitant of depression and has an important role in the patient's marriage and attitude toward sex. Many women dwelled on their past or current misdeeds, which were magnified out of proportion and had little reality in fact. In this context there were a significant number of women who related their illness to previous sexual misconduct and saw the illness as reasonable punishment for their sins. No amount of persuasion could convince them of the unreasonableness of their assumption. If one did not listen closely to the context of the presumed sexual misconduct, one could be persuaded that the guilt had some justification. It was useful to encourage the patient to discuss the sexual involvement without actively accepting it as a basis for guilt. Often with these discussions the guilt of the affair diminished and the patient could begin to consider more central issues. Some of the problems our patients raised as serious sexual misconducts and felt extremely guilty about included: masturbation when unable to achieve sexual gratification in the marriage, sexual fantasies towards a respected priest, verbal but not physical relations with the man next door.

Several women did become depressed after the breakup and disclosure of an extramarital affair. It was rare that affairs began in the context of a mutually satisfying marriage; they had to be viewed in terms of the ongoing marital relationship. Often the disclosure of an affair did not come as a surprise, as the marital relationship had been deteriorating for some time. However, overt recognition emphasized the woman's feelings of inadequacy as a sexual partner. Along with depressive feelings, overt expressions of rage and resentment aimed directly at the spouse, as well as the other woman, were common features.

One woman alternated between depressive feelings and explosive rages when she learned about her husband's affair. Apparently, he left the home each day at 7:00 A.M. but, unknown to his wife, did not have to report to work until 11:00 A.M. He visited his mistress every day between those early hours. When he broke off the affair and "confessed," his wife became depressed and her symptoms included early morning awakening. Thinking about what her husband had been doing, she would get up every morning at seven o'clock and engage in tirades against him until it was time for him to leave for work. She was at a loss to control this behavior and it was driving her husband further away from her.

Premorbid Marital Adjustment

While marital and sexual relations were usually impaired during the depressive episode, not all the depressed women had poor marriages prior to their illnesses. We found a number of marriages where free and easy communications, mutual sensitivity to each other's needs, and satisfying sexual relations had existed prior to the depression. The illness put considerable strain on the relationship, but the husband continued to be supportive, although somewhat distressed by his wife's withdrawal.

Assessments of premorbid marital adjustment were made from knowledge of patients and case material by the treating psychiatrists during the initial interview and by the research interviewer at the end of the study. The two judgments were independent but showed almost complete concordance. Using these assessments, the twenty-eight depressed patients were divided into two groups. Thirteen were judged to have stable, adaptive, mutually supportive marriages prior to the depressive illness (adaptive marriages), and fourteen women were judged to have at least moderately unstable, maladaptive premorbid marital adjustment (maladaptive marriages). Rating of premorbid adjustment was not available on one patient. The marital adjustment of the two groups was compared. Since the N's were low, the 10 percent level of significance was accepted. There were significant differences on four of the eleven variables between depressed patients with adaptive premorbid marital adjustments and those with maladaptive premorbid marital adjustment (table 7.2).

As expected, an adaptive premorbid marriage tended to be associated with reduced marital strains during the illness. Those

TABLE 7.2. SOCIAL ADJUSTMENT SCORES IN MARITAL ROLE.
COMPARISON BETWEEN THOSE DEPRESSED PATIENTS WITH
ADAPTIVE OR MALADAPTIVE PREMORBID MARITAL ADJUSTMENT

Variable	Adaptive N = 13		Maladaptive* N = 14		Significance of Difference
	Mean†	S.D.	Mean	S.D.	
Reticence	1.08	0.28	1.50	0.76	<.10
Domineering Behavior	2.85	1.07	2.14	0.77	<.10
Submissiveness	1.77	0.83	2.79	1.19	<.05
Dependency	2.62	1.26	2.07	1.21	NS
Diminished Sexual Intercourse	1.75	0.75	1.92	1.08	NS
Sexual Problems	2.62	0.87	2.69	0.75	NS
Disinterest in Sex	2.75	1.06	2.53	0.99	NS
Lack of Affection	3.15	1.14	2.86	1.29	NS
Guilt	2.69	1.25	2.44	0.81	NS
Resentment	1.46	0.52	1.88	1.15	NS
Friction	2.31	1.03	3.14	1.35	<.10

† The scale range is 1–5 for all variables. Higher scores indicate greater impairment.
* One patient was excluded as her premorbid marital adjustment had not been rated. Therefore, total N = 27.

patients with adaptive premorbid marriages tended to be less reticent, more domineering, less submissive, and to have less marital friction when depressed than those patients with a maladaptive premorbid marriage. These findings suggest that those patients with adaptive premorbid marriages, when depressed, show less of the disturbance found to characterize the marital relationship of the depressed woman. There was still a good deal of impairment. Regardless of her premorbid marital adjustment, the depressed woman experienced sexual problems, felt dissatisfaction, guilt, and resentment towards her spouse.

The depressed woman with an adaptive premorbid marital adjustment usually described a mutually supportive relationship with her spouse, including an interest and enjoyment of sexual relationships prior to the onset of her depression. She saw the illness as being caused by problems which arose outside the marriage. When depressed, she withdrew emotionally and sexually in an attempt to protect her husband from her thoughts and "bad" feelings. This protection only increased isolation from him and made him feel rejected by her.

B.R. was a 39-year-old woman. She and her husband had a strong relationship in which feelings and problems were discussed openly. They had a mutually satisfying sexual relationship throughout the 17 years of their marriage. Within the two years prior to the onset of depression, her husband's business began to fail, making it necessary for her to work outside the home full time. At the same time, B.R. was troubled by the reactivation of an orthopedic problem. She did not want to add to her husband's worries and, in order to protect him, began to hold in her concerns rather than discuss them with him. As she grew increasingly depressed, she became unable to tolerate physical contact, and withdrew. She could not understand her own feelings as she had previously found comfort in their relationship. She was frightened and felt that her withdrawal would protect her already overburdened husband. Her husband, however, interpreted her withdrawal as rejection of him.

In those patients with a chronically poor marriage prior to the illness, the marriage became an arena for the depressive symptoms. Whereas the women with adaptive marriages saw the illness arising outside the marriage, those with maladaptive marriages saw the marital relationship as the prime cause of the illness. During the illness in the maladaptive marriage, the patient's clinical status was often directly related to the degree of marital disharmony. It was difficult to determine cause and effect in marital interactions. Some patients provoked friction when they were feeling poorly, while others seemed clearly to be reacting to provocation by symptoms. Depressive symptoms were used at times to exploit the spouses' feelings of guilt and responsibility. Most patients with poor marriages prior to the illness had a history of poor sexual relations.

R.T. was a 40-year-old married woman who, prior to her illness, had a history of marital problems. The patient saw her husband as having contributed to causing her illness because of his frequent job changes and his attachment to his mother. The patient's concept of marriage included the belief that, if she could keep her husband satisfied sexually, all other things would take care of themselves. She also believed that, if her husband loved her, he intuitively would know her needs. She saw no reason to tell him how she felt because she thought he should know what things displeased her. Instead, she communicated her attitudes by giving or withholding sex or by brooding, crying, or withdrawing. While her husband might initially respond to her martyred affect, he eventually resented it and burst into rage.

Autonomy and Intimacy in the Marriage of Depressives

Marriage makes strong demands for commitment to an adult identity which includes an ability to achieve autonomy and to share emotional and sexual intimacy. The depressed woman showed striking deficiencies in her autonomy and capacity for intimacy even though she maintained some outward performance of marital tasks. Her deficiencies were acts of omission rather than commission and resulted in increased tension with her husband. Her impaired ability to communicate made shared emotional intimacy with her husband difficult. She was withdrawn and reticent, unable to discuss her feelings or make her needs known or understood, though her expression clearly indicated that she was suffering and was ungratified. This impaired communication resulted in misinterpretation and increased tensions. Problems not expressed were not resolved, and therefore built up.

Other investigators have discussed impaired communication of the depressive, and have described it as resistance and manipulation to obtain wishes (Stuart 1967; Bonime 1962, 1965; Becker 1962) and a major target symptom to be dealt with in therapy (Spiegel 1960; Cohen 1954). Our findings also suggest that, whatever its origins, impaired communication was a pervasive problem for the depressed woman. The effect of this impaired communication was particularly disastrous in the marital relationship where unspoken diffuse misery was conveyed to the spouse with the implication that it was either caused by or should be alleviated by the spouse.

The depressed woman's lack of autonomy in the marital relationship was characterized by submissiveness and dependency. Not only did she depend on her spouse for the physical accomplishment of her usual household tasks, but she required his assistance in making minor decisions. She was indecisive and ambivalent to the point that simple daily household routine was hampered. Her marked need for approval and reassurance from her husband resulted in her inability to assert herself directly on even minor issues.

Her continued sexual relations in the face of disinterest and unresponsiveness exemplified the level of her submissiveness.

Despite only slightly diminished sexual relations, she had considerable physical problems in such relationships including pain and an inability to achieve orgasm. She continued relations rather than being assertive enough to say "no." At the same time this continuation did not contribute to marital intimacy but built up her resentment towards her husband.

The stereotyped social performance of the depressive and the difficulty in intimate and empathetic relations have also been described (Cohen 1954; Gibson 1958). The depressed woman's sexual performance is consistent with this view. While her sexual participation might continue, it did not represent an intimate and involved exchange with her husband but furthered her estrangement and resentment.

Implications for Treatment

Our findings highlight the impact of a depressive illness on the marital relationship. In many instances the involvement of the spouse in the treatment of his depressed wife is important. The degree and direction of the involvement depends on the degree of pathology in the relationship, the premorbid marital adjustment, and the direction of the depressed woman's symptoms. In those women with adaptive premorbid marital adjustment, treatment might gear itself to educating the spouse about the illness. In this way the depressed woman does not feel the need to hide her symptoms from her husband and can continue to gain support from him. Reassurance and support, practical advice, community resources to help with the children may also be helpful to the spouse and patient with an adaptive premorbid adjustment, so that the spouse can cope with the extra load.

In those patients with a maladaptive premorbid marriage, especially where the depressed woman views her illness as caused by her spouse, intensive family and individual therapy may be indicated. Overall, these findings point to marriage as an important focus of depressive disturbance.

8
Parenthood

A mother with a psychiatric disorder has a certain urgent appeal when one considers the short-term effects on her children or the long-term ones in the development of pathological or deviant behavior. In this chapter we will explore the interaction between depressed women and their children.

Background of the Study

Beginning with the classic studies of John Bowlby (1951), which highlighted the child's need for a warm and continuous relationship, the concept of maternal deprivation has gained wide acceptance. Disruption of the maternal bond by physical or emotional separation has been held to be the cause of a variety of psychiatric malfunctions in adulthood. There have been a number of criticisms of the simplicity of this theory and of the methodology on which it is based. (Rutter 1972). These observations have encouraged a closer look at the relationship of mother and children and the impact of this relationship on later development. A generation of studies has led to the conclusion that maternal discord and disaffection increase the likelihood of the children showing disorders of conduct and that this effect is not only associated with the early childhood but can be important for the child of any age (Rutter 1972; Robins 1970). Rutter has noted that the concept of maternal deprivation is too heterogeneous to be useful and that a more precise delineation of the aspects of poor maternal care is now needed (1972). One way to approach more precision is to examine the mothering of women with a specific psychiatric disorder. In this regard there have been scattered observations of the difficulties arising between depressed mothers and their children (Fabian and Donohue 1956; Post and Wardle 1962; Rutter 1966, 1972; Walzer 1961; Deykin et al. 1966; Jacobson and Klerman, 1966).

Fabian and Donohue found that a third of the mothers of the children who were referred to their child guidance clinic were depressed. They felt that maternal depression was a family catastrophe since all family members suffered and that the effects on infants and children were disastrous. They noted instances of "murderous hostility" by the mother towards the child, as well as caricatures of overcautious behavior. The symptoms noted in the children included the younger children's failure to adjust to school and deviant personality patterns in the older age-groups (Fabian and Donohue 1956). Walzer, working at a child guidance clinic, also noted the frequency of mild depression in the parents of children referred to it and suggested treating the parents in order to help the children.[1]

In a study of the intra- and extrafamilial relations of psychiatric patients, Post (1962) found that the most disturbance occurred in the social relations of patients with chronic or recurrent affective disorders. Eighty percent of the children of these patients were judged to have psychiatric problems, and 34 percent were regarded as seriously disturbed. Children of patients termed psychotic were often less affected than children of nonpsychotic depressed patients.

The most comprehensive study of the children of psychiatrically disturbed patients was carried out by Rutter in 1966. He investigated the adjustment of children of depressives, schizophrenics, and normal parents. He found that affective

---

1. For a review of studies of parents of children with psychiatric disorders, see M. Rutter, *Children of Sick Parents* (Maudsley Monographs, London, 1966), pp. 9–11.

symptoms occurred more frequently in parents of disturbed children than in parents of normal children. In his study, several of the mothers' symptoms directly involved their children and included hostility towards the children. Parents with personality abnormalities most often had children with neurotic or behavioral disorders. Only a few schizophrenic mothers were noted to have disturbed children, possibly, Rutter suggests, because the children of schizophrenics tended to be cared for by people other than the mother.

Resnich, in a review of 131 cases of parental child murders, found that 71 percent of the mothers were depressed (1969). He noted that psychiatrists should be alert to the homicidal potential of depressed mothers. The danger is increased with evidence of hostility towards the favorite child of a loathed spouse; where the mother is fearful about harming the child or overly concerned about his health; where the suicidal mother has a strong identification with an "overloved child"; or when the mother has what McDermaid and Winkler termed a "child centered obsessional depression" (1955). A clinical report by an English psychiatrist describes a relationship between maternal depression and child abuse (Isaacs 1968). However, it is not possible to determine from this report if depression occurs more frequently than other diagnoses.

Assessments

Since the requirements of parenthood change as children mature, the areas assessed were those which appeared to transcend any specific age and might be considered the essentials of mothering and of any close human relations. These include: emotional involvement, interpersonal communication, friction, and feelings. The assessments were made only for mothers with children living at home.

Lack of emotional involvement was assessed by rating the degree to which the mother was concerned in the day-to-day care of her children. For younger children this would pertain to her involvement in their play, education, and physical care. For older children it would include her involvement in their school progress and social activities, as well as the discussing and dispensing of discipline or work around the house. Lack of communication was assessed by the degree to which the mother was able to talk with and listen to her children. In the rating of friction the mother was asked if and how much the children had been annoying her. Particular attention was paid to frequency of arguments and criticisms, fighting and tensions.

Four items assessed feelings. The first was the degree to which the mother experienced warm and affectionate feelings towards the children. The remaining three concerned feelings of excessive guilt, of worry and anxiety, and of resentment. These three were assessed in connection with the family unit as a whole, but since their main impact in fact concerned the children, they will be considered in this chapter.

Information on the patients' children was available in both the psychiatrist's and social worker's detailed case records. In most cases the records were based on direct observations of the children. This information was found to be extensive in most records, as it was often a significant focus of the treatment. These records were made independently of the social adjustment assessments of the mother and without knowledge of the results of these assessments. Information on the children of the normals was available in the narrative case summaries of the raters. While these summaries were not independent of the mothers' ratings, they were often based on direct observation of the children during the home interview. A content analysis of all available records was made by the authors, who had not made the mothers' ratings. The observations on the individual children were categorized by the age of the child and the type of problem noted.

Comparison with Normals

Thirty-five of the forty patients and twenty-seven of the normals had children living at home. The average number of children for both the patients and the normals was about 2.5.

The depressed women were considerably more impaired as parents than the normal women (table 8.1). The depressed women were only moderately involved in their children's daily life, had difficulty communicating with them, and were aware

TABLE 8.1. SOCIAL ADJUSTMENT SCORES IN PARENTAL ROLE

Variables*	Depressives N = 35		Normals N = 27		Significance of Difference
	Mean	S.D.	Mean	S.D.	
Lack of Involvement	2.71	0.99	1.63	0.84	<.001
Impaired Communication	2.32	0.91	1.67	0.68	<.01
Friction	3.09	0.95	1.93	0.62	<.001
Lack of Affection	1.94	1.06	1.19	0.40	<.001
Guilt	2.97	1.15	1.30	0.46	<.001
Worry	2.31	1.05	1.89	0.75	NS
Resentment	2.03	1.12	1.33	0.48	<.01
Overall Evaluation†	3.80	0.90	2.12	0.71	<.001

* Higher scores indicate more impairment.
† Scale range is 1–7. Range for remaining variables is 1–5.

of loss of affection for their children. Particularly striking is the fact that they reported considerable friction with their children —a contrast to the relatively harmonious, involved, and affectionate relations the normal women reported having with their children. The depressed women also reported moderate degrees of guilt about the adequacy of their role in the nuclear family and expressed considerable resentment and ambivalence towards family members, feeling that the nuclear family had "let them down" or "been unfair." Although they worried occasionally about their families, the degree of worry was not significantly different from that reported by the normal women. Overall, the interviewer evaluated the depressed women as moderately maladjusted, while the normals were evaluated as having minor or no maladjustmnt.

In terms of the family life-cycle, these trends received considerable amplification in a more detailed clinical study.

Family Life-Cycle and Depression

Paralleling the concept of normative psychosocial stages in individual development, stages in the life cycle of the nuclear family have been explored by a number of authors (Fleck 1966; Nye and Berardo 1966; Lidz 1968; Parsons and Bales 1955). Such stages in the family life-cycle may be characterized in terms of the family's sociobiological functions:

TABLE 8.2. FAMILY LIFE-CYCLE, ADAPTIVE ROLES, AND IMPAIRMENT IN DEPRESSION

Stages in Family Life-Cycle	Adaptive Performance Maternal Role	Child's Role	Impairment In Depression Maternal Role	Child's Impairment
Nuturing (Infancy)	Provide physical care and closeness Teach child to observe and communicate inner and outer experience and to master separation	Dependent and helpless	Helplessness Overindulgence or hostile Excessive concern Inability to separate self from child	Tyrannical behavior Inability to separate from mother—poor ego boundary Vulnerable to subsequent separations Potential damage to later development
Enculturation (Younger children)	Teaching instrumental modes of the culture and social skills, cultural mores Facilitating peer relations Providing positive models of identification by example rather than explicitly	Learning social, instrumental, and communicative skills Making friends	Emotional and physical uninvolvement or over-involvement Friction, irritability Self-preoccupation Withdrawal and emotional distances Ambivalent affection Inability to be a positive identification mode	Rivalry with peers and sib for attention Feelings of isolation or depression Hyperactivity School problems Enuresis or other symptoms Potential for learning idiosyncratic behavior
Emancipation (Adolescents)	Tolerance and resilience in allowing adolescent to experiment with independent behavior-guidance	Developing independence Sexual, occupational, educational exploration	Impaired communication Friction or withdrawal Resentment Worry Guilt Envy and competition	Deviant behavior Rebellion rather than ex-ploration Withdrawal
Termination—Empty Nest (Child leaves home)	Gratification from roles other than maternal	Independence Some sexual and occupational resolutions Ready to begin own family	Persists in maintaining maternal role Friction, latent or overt Resentment	Rebellion Guilt Conflict with parents may interfere with own new roles

1. Care of the newborn—the postpartum stage.
2. Nurture of the infant—the infancy stage.
3. Enculturation of the young child—the childhood stage.
4. Emancipation of the offspring from the family—the adolescent in the family.
5. Termination of child rearing—the "empty nest."

At each stage specific maternal tasks are called for. Impairment in the mothers' performance may be viewed in the framework of individual and family pathology. Table 8.2 describes the family life-cycle and the impairments in depression. The affective life of the family depends largely upon the mother, who, in our society, is usually responsible for the emotional climate of the family, despite currently changing family roles.

We first divided the thirty-five depressed mothers according to the stage of evolution the family had reached. This division can be seen in table 8.3, which also shows the number of mothers who were having problems with children during a particular stage, and the number of children involved in the problems. As might be expected, many of the mothers had children at different stages, since the evolution of the family is a slow process during which the growing children span a range of development.

Pathology was evident at all stages of development. It was most marked at three points—in the postpartum stage (where, however, the group was very small), in infancy (nurturing stage), and during the adolescent phase (emancipation). Disturbance of maternal role around the enculturation and termination stages was less marked. We will discuss in detail the expectations and disturbances found at each stage of the cycle.

Care of the Newborn

Three of the thirty-five mothers were currently experiencing postpartum depressions and were immobilized in caring for their newborn infants.[2] All three women were in their twenties and

2. Considerably more has been written than elucidated about postpartum depression. For a guide to the literature one might read W. A. Brown and P. Shereshefsky, "Seven women: A prospective study of postpartum psychi-

TABLE 8.3. FREQUENCY OF CONFLICT BETWEEN DEPRESSED MOTHERS AND THEIR CHILDREN

Stages in Family Life-Cycle	Mothers with Children Currently in Stage N*	Mothers with Problem N	%	Children Currently in Stage N	Children Involved in Problem N	%
Postpartum (Newborn)	3	3	100	3	3	100
Nurturing (Infancy)	11	8	73	16	13	81
Enculturation (Childhood)	20	10	50	38	20	52
Emancipation (Adolescence)	16	13	81	26	17	65
Termination (The Empty Nest)	15	9	60	26	10	38

* Since an individual mother usually has more than one child, the number of mothers and children in this table exceeds the total of forty interviewed mothers.

had one or two other preschool children. Helpless and over-whelmed by the care required by the newborn infant, they often became overindulgent, overprotective, or compulsive mothers. Their unreasonably high standards left them feeling inadequate to cope with the needs of the new and, perhaps, unwanted baby. This new burden was coupled with the continuing demands of their other children. Moreover, the mothers' inability to cope with their new infants was seen in their tendency to overfeed the infants, in their fear of doing psychological damage to them, and in their anxiety on holding or leaving them. Aware of their difficulties, these women expressed considerable guilt and in-adequacy over their performance.

B.P., a 26-year-old woman, married into a close-knit family with whom she lived in close proximity and had some conflict. Her first child was a boy aged 4. Two weeks following the birth of her second child she felt depressed, unable to eat or sleep, or do her housework, and helpless in providing care. She became excessively preoccupied

atric disorders," *Psychiatry* 35: 139–59, May 1972; or H. F. Butts, "Postpartum psychiatric problems: A review of the literature dealing with etiological theories," *Journal of the National Medical Association* 61: 136–39, 204, March 1969.

with his care, felt her in-laws were critical of her as a mother, and that someone other than she should rear her children.

In her desire to make up to her children for what she missed in her childhood, she had been an overindulgent mother. This had some negative repercussions in limiting her from free social outlets with her husband, and producing tyrannical, demanding behavior in her older boy to whom her behavior was slavish and compliant.

While this case exemplified the overindulgent and over-protective pattern, there were other women who expressed overtly hostile feelings. Two mothers had tried to choke their babies in previous episodes. It is well known that infanticide is a rare but tragic outcome of severe postpartum psychotic states (Lukianowicz 1971; Resnich 1969, 1970; McDermaid and Winkler 1955; Evan 1968).

Nurturing Tasks

The nurturing tasks involve the care, feeding, and physical close-ness required of the mother by the dependent and helpless infant. As the infant grows, the mother must assist the infant to observe and communicate his inner and outer experiences and to master separation. While these tasks are traditionally assigned to the mother, she requires strong emotional support from her spouse to carry them out effectively. The depressed mothers of infants were either overconcerned, helpless, and guilty, or di-rectly hostile—laying the groundwork for future psychological damage to the offspring or producing tyrannical behavior in their children. Eleven of the mothers had a total of sixteen chil-dren in this developmental stage. Eight of the eleven mothers (73 percent) with children in this stage showed impaired ma-ternal function and thirteen of the sixteen children (81 percent) were affected by the mothers' symptoms (table 8.2).

O.P. was a 29-year-old woman who came to the United States six years ago from a rural area of Hungary. She lived with a somewhat unsympathetic relative for the first year and then married. Her two children were born close together and, although she was reluctant to admit it, she found it difficult to cope with the responsibility of their care. To compensate, she became overprotective and at times would force-feed the children. She bribed her already overweight three-year-old to eat more. She would sit with him through endless meals, finally spoon-feeding him if he resisted. She could not tolerate the boy's crying and, if he woke during the night, she would bring him into her room, or try to feed him. Consequently, the child never slept through the night without awakening. Her depression served to increase her hypersensitivity and she interpreted the boy's refusal to eat or his crying as rejection and proof that she was a bad mother.

M.D. was a 28-year-old woman, married five years, with one son, aged three and a half. She and her husband had been involved in marital conflict for most of their marriage. However, Mrs. D. became depressed when she and her husband separated briefly. During the height of her depression she was unable to provide more than minimal physical care for her son. The patient felt that the boy was aligned with the husband against her and misinterpreted normal childhood behavior. For example, when Mr. D. came home from work, the child would run to his father. Mrs. D. saw this as the child's preference for the father. The youngster reacted to the mother's rejection by soiling his pants, which infuriated the mother but gained her attention.

Enculturation of the School-Age Children

The enculturation stage calls for the mother's emotional and physical involvement in assisting her child to learn social skills and customs, as well as how to get along with others, especially peers.

Ten of the twenty depressed mothers with children in this stage had problems in enculturation tasks. These depressed mothers were unable to become deeply involved in their children's lives. Irritability, sensitivity, self-preoccupation, and anergia prevented them from meeting their children's normal demands for attention and communication. The mothers' low self-esteem and hopelessness impaired their ability to be positive models for their children. The children's meals, dressing, accounts of school activities, requests for help in homework, their playful noise and friends were met with the mother's lack of involvement and withdrawal. Some women withdrew not only emotionally but physically from daily tasks. Household chaos became the norm in these families. Their children often looked physically uncared for and suffered more than the usual number of accidents, probably as a result of the maternal inattention and general confusion in the house. Nearly all these depressed women complained about being intolerant of their children's noise. The children reacted to the mothers' withdrawal by becoming more demanding or by fighting among themselves. Mothers who had relatives and friends readily available would often ask assistance in child-care. Those who did not have such assistance would either leave the children alone or might retire to bed during the day. A few with financial resources relinquished their children to maids. One mother receiving state aid asked the welfare department to have foster care arranged for her children.

Limited involvement with their children by means of emotional distance and control was another pattern observed among the depressed women. One mother would leave the house so that her children could have unsupervised play that she would not have to hear. Another mother regimented household activity so that the children were allowed specified times for meals, snacks, homework, and television viewing, and any deviation from this schedule elicited the mother's harsh reprisal.

There was also a pattern of overinvolvement in which the depressed women would engage in a frenzied pursuit of activities with their children. On the surface this activity was interpreted by less intimate associates as "togetherness," but closer observation showed that such overinvolvement actually diluted emotional closeness and appeared to compensate for a sense of guilt and deeper disinterest.

P.T. was a 30-year-old mother of three children ranging in age from four to eight. Prior to her depression she had taken part in many voluntary activities. As she became depressed, these activities increased in an unselected fashion. She felt unable to refuse. As she said, "They help me to get away from myself." She had considerable difficulty managing the daily care of the children and frantically drove them around to clubs, to the library, and to movies. She became a classroom mother, ran a PTA party, served at the school lunch program, drove the nursery school car-pool. However, individual contacts with the children were cold and brittle. Her activities were usually aimless and without gratification. She openly spoke of resenting the dependency of the children and feeling trapped by them. Her excessive activity with the children was punctuated by her screaming and slapping them.

T.L., although from a different socioeconomic group, was quite similar in behavior. An intelligent 29-year-old unmarried woman, she was raising four children, aged three to eleven, on Aid to Dependent Children payments. While experiencing depressive symptoms, she maintained active involvement in a neighborhood community program and took considerable responsibility in organizing a summer play program. She maintained high standards of educational achievement and made weekly trips with her children to the Salvation Army or library to find books and toys. She took them to neighborhood craft programs while expressing considerable irritation and anger at their demands and slapping them if they complained.

While emotional uninvolvement and overall irritability contributed to the majority of the depressed women's problems with their children, in two cases there was evidence of more serious overt and unequivocal hostility directed toward one particular child whom the mothers blamed for their illnesses. Both instances involved families with girls in early adolescence, and no overt conflict existed between the mothers and the other child.

R.T. was a 36-year-old housewife with three previous episodes of depression, all occurring in the summer and which she related to her 10-year-old daughter being home from school. She considered the child spoiled and self-centered, openly resented her, and stated she did not love her. She suffered guilt and remorse for these hostile feelings but was unable to control them.

S.J., a 44-year-old, twice divorced, lived with her seventeen-year-old son and twelve-year-old daughter. The daughter was from her previous marriage and her ex-husband refused to pay maintenance for her. The mother had had a number of depressive episodes, the most recent precipitated by the loss of a boyfriend who, she felt, left because of her instability in handling her daughter. She openly rejected the girl and tried to send her back to her father. When her older child left for college, she felt hopeless about her own ability to care for the younger girl and felt she needed care herself. The daughter was now receiving treatment for migraine headaches.

Most of the children experienced the impact of their mother's persistent irritability, withdrawal, and subtle rejection. The women were handicapped in dealing with their family's affectional needs and in providing adequate role models for their children. Although the children's difficulties were subtly apparent in early latency, most of these children might not have come to the attention of mental health or school personnel until the age of puberty. The children's symptoms were usually hyperactivity and/or excessive sibling rivalry. It is interesting to note that childhood hyperactivity has been compared to agitated depression (Zrull et al. 1970). Of the thirty-eight children in this age group, twenty (52 percent) were showing some impact from the mother's illness and several developed acute symptoms during their mothers' depressive illnesses. One seven-year-old boy became enuretic and began having nightmares. Another nine-year-old was failing in school and became a behavior problem. A ten-year-old girl lost considerable weight, appeared depressed, and was referred to a child-guidance clinic.

Emancipation—The Adolescent

While the emancipation of the child from the parental family is a gradual process, adolescence provides the culmination of the many earlier steps. During adolescence, the mother should have tolerance and resilience in allowing the adolescent to experiment with independent behavior, yet should provide guidance when needed. If the child has learned maladaptive or idiosyncratic patterns, he will be seriously handicapped in sexual, occupational, and educational explorations during this period.

Problems with the emancipation of their teenage and young adult children were noted in thirteen of the sixteen depressed women (81 percent) with children in this age range. While these thirteen women had children of other ages living at home, the overt problem was manifested most often by the adolescent child. One mother of six children had serious problems with her three teenagers, while the three younger children were apparently uninvolved. In many cases, the uninvolved children were the youngest members of the families; often these children acted as the dutiful offspring who would take over for mother without complaining. In two families, the departure or change in behavior of the "good" child, who had been the mother's ally against the adolescent problem-child, even seemed to exacerbate familial conflict and be associated with the onset of the mother's depressive illness. Frequently, friction between depressed mothers and their adolescent children was open and severe. Anger, resentment, and intolerance of their children's growing independence and an inability to set limits characterized the mothers' behavior. They either over- or undercontrolled their adolescents. Family problems were handled by the mothers' angry outbursts or withdrawal and with little resilience.

With few exceptions the adolescents' emancipation was characterized by rebellion rather than exploration. Their serious difficulties with authority and deviant behavior included truancy, school dropout, drug abuse, theft, and promiscuity. School problems occurred most frequently and were usually an early sign of the adolescent's problem.

The role of the depressed woman's spouse was often crucial in the perpetuation of the conflict. If the spouse aligned himself with the adolescent against the mother, the child's abusive behavior towards the mother increased and was difficult to reduce even when the mother recovered.

R.P. lived with her husband, an engineer, her sons aged 5, 11, and 12, who presented no immediate problems, and her daughters aged 14, 17, and 18. Mrs. P's depression was preceded by a gradual family deterioration in which Mr. P. lost his job, the family moved and subsequently lost its savings when Mr. P. could not find work. Mrs. P. began an affair, culminating in her depression and suicide attempt. At the height of the mother's illness, two of the girls dropped out of school, spending their days at home in bed and their evenings playing music loudly and inviting strange men to the house. They refused either to work or to return to school. Later they began taking psychedelic drugs and one girl became involved in a homosexual relationship. Mrs. P. was moderately depressed for about six months, spending much of her day in bed. There were considerable arguments between the mother and her daughters in which Mr. P. allied himself with the daughters. Mrs. P. came for psychiatric treatment after a serious fist fight with her oldest daughter, and when her 14-year-old was found to be truanting from school. The relation with the boys, while less hostile, was quite disengaged, and the patient never seemed able to discuss them individually, referring to them only as "the boys."

In two cases, depressives' children were involved with the law.

L.D.'s 14-year-old hyperactive boy was having difficulties in school. At the height of the mother's depression, he stole a bicycle and was placed on probation. Her other children, ages 8 and 10, were dutiful, keeping house and preparing meals for her while she remained in bed.

Mrs. M., a 48-year-old, separated from her husband for the last four years and living on welfare, was involved in an extremely hostile relationship with her 17-year-old son. The patient was blamed by the son for the breakup of her marriage. He was rebellious and threatened her, at times evicting her from the house by physical force. The patient had had symptoms intermittently for a few years which increased with growing difficulties with her son. Her son was arrested for carrying a blackjack, and her symptoms improved when he left the home for jail, only to return when he was not convicted. A few months later she learned that he was a heroin addict.

In some cases where no deviant behavior was observed, the mother anxiously anticipated difficulty, especially sexual promiscuity. The adolescent's normal movement toward independence stirred up conflict. Several of the mothers were envious of their daughter's developing sexuality as well as being competitive with the girl for the attention of the spouse (Deutsch 1965).

One patient, D.L., became depressed while on vacation when her 15-year-old began dating for the first time. Although the youngster gave no evidence of unruly behavior, the mother secretly followed her around to observe her conduct, enlisting the aid of her bewildered husband and ruining everyone's vacation. When asked what her fears were, she related them to worrying about the girl becoming sexually involved. Underlying the mother's concern was envy and competition with her daughter.

Two of the mothers improved symptomatically when their teenage children left home, although the departures were not the outcome of constructive family negotiations. One child ran away and another was jailed.

Although the mother's depressive symptoms gained sympathy from some of her younger children, adolescents tended to exploit their mother's helplessness. While the depression might be interpreted as a reaction to having to deal with adolescent problem-children, the clinical material suggested otherwise. In almost all instances, the mother had previously been treated for depression or had shown chronic or intermittent symptoms while her children were younger and not observed to have behavior problems.

Changes that occurred with clinical improvement will be dealt with more extensively in later chapters. It is relevant here to note that as the depressed woman's symptoms and social performance improved on follow-up, so did the behavior of the adolescents (see chap. 11). This would support the view that the disturbed adolescent behavior was more often a consequence than a cause of the maternal depression. The ability of the mother to pull herself together, to set limits, to negotiate with the adolescent, and to show genuine interest when she had recovered, usually had a salutary effect on the child. Obviously, the youngster on heroin did not stop his habit. However, he did stop his physical abusiveness toward his mother when she had enough energy and self-confidence to make it clear that she would not tolerate it. One fourteen-year-old had refused to return to school during her mother's illness. When her mother felt better, she began to listen to what was disturbing the youngster in school. The mother was then able to discuss the problems with school officials and worked out a more satisfactory school placement.

Another seventeen-year-old responded to her mother's recovery by mobilizing herself to look for employment. The depressed mother's pessimism about the girl's future and chances of ever finding employment had deterred the girl from making any plans. The youngster on probation for stealing a bicycle took a paper route to buy his own bicycle and joined a boy's club. The girl involved in a homosexual relationship returned home when the mother was well enough to encourage her to return. Although the girl continued the homosexual relationship, she was not living with the woman and had begun involving herself in heterosexual relationships also.

A number of authors have suggested that adolescent deviant behavior such as temper tantrums, school dropout, truancy, running away, drug use, disobedience, and promiscuity may in fact mask underlying depression (Burke 1962; Anthony 1968; Gould 1965; Lesse 1968; Chwast 1967; Malmquist 1971; Glaser 1967; Kaufman 1959; Gallemore and Wilson 1972). Gang contacts may mask helplessness and prevent these feelings from becoming overt (Chwast 1967). Aggressive behavior may ward off feelings of depression and may be considered justified by the adolescent for past grievances toward the parent (Malmquist 1971).

Feelings of loss may have been important in precipitating the difficulties noted in the adolescent children. The identification process is considered critical in preventing delinquency among adolescents and, the loss of a parent through death has been observed to interfere with the development of an effective superego (Koller 1971). While a depressed mother may be physically present, her detachment may be experienced as a loss by the vulnerable adolescent. Not only is there a loss of the mother's nurturing and interest, but also of her direction and control (Hill 1969; Poznanski 1970). She may not be psychologically available for guidance to lend interest or comfort.

It is beyond the scope of this study to determine the degree of covert depression in the adolescents, since contacts were primarily with the mothers. However, certain trends were suggestive. The adolescents did experience a loss in the withdrawal of their mothers during their depressive episodes. For many of these women this was not their first depressive episode, so that their children had been through this before. A number of the adolescents did appear to have a quality of hopelessness, characteristic of depression. While there was suggestion that the deviance was a form of masked depression in many of the adolescents, more direct clinical study would be necessary to confirm this.

"The Empty Nest"

The termination of an active maternal role occurs gradually as the child becomes a young adult. The termination is highlighted by the child physically moving out of the home. While thoughts of and feelings for the absent children continue, the children no longer take much of the mother's time and effort. The mother must now find a new way of life, expand old interests, and seek gratification through roles other than the maternal one. The inability to deal successfully with the termination of child-rearing and to adjust to the childless-mother status can contribute to a depression in middle-aged women and has been described as the "empty nest" syndrome. Deykin et al. (1966) described this conflict as either overt or latent and noted that difficulties were more common in less-educated women from traditional backgrounds, and where the spouse was absent (see chap. 3).

In this sample, nine of the fifteen patients (60 percent) with children who were leaving home developed a depressive pattern which was similar to the "empty nest" syndrome. Their children were in their later teens and early twenties and had left home to go to college or to marry. In most cases, the illness followed departure of the only child or of the youngest children of mothers who were either divorced or widowed or having severe marital problems that rendered their husbands emotionally "unavailable." Typically close dependent relationships had existed between the depressed mothers and their children, and the children's departure exacerbated the mothers' feelings of social isolation and emotional loss.

Following the typology proposed by Deykin et al., three of the depressed patients could be characterized as having overt conflict and six as having latent conflict with their grown children. Our sample was too small to search for predictors; however, the familial patterns were similar to those described by Deykin et al.

P.R., a 54-year-old Italian widow with very limited intellectual capacity and a grade-school education, was typical of the overt-conflict patient. She lived with her 20-year-old daughter. An older daughter was married. The younger girl was very much bound to the mother, going out very little until she recently met her fiancé. Three weeks before the patient was admitted for depression, her daughter announced she was getting married. The patient quarrelled with her and then became anxious, depending upon relatives, and ringing them for help at very awkward hours. During the course of her illness, she fought frequently with the daughter, blamed her for making her ill, and was unable to plan a wedding for her.

L.J. was a hard-working, intelligent, divorced woman who worked as a nurse and became depressed when her 17-year-old daughter left for college. The mother took pride in her daughter's ability and offered her considerable financial help and emotional encouragement to go. But when the girl left home, the patient stated sadly that now she would have to make a life of her own. Prior to the girl's leaving for college, the patient had some minor surgery which served to highlight her own vulnerability and ultimate dependency on the girl.

Although overt or latent conflict existed between the mothers and their older children who left home, the children were able to make the break from home and to weaken the relationship by the physical distance between mother and children. The possibility remained that the children might experience problems in their new roles because of their unresolved conflicts with the mother.

Conclusions

The main points that emerge from these comparisons are that the acute symptoms of depression conflict with the demands of being a mother and produce a widespread negative impact on the children. At the simplest level, the helplessness and hostility which are associated with acute depression interfere with the ability to be a warm and consistent mother. Depressive symptoms put the mother in an untenable position of having to give when she needs to get. The need of the depressed mother for help, guidance, and affection is frustrated by similar demands made upon her by her children (Abraham 1927; Rado 1968; Bibring 1953). The hostility between depressed women and their children is a central theme and one we will return to in chapter 10.

9
Dimensions of
Social Adjustment

This chapter explores alternative approaches to the description of our findings. Since it deals with scoring methods and statistical approaches, it is more technical than previous chapters. In the preceding chapters we presented in considerable detail a comparison of role performance between acutely depressed and normal women. In this chapter we will look at consistent patterns of behavior which underlie performance, in order to summarize the patients' main maladjustments. Most discussions of social adjustment in the literature and most scales for its measurement have followed a role performance framework. An alternative conceptual framework, which was also employed in the organization of our scale but has not so far been used, is that of qualitative categories. These categories include performance and interpersonal behaviors, friction, feelings and satisfactions, and the overall patient evaluations. This organization extends across roles and is largely independent of them.

The two conceptual frameworks described were derived on theoretical and a priori bases. Another way of proceeding might be the empirical one of allowing the data to suggest appropriate dimensions. One suitable statistical tool available for this approach is factor analysis.[1]

As discussed in chapter 2, the application of factor analysis to the dimensions of social and interpersonal functioning has been limited (Gelder et al. 1967; Mandel 1959; Miles et al. 1951).

Therefore, we set out to explore the interrelations between the different aspects of social function, using factor analysis in addition to the scoring systems based on role areas and qualitative categories. In order to produce an adequate range of heterogeneity and thus facilitate the isolation of rating dimensions, the scores for the depressed patients and normals were combined for the correlational analyses and factor analysis to be reported here.

Scoring by Role Areas

Prior to factor analysis the two theoretical scoring systems implicit in the construction of the scale were investigated. The most important of these was that derived by summing in each of the role areas of work, social and leisure, extended family, marital as spouse, parental, and marital family unit. Since the number of items scored in each role varied from patient to patient, a simple total score for each role was not appropriate. To indicate the score for each role, a mean was calculated consisting of the total summed score of items divided by the number of items rated. The overall judgments were not included in the summed scores. Within each role, correlations of each item to

1. For the reader who is unfamiliar with factor analysis, this is a statistical technique for reducing and simplifying a pattern of intercorrelations between variables. A number of different methods are available. All produce as their end product a set of dimensions known as factors. These correspond approximately to constructs underlying and explaining the variables. For example, we might take a number of measurements between points on many human bodies and, by factor analysis, reduce them to such overall dimensions as height, breadth, or trunk circumference. Factors are hypothetical rather than real, but provide useful ways of summarizing possible underlying dimensions. They are described in terms of factor loadings of the individual items. These correspond to correlations; they can theoretically vary between +1.0 (complete correspondence) and −1.0 (a complete inverse relationship), but in practice will always be lower. Derivation of factors by factor analysis depends on complex procedures of matrix algebra. For details of the mathematics the interested reader is referred to technical works such as Harman (1960).

the mean of all items for that role were then examined. These item-to-mean correlations are set out in table 9.1.

TABLE 9.1. SCORING BY ROLE AREAS

	N	Correlation
Work: Time lost	79	.77***
Impaired performance	79	.82***
Friction	79	.39***
Distress	79	.74***
Disinterest	79	.82***
Feelings of inadequacy	79	.80***
Social and Leisure: Diminished contact with friends	80	.62***
Diminished social interactions	80	.62***
Impaired leisure activities	80	.62***
Friction	79	.13
Reticence	79	.38***
Hypersensitive behavior	79	.40***
Social discomfort	79	.63***
Loneliness	80	.48***
Boredom	80	.61***
Diminished dating	12	.55***
Disinterest in dating	14	.33**
Extended Family: Friction	74	.53***
Reticence	79	.61***
Withdrawal	77	.67***
Family attachment	78	.12
Rebellion	78	.49***
Guilt	79	.49***
Worry	79	.17
Resentment	79	.75***
Marital as Spouse: Friction	61	.56***
Reticence	61	.70***
Domineering behavior	61	.09
Dependency	61	.22
Submissiveness	61	.26*
Lack of affection	61	.26*
Diminished intercourse	61	.54***
Sexual problems	54	.60***
Disinterest in sex	60	.77***
Parental: Lack of involvement	62	.81***
Impaired communication	61	.73***
Friction	62	.74***
Lack of affection	62	.83***
Marital Family Unit: Guilt	74	.76***
Worry	73	.55***
Resentment	74	.60***

*** p < .001
** p < .01
* p < .05

For this scoring system to be adequate, we would hope the correlations to be moderately high, indicating that within each area the individual items were all related reasonably closely to each other and to the sum total of them all. We would not expect very high correlations, which would indicate that all items were in effect identical so that inclusion of many items added very little. We would certainly wish to avoid low correlations, which would indicate that some items showed very little variation in common with the area score in which they had been incorporated. As shown in the table, correlations were in fact moderate in magnitude. However, in each role, except the two small ones of parental role and family unit, some items correlated below .45 with the mean. The heterogeneity of items was most pronounced for extended family and marital roles. The work role appeared fairly uniform. The correlations in general suggested that while the grouping by role areas served to summarize many common elements among items, it did not group them in a way completely consistent with their interrelationships.

Scoring by Qualitative Categories

Similar item-to-means correlations were calculated for the qualitative categories, which provided an alternative, although less familiar, theoretical grouping of items. The three behavioral subcategories were scored separately, giving five categories in all. Findings are set out in table 9.2. A similar pattern was evident in the grouping by role areas, but with greater homogeneity. Some categories appeared to be quite homogeneous, particularly that of friction. The overall category also showed high item-to-mean correlations, but was of less interest as it reflected somewhat intuitive and unstructured judgments which might well interrelate due to halo effects. The category of performance appeared moderately homogeneous, with only two correlations below .45 (one for diminished dating, which involved a very low N of unmarried subjects). Satisfactions and feelings, although less homogeneous, still contained only a few low correlations in proportion to the large number of items entering into the category. The interpersonal behaviors appeared to contain a selection of items that was quite heterogeneous. Overall, this

TABLE 9.2. SCORING BY QUALITATIVE CATEGORIES

Items	N	Correlation
Performance: Time lost (W)†	79	.72***
Impaired performance (W)	79	.67***
Diminished contact with friends (SL)	80	.60***
Diminished social interactions (SL)	80	.66***
Impaired leisure activities (SL)	80	.58***
Diminished dating (SL)	12	.28
Diminished intercourse (M)	61	.56***
Sexual problems (M)	54	.52***
Lack of involvement (P)	62	.59***
Interpersonal Behaviors: Reticence (SL)	79	.57***
Hypersensitive behavior (SL)	79	.43***
Reticence (EF)	79	.70***
Withdrawal (EF)	77	.66***
Family attachment (EF)	78	.15
Rebellion (EF)	78	.39**
Reticence (M)	61	.56***
Domineering behavior (M)	61	.06
Dependence (M)	61	.39**
Submissiveness (M)	61	.29*
Impaired communication (P)	61	.45***
Friction: Work	79	.63***
Social and leisure	79	.69***
Extended family	74	.74***
Marital as spouse	61	.77***
Parental	62	.75***
Feelings and Satisfactions: Distress (W)	79	.82***
Disinterest (W)	79	.76***
Feelings of inadequacy (W)	79	.74***
Distress (SL)	79	.69***
Loneliness (SL)	80	.46***
Boredom (SL)	80	.73***
Disinterest in dating (SL)	14	.35**
Guilt (EF)	79	.48***
Worry (EF)	79	.13
Resentment (EF)	79	.64***
Lack of affection (M)	61	.33**
Disinterest in sex (M)	60	.63***
Lack of affection (P)	62	.56***
Guilt (FU)	74	.76***
Worry (FU)	73	.38**
Resentment (FU)	74	.45***
Overall Evaluations of Each Role: Work	78	.81***
Social and leisure	79	.83***
Extended family	78	.75***
Marital as spouse	60	.71***
Parental	61	.88***
Overall adjustment	79	.95***

† Role areas are indicated by abbreviations in brackets: W, work; SL, social and leisure; M, marital as spouse; P, parental; EF, extended family; FU, family unit.
*** p < .001
** p < .01
* p < .05

theoretical categorization, although indicating important common elements cutting across role areas, was still not of sufficient internal consistency to be completely satisfactory.

Factor Analysis

Results so far suggested that the two a priori scoring systems had considerable value as data condensations, but that neither system produced completely homogeneous rating dimensions. Therefore, a factor analysis appeared to be indicated. For this, thirty-seven of the rating variables were selected. The six overall ratings and the rating of economic inadequacy were conceptually inappropriate and were consequently excluded. Four other items, frequency of dating, interest in dating, rebelliousness (extended family) and frequency of intercourse, were excluded because of low N's or highly skewed distributions.

Intercorrelations were computed on the remaining thirty-seven items and subjected to principal component analysis (Harman 1960). Six principal components were utilized; the latent root of the last was 1.66. Rotations to the normal varimax criterion were then performed (Harman 1960). The six-factor rotation was selected for further study. Loadings above .45 on these factors are shown in table 9.3. They accounted for thirty-three of the thirty-seven items, with overlap between two factors on only one item, disinterest in sex. The factors were easily interpretable and conceptually meaningful. Suggested names were based on their item content.

Factor 1 appeared to reflect work performance. Five of the seven relevant items came from the work role. A sixth, feelings of guilt towards family unit, dealt with feelings of inadequacy as parent or spouse, obviously closely related to instrumental role performance for women. The last item, disinterest in sex, seemed less appropriate but loaded almost as highly on factor 6.

Factor 2 was the clearest and most easily interpretable, as interpersonal friction. The four items reflecting friction loaded here, as did feelings of resentment to family unit and extended family, and hypersensitive behavior in social relations.

The items in factor 3 referred particularly to inhibited communication and included ratings of reticence towards extended family, friends, and husband, impaired communication with children, diminished contact with friends, and withdrawal from extended family. Domineering behavior towards husband also loaded on this factor.

TABLE 9.3.   LOADINGS ABOVE .45 ON ROTATED FACTORS

Factor 1: Work Performance 11.4% of variance		Diminished contact with friends (SL)	.48
*Items**	%	Withdrawal (EF)	.47
Impaired performance (W)	.81	Reticence (M)	.46
Time lost (W)	.71	**Factor 4: Submissive Dependency** 8.5% of variance	
Disinterest (W)	.64		
Disinterest in sex† (M)	.59	*Items*	%
Feelings of inadequacy (W)	.54	Dependence (M)	.81
Guilt (FU)	.53	Submissiveness (M)	.65
Factor 2: Interpersonal Friction 12.6% of variance		Guilt (EF)	.58
		Factor 5: Family Attachment 6.6% of variance	
Items	%		
Friction (SL)	.78	*Items*	%
Friction (EF)	.76	Family attachment (EF)	.68
Friction (W)	.69	Diminished social interactions (SL)	.60
Resentment (FU)	.66		
Friction (M)	.56	Sexual Problems (M)	.56
Friction (P)	.56	**Factor 6: Anxious Rumination** 8.9% of variance	
Resentment (EF)	.54		
Hypersensitive behaviour (SL)	.46	*Items*	%
Factor 3: Inhibited Communication 8.9% of variance		Worry (FU)	.59
		Worry (EF)	.58
Items	%	Lack of affection (P)	.53
Reticence (EF)	.73	Boredom (SL)	.52
Reticence (SL)	.62	Disinterest in sex† (M)	.51
Impaired communication (P)	.58	Social discomfort (SL)	.50
Domineering behaviour (M)	.52	Lack of involvement (P)	.49

* Role areas are indicated by abbreviations in brackets: W, work; FU, family unit; SL, social and leisure; EF, extended family; M, marital as spouse; P, parental.
† Disinterest in sex was scored only on factor 6—anxious rumination.

Factors 4 and 5 each contained only three items loading above .45. Factor 4 appeared to reflect submissive dependency, as measured by dependency and submissiveness in the marital relationship together with guilt towards extended family. Factor 5 was the least clear factor. It was interpreted as indicating the degree to which the subject was attached to the family and withdrawn from outside activities. Items loading on this factor were: the rating of family attachment in extended family, diminished social interactions outside the home, and, less appropriately, sexual problems in the marriage.

Interpretation of factor 6 was easier. Six of the seven loadings were on items measuring satisfactions and feelings. High scores on this factor indicated anxious ruminations, as reflected by excessive worrying about marital and extended family; disinterest and boredom for leisure activities; disinterest in sex; lack of affection for children, together with lack of involvement in activities with children.

The factorial dimensions emerging from this analysis by and large did not correspond to the role framework. Only one factor, work performance, would be clearly identified with a role (although even here the friction element was separated and incorporated in the factor of friction). The remaining factors cut across roles, uniting common elements in several roles.

There was more overlap between factors and the grouping by qualitative category, which cut across role areas. The resemblance was clearest for the friction factor, which contained all of the variables in the friction category together with some other related items. Factor 6, anxious rumination, consisted almost entirely of feelings and satisfactions, and factor 1, work performance, derived mainly from those items reflecting concrete performance. The category of interpersonal behaviors was, however, too diffuse; its items fell into three more specific patterns —inhibited communication, submissive dependency, and family attachment.

Two major distinctions of great importance were reflected in the factors—that between actual behavior and subjective distress, and that between instrumental performance and interpersonal relations. The first of these distinctions we tried to make in the rating procedure. Our technique depended solely on information obtained from the patient at interview; nevertheless, the raters tried strenuously to separate judgments as to actual patient behavior from the patient's statements as to feelings and satisfactions. Their ability to do so was upheld by the factorial separation. One factor, anxious rumination, reflected subjective distress and dissatisfactions; the others all concerned behavior.

This distinction is particularly important for depressed patients, whose self-perception, disturbed by worthlessness and guilt, need not parallel actual behavior.

Within the realm of actual behavior, rather than feelings or satisfactions, there was much diversity, reflected in the other five factors which emerged. A further important distinction lay within these factors. This was the contrast between factor 1, measuring work performance, and factors 2 through 5, which referred to various aspects of interpersonal relations—interpersonal friction, inhibited communication, submissive dependency, and family attachment. This distinction closely overlaps with the difference between instrumental and expressive roles described by Parson and Bales (1955) (see chap. 2). Work performance refers to the instrumental role: the remaining factors, although not identical with roles, correspond to the element of expressive role function. Friction in the work role, an element which is expressive rather than instrumental, was separated from work performance and incorporated in interpersonal friction. This distinction also overlapped with another, included in the qualitative categories used in our scale construction. The subcategory, labelled performance, included a number of concrete behaviors such as performance at work, number of days off, details of housework, or number of visits outside the home, which are easily and reliably quantified. These refer especially to the work role, and they fell particularly in the factor of work performance. Perhaps because of their easy quantification, variables of this type have been widely used and form the greater part of the item content of some published scales, particularly the earlier ones. Only more recently has attention been paid to subtler disturbances in interpersonal relationships such as dependency, hostility, and withdrawal (Gurland et al. 1972a; Parloff et al. 1954; Linn et al. 1969). These made up our category of interpersonal behaviors and they largely concerned expressive role function.

Overall, then, the factors from this analysis spanned a range of phenomena. One referred to subjective distress, five to behavior. Among those describing behavior, one concerned instrumental behavior, three interpersonal relations. We will see that this factorial framework provided a particularly suitable method of summarizing the disturbances of these depressed women.

Differences between Patients and Normals

We next compared scores for patients and normals on the three sets of derived scores—by role areas, qualitative categories, and factorial dimensions. For role areas and qualitative categories, scores had already been obtained as described earlier in this chapter. For factors, scores were derived by summing with unit weight the items shown in table 9.3 loading above .45, and dividing by the number of items to reduce all factor scores to the same range of 1–5. Differences between the two groups were tested for significance using the t test. Findings are shown in table 9.4.

Findings for the role areas reflected the general trends discussed in previous chapters. There was a general tendency for depressed patients to be impaired on all scores. The most disturbed role was clearly that of work, for which the difference was largest in magnitude. The least differences were in relationships with extended family. Neither patients nor normals showed much evidence of disturbance in this area; nevertheless, the differences were statistically significant.

The qualitative categories showed differential trends, mostly in keeping with the factors, as will be discussed. The most striking differences were found on the overall evaluations. Unlike the other items, these were rated on expanded, seven-point scales, so that direct comparison with the other scores may be misleading. Moreover, the ratings were on bases which were unstructured and intuitive, so that rater bias that depressives should be disturbed might have exaggerated the differences. The scores based on the more specific items are therefore of greater interest. The most marked differences were on performance and satisfactions and feelings, corresponding to work performance and anxious rumination. The differences on interpersonal behaviors and friction were less marked. All differences between the two groups were, however, highly significant.

The factors provided an overview of depressive malfunction which appeared particularly apt for summarizing the main dis-

TABLE 9.4. DERIVED SCORES: MEAN SCORES FOR PATIENTS AND NORMALS

	Depressed Patients* N = 40	Normals N = 40	t-Value	Significance of Difference
Factor Scores				
Work performance	2.81	1.31	10.16	<.001
Anxious rumination	2.35	1.54	7.14	<.001
Interpersonal friction	2.07	1.41	5.74	<.001
Inhibited communication	2.58	1.97	4.07	<.001
Submissive dependency	1.92	1.51	2.60	<.05
Family attachment	2.44	1.81	3.27	<.01
Role Areas				
Work	2.65	1.33	11.15	<.001
Social and leisure	2.60	1.85	6.75	<.001
Extended family	1.89	1.48	4.51	<.001
Marital	2.34	1.72	6.06	<.001
Parental	2.51	1.60	5.93	<.001
Marital family unit	2.44	1.52	7.74	<.001
Qualitative Categories				
Performance	2.78	1.86	7.33	<.001
Interpersonal behaviors	2.20	1.69	5.19	<.001
Friction	1.98	1.39	4.96	<.001
Feelings and satisfactions	2.39	1.46	10.15	<.001
Overall evaluation†	3.94	2.21	12.06	<.001

* Higher scores indicate greater impairment.
† Scale of 1–7. Remaining items were rated on a 5-point scale.

turbances. The most marked patient-normal differences were in work performance and anxious rumination. Both these disturbances appear closely related to the characteristic symptoms of depression. As we discussed in chapters 3 and 5, impaired work performance has in the past been regarded as sufficiently characteristic of depression for items assessing it to be included in such symptomatic rating scales as that of Hamilton (1960). It may readily be related to the general inhibition, psychomotor retardation, impairment of concentration, and loss of confidence that accompany depression. The factor of anxious rumination contained items measuring subjective distress and dissatisfactions in many roles. These elements may readily reflect the hopelessness, helplessness, worthlessness, and anxiety that are typical of depressive thinking. We should note, however, that both these factorial dimensions belong to the realm of social adjustment and that neither measures symptoms directly. Work performance refers to functional behavior in the social role of work. Anxious rumination refers to subjective satisfaction and concerns a variety of expected performances and interpersonal relations which, although they may be colored by the mood of depression, are distinct from it.

The remaining disturbances concerned interpersonal relations. Two more dimensions showed impairment which, although not quite as striking as for the two previously dealt with, was at least moderate in degree. These were inhibited communication and interpersonal friction. Inhibited communication was only a clear dimension in the factorial system. In the qualitative categories it was buried in interpersonal behaviors, and in the roles system, in various roles. This impaired communication has not received much specific comment in the literature on depression although Spiegel (1960) referred to it (chap. 3). It might perhaps be related to the general inhibition characterizing depression.

Friction across roles was consistently increased both on the factor dimension of interpersonal friction and on the qualitative category, which closely corresponded to it. This finding is of considerable interest and is consistent with findings in previous chapters. Rather than the inhibition of overt hostility, which might be inferred from some theories relating depression to hostility directed inwards on the self, overt hostility was in fact increased. Because of the importance of this finding, we will examine it in greater detail in the next chapter.

The remaining two factors, family attachment and submissive dependency, were also interpersonal. They showed the least disturbance, although for both it was statistically significant. Nevertheless, both these disturbances seem consistent with previous literature on depression and the characteristics of our patients. Family attachment summarized a pattern of diminished social interactions combined with undue attachment to the extended family. Social withdrawal might easily accompany the general reduction of activity of depression. The patterns of close relationships with extended family described in chapter 6 would lead us to expect that the extended family would be spared this withdrawal.

The least abnormal specific dimension was that of dependency. In the past this has often been regarded as characteristic of depression, with its withdrawal and reduction of functional capacity, and emphasis has been laid on it by psychoanalytic writers (see chap. 3). It emerged as a separate factor and differentiated the two groups significantly, but it did not do so strikingly. This finding may partly reflect the fact that this depressed sample was largely outpatient, and moderately rather than severely ill.

One technical aspect of factor analysis requires comment here. The intercorrelation matrix was based on the pooled sample of eighty subjects. A major source of the variance in these intercorrelations must therefore be the contrast between depression and normality. We would therefore expect the factors to reflect this difference. This was, of course, the reason for selecting the sample for analysis in this way. Therefore it is not surprising that some of the factors show large patient-normal differences. What is worthy of comment is that the differences between patients and normals are truly multidimensional. In these circumstances, where we might have simply obtained one large dimension equivalent to depressive malfunction, we did in fact obtain a number of orthogonal dimensions. For some of them, patient-normal differences were relatively weak, suggesting they did not solely depend on depressive function but had greater generality. We are not dealing here merely with depressive symptoms: these are disturbances in the social field. Although we can interpret them in terms of known disturbances of depression, they are empirical findings. We could not have predicted with any ease that these dimensions, rather than others, would have emerged from the ratings analyzed so as to characterize the depressed woman.

The findings described in this chapter refer only to the depressed state. Although we can say which disturbances most characterize the depressive, we cannot say at this stage which of the dysfunctions are secondary consequences of symptomatic depression and which may be shown by the depression-prone patient even when well. In order to explore this issue we will later examine the changes found on follow-up.

Dimensions of Social Maladjustment

The question arises as to what generality these factors may have beyond depression. Do they merely summarize disturbance of the depressed woman or do they tell us something about social function in general? We cannot answer this question empirically from the present data, but we can look for similiarities in other studies in the literature.

We first note resemblances to the theoretical frameworks in other instruments that used categories cutting across roles. Gurland et al. (1972a) used four categories: deviant behavior, friction, distress, and inferential. Our categories of interpersonal behavior, friction, and feelings and satisfactions were based on the first three of these. Friction and distress emerged as clear factors in our factor analysis. Parloff et al. (1954), in their Social Ineffectiveness Scale, were among the first to utilize clinical rating dimensions of social adjustment that cut across functional roles. They assessed seven pairs of inappropriate behaviors in interpersonal relationships. Two of these emerged clearly in our analysis: overdependency and withdrawal. Interpersonal friction, work performance, and anxious rumination were not clearly represented in the item context of the Social Ineffectiveness Scale.

The factors isolated resembled factorial dimensions described in some other published studies. Linn et al. (1969), in a similar study to ours, but rating psychotic patients, reported five factors —apathetic detachment, dissatisfaction, hostility, health-finance concern, and manipulative dependency. The parallels between dissatisfaction and anxious rumination, hostility and friction, are clearest. The Linn manipulative dependency factor parallels our factor of emotional dependency.

Gurland et al. (1972b) have very recently reported a factor analysis of the SSIAM based on ratings of mixed adult patients who were considered suitable for outpatient psychotherapy. Six factors emerged, interpreted as social isolation, work inadequacy, friction with family, dependence on family, sexual dissatisfaction, and friction outside family. The clearest resemblances are between work inadequacy and our dimension of impaired work performance, and dependence on family and our dimension of family attachment. Friction was split into two dimensions in this analysis.

Katz and Lyerly (1963) described ratings of schizophrenics made by relatives, rather than interviewers, and including, as well as social behavior, a comprehensive list of minor and major psychiatric symptoms. In spite of these methodological differences from our study, some similar dimensions emerged. The authors grouped items into twelve clusters on the basis of intercorrelations. One of the item clusters, helplessness, included helpless, dependent behavior with depressive overtones akin to our factor of emotional dependency. Another, belligerence, described acts of manifest hostility related to interpersonal friction. A factor analysis performed on these clusters also isolated one dimension of social obstreperousness.

Strupp and Bergin (1969) described dimensions which had tended to emerge in a number of factor analyses of outcome measure in psychotherapy studies. The reviewed analyses differed from the present one in that they included not only measures of social functioning but a variety of scales measuring other areas. Partly as a result, factors emerging tended to reflect measurement method rather than dimensions across scales. The dimensions corresponded approximately to client self-evaluation, therapist evaluation, TAT and other fantasy evaluations, indices of concrete specific behavior, and other factors associated with specific instruments.

These comparisons with other studies based on nondepressive samples suggest that the factors described here have some generality. However, factors emerging from factor analysis depend to a considerable extent on the nature of the samples employed. It is unlikely that our depressive sample would represent the full gamut of potential disturbances. Additional factors, such as dominance, impulsiveness, sociopathic behavior, might emerge from other samples: the present factors probably represent that part of the spectrum characteristic of depression.

Conclusion

We have explored in this chapter three alternative systems of organizing and conceptualizing social adjustment—by role areas, by hypothetical qualitative categories, and by empirically derived factor analysis. Six dimensions of social adjustment were identified. They were interpreted as work performance, interpersonal friction, uninhibited communication, submissive dependency, family attachment, and anxious rumination. The factors appear to have many advantages as a scoring system. Their derivation renders them relatively "pure" in terms of item variance. They are conceptually meaningful and were able to show differential patterns. This does not mean that the other two frameworks should be abandoned. The qualitative categories overlapped with the factor system and might be regarded as an alternative in which types of items are more precisely distinguished but different specific patterns within interpersonal behaviors are not clearly distinguished. The role framework is more clearly a different one than categories or factors. It is a familiar framework and the earlier chapters in this book bear testament to its utility. It is true that the factorial dimensions, except for work performance, cut across roles. This does not necessarily refute the validity of the more familiar framework. Factors have no real existence; they are only hypothetical dimensions useful for systematizing the shared variance in items. Many other alternative factors could be obtained by further appropriate rotation, and some of these might correspond more closely to roles. Those emerging most readily did not do so, however. While role theory might provide a useful framework for making overall judgments of function, when function within these roles is broken down into its many components, common elements across roles also can be found.

10
Hostility in Depression

Opinions still differ on the presence, direction, and etiology of hostility in depression. In this chapter we will explore the dimension of hostility, which cuts across social roles, using several different assessments of hostility. The results of these assessments clarify the discrepancies found in the literature about hostility in depression.

We have already shown that acutely depressed women are more, not less, overtly hostile than the normals in all roles with the exception of their extended families (chaps. 5, 7, 8). Even here differences between patients and normals were in the same direction of increased hostility in the depressives and were not far from significant.[1] The finding of increased hostility requires further exploration since it contradicts a common view that externally expressed hostility should be diminished in depression. The relevant theories were reviewed in chapter 3. Hostility is central to the classical psychoanalytic model, which viewed hostility reverted away from the object world toward the self as

1. Increased overt hostility in the depressives was also reflected in the qualitative category of friction and the factorial dimension of interpersonal friction, which included all friction ratings together with some related variables (see chap. 9).

crucial in the formation of a depressive illness (Abraham 1927; Freud 1916; Rado 1928). It has often been inferred from this observation that externally directed hostility ought to be reduced in depression. Empirical studies have been few. One recent study, as noted in chapter 3, did report a diminution of outwardly expressed hostility in acutely depressed patients when compared to normals (Friedman 1970). This study, however, found that the hostility decreased even further during the patient's recovery, indicating that redirected hostility outward was not essential to recovery. Similarly, another study found that the expression of hostility outward was not correlated with symptomatic improvement in depression (Klerman and Gershon 1970). Contrary to the theory that "hostility-in" equals depression in all depressed patients, clinical experience suggests that depressed patients are often quite hostile. Even Rado in 1928 described the depressive as "irritable and brittle, easily taking offense."

One source contributing to the disagreements in the literature may be imprecision in definitions of the concepts. Depressed patients are heterogeneous, and the overt hostility appears to characterize certain subgroups, especially those with a high incidence of hysterical and other personality disorders (Lazare and Klerman 1968; Paykel 1971; Gershon et al. 1962) and a tendency to make suicide attempts (Paykel and Dienelt 1971; Phillip 1970; Weissman et al. 1973). Buss and Durkee (1957) have pointed out that the term "hostility" covers many diverse behaviors and attitudes that require separate assessment. Moreover, the expression of hostility in depressed patients may be elicited only in certain situations and in relationship to specific persons. The effects of these circumstances in modifying hostility and its expression have not been studied. Since, in our study, multiple assessments of different hostile expression were recorded, there was an opportunity to examine hostility in depression under various conditions.

Assessments

The ratings from the social adjustment scale were supplemented for these analyses by data derived from the initial psychiatric symptom interview. At initial interview all depressed patients were seen for at least one hour by an experienced psychiatrist responsible for their ongoing treatment, who administered the Clinical Interview for Depression (clinical interview) (Paykel et al. 1970), a modification of the Hamilton Rating Scale, and the Brief Psychiatric Rating Scale (BPRS) (Overall and Gorham 1962). Since the normal subjects were selected to be symptom-free at interview, they were not given the preceding clinical status assessments.

These ratings could be divided into two groups: ratings of hostile behavior at interview and patient's report of hostility to others.

A. *Ratings of Hostile Behavior at Interview.* Two ratings referred to hostile behavior manifested at interview. *Uncooperativeness (BPRS).* The psychiatrist assessed resistance, unfriendliness, resentment, and uncooperativeness, based solely on patient's behavior in the interview situation and not on reported hostility outside it.

Hostility (clinical interview). The psychiatrist rated the extent to which the patient spontaneously evidenced hostility by complaining of staff, procedures, or interviewer, demanded special attention, was uncooperative, or was overtly hostile at interview.

B. *Report of Hostility to Others.* These ratings did not refer to the patient's overt behavior, but to her reports of hostile behavior or feelings to others.

Hostility (BPRS). The psychiatrist rated patient's animosity, contempt, belligerence towards others outside the interview, based on the patient's verbal report.

Irritability (clinical interview). The psychiatrist rated hostile behaviors such as getting irritated with others, losing one's temper, shouting, slamming doors, hitting, based on patient's reports and not manifest behavior at interview.

Friction (SAS). The social adjustment scale items assessed overt hostility at work, with friends and extended family, with spouse and children.

Interview Hostility and Hostility to Others

There was a difference between the ratings of hostile behavior at the interview and the ratings of the patients' reports of hostile

TABLE 10.1. RATINGS OF HOSTILITY FOR
FORTY DEPRESSED PATIENTS

Rating Scale*	Mean†
Hostility at interview	
1. Uncooperativeness (BPRS)	1.60
2. Hostility (Clinical Interview)	1.55
Reported hostility to others	
3. Hostility (BPRS)	2.43
4. Irritability (Clinical Interview)	2.85
5. Friction (SAS)	1.98

* Scale range is 1–7 for all ratings except friction,
where the range is 1–5.
† Higher scores indicate greater impairment.

behavior to others outside the interview (see table 10.1). Hostile
behavior at the interview was rated at the very low part of the
scale range, little above the zero point (that is, number 1 in these
ratings). Hostility to others was rated higher, in the moderate
range. Although the ratings were not on identical scales and caution is necessary in comparing them, this difference appeared to
be consistent over the two ratings of hostile behavior and the
three ratings of hostility to others, strongly suggesting differences between them. The discrepancy might explain the reports
in the psychiatric literature of diminished hostility in depressives. Depressives did show low hostility to therapists but not to
those outside the therapy situation.

Continuum of Intimacy

Further evidence of differences in the expression of hostility to
different persons in the social field was obtained when findings
were examined separately for the interpersonal friction ratings
in the five roles. Since these ratings had also been made on
normals, comparisons were possible. Findings are shown graphically in figure 10.1.

The five areas were ranked and are displayed along a continuum of social distance or intimacy, ranging from work at the
most distant, through social leisure (friends), extended family, to
spouse and children at the intimate pole; (since all subjects
were females, children rather than spouse were ranked as the
most intimate, but this judgment may be debatable). That this
concept was meaningful was demonstrated by the findings.

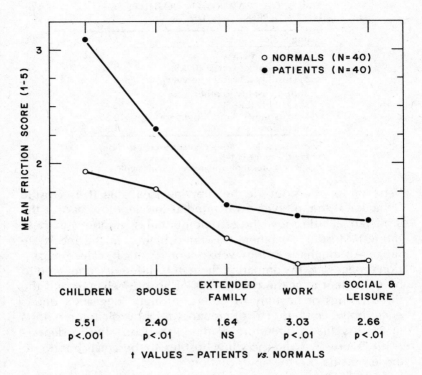

FIG. 10.1.   Degree of friction as a function of social distance or intimacy.

There was an increase in friction as the intimate pole was approached for normals. This was much more marked for depressives. While patients' friction as compared to normals was actually a little increased in all roles except with extended family, it was most markedly so in the intimate areas, particularly in relationship with children.

These findings are consistent with the findings for interview hostility, but serve to extend them. The expression of hostility in depressed patients varies along a continuum. At one pole, hostility to close relations (spouse and children) is markedly increased. At the other pole, hostility at work shows only a little increase. Hostility manifested at interview may not be increased at all. We cannot be sure since we have no normals for this rating by the psychiatrist. Although ratings were a little above the zero point, so might they be for normals. It is at least probable that other kinds of patients may score higher.

Intercorrelation

To further explore the variation in hostility ratings, the five ratings on the depressed patients were intercorrelated (see table 10.2). Not only was there a difference in mean level between hostility at interview and to others, but, to some extent, the two kinds of hostility were separable on intercorrelations. Within the group of reported hostility to others there were three possible correlations, and all were significant. Within hostility at interview there was only one possible correlation—between the two items—and it, too, was significant. Thus all of the four possible correlations within item groups reached statistical significance. Between items of one group and of the other, there were six possible correlations, and only two reached statistical significance—those between hostility at interview (rating interview-hostility) and hostility (BPRS) and friction (both rating hostility to others). These correlations are probably explicable in terms of detailed rating instructions for hostility at interview (clinical interview). Although this variable rated interview behavior primarily, it also included animosity shown to staff outside the interview situation. A limited overlap with hostility to others was, therefore, implied. In general it appeared that items in the two kinds of hostility tended to vary in separate groups, further supporting their differentiation.

Implications for Assessing Hostility

These findings have several implications for the assessment of hostility. The depressed patient's behavior at interview is a poor sample of her actual behavior outside. In the initial psychiatric interview she is cooperative, compliant, and not hostile. The psychiatrist is, in a sense, correct in regarding her as lacking in overt hostility.

Had her behavior with the psychiatrist been used to assess her interpersonal difficulties outside the interview, a distorted

TABLE 10.2 INTERCORRELATION OF HOSTILITY VARIABLES AT INTERVIEW AND AS REPORTED TO OTHERS FROM BPRS, CLINICAL INTERVIEW, AND SAS

| | | Hostility at Interview | | Reported Hostility to Others | | |
		Uncooperativeness (BPRS)	Hostility at Interview (Clinical Interview)	Hostility (BPRS)	Irritability (Clin. Int.)	$\overline{X}$ Friction† (SAS)
Hostility at Interview	Uncooperativeness (BPRS)	1.000				
	Hostility (Clinical Int.)	.375*	1.000			
Reported Hostility to Others	Hostility (BPRS)	.122	.511**	1.000		
	Irritability (Clin. Int.)	.253	.307	.536**	1.000	
	$\overline{X}$ Friction† (SAS)	.173	.389*	.424**	.529**	1.000

* p < .05
** p < .01
† Mean of five separate ratings

view would have been presented. The psychiatrist during early interviews, like the patient's acquaintances, was not the recipient of the hostility. There would be considerable discrepancy between the family's complaints about the patient's irritability and the psychiatrist's experience. Although the patient's global reports of hostility outside the interview showed a moderate increase from that shown at interview, this gave a limited picture of the range of hostility. Such overall evaluations concealed the full picture. The patient was having considerable friction with some people, none at all with others, and none with the therapist. Assuming she took the full range of her relationships with different persons into account, at best her overall assessment would have described an artificial average which represented neither the extreme friction she might have with her children nor the relatively harmonious relations she might have with her neighbors.

Others have commented on the need for supplementing overall estimates of intensity of hostility with estimates of the intensity of the various subhostilities (Buss and Durkee 1957). These data suggest that assessments of hostility include systematic inquiry into the patient's specific relationships especially with close family. The overt presence of hostility at interview may also be influenced by the timing of the interview and the rater's therapeutic involvement.

The Object Choice of Hostility in Depression

Outside the psychiatric interview, a different picture of the depressed patient's behavior emerges. She has significantly more friction than normals in most relationships. The psychoanalytic model of depression emphasizes a redirection of hostile feelings inward on the self (chap. 3). This has been associated by many with the implication that outwardly directed hostility to others must be reduced. These findings leave little doubt that this is a misconception. The depressed woman studied here showed significantly more overt interpersonal hostility in most relationships, and the intensity of these hostile feelings ranged from resentment, general irritability, through arguments of increasing intensity, to physical encounters. With the therapist, however, she was withdrawn, compliant, and often obsequious.

E.B.'s behavior illustrates this. She cried throughout the interview, had thoughts of suicide, was hopeless about the future, and said she was a failure. She was willing to go along with whatever treatment was prescribed. As we got to know her, we learned that she was involved in an extremely hostile exchange at home with her husband and children. In an explosive rage she had thrown a set of dishes at her husband, and then had thrown her 15-year-old daughter down the stairs. However, she maintained harmonious relationships with her friends and work associates throughout her illness.

Increased hostility with intimate associates in depression is partially consistent with the psychoanalytic observations. Presumably, depression occurs when the individual cannot directly express this anger towards the disappointing love-object for fear of losing support. Therefore, overt anger is shifted from the love-object to anger against the self and verbalized appreciation of the object. The overt expression of this anger is presumed to be therapeutic when it occurs. Depressive symptoms secondarily obtain care and attention for the patient.

Following this line of reasoning, it is consistent that the depressed patient is not hostile during initial interviews. The patient's disappointments are not with the therapist. Rather than frustrating needs for love and dependency, the therapist is offering assistance. As Ostow (1970) has pointed out, the therapist in his attempts to comfort is assuming a role that has been relinquished by the patient's love-object. However, the amount of direct expression of hostility we observed was inconsistent with the psychoanalytic theory. Furthermore, this direct expression occurred despite symptoms and was not necessarily therapeutic. In long-term treatment the therapist might assume in the transference a role similar to close family, and the patient's overt hostility might become apparent. This hostility has been described by those engaged in intensive psychotherapy with depressed patients (Spiegel 1967). Hospitalized depressives probably exhibit more hostility to staff members, especially nurses, who assume an intimate care-taking role.

Psychoanalytic theory suggests that the depressed patient's own mother should be a source of hostility. If this were so, the question would arise as to why more hostility is not shown with the extended family that included the patient's parents. The sample was middle-aged and many of their parents were not living, so that extended family relationships were only with siblings. While the hostility to parents may have existed on an unconscious level, it was not detected by these assessments.

Question arises as to why children are the objects of the most hostility, even greater than that found towards the spouse. Clinical data suggested that the spouse in a small number of cases was providing emotional support; therefore the patient did not feel hostile toward him. More often, the patient was hostile and tempered direct expression toward the spouse out of fear of the consequences. She was less fearful of the immediate consequences with the children, and they became the misdirected targets of her unexpressed rage towards her spouse. The children were vulnerable, in that they did not supply the mother with a dependent relationship but made their own demands for dependency.

When Mrs. D. came for her weekly appointment she could barely speak above a whisper. Always on time, never missing an appointment, when she arrived today she was even earlier and more quiet than usual. It was only at the end of the hour that she described what had gone on the night before. With a trembling voice she said that she had held a knife up to her daughter's throat and had the girl moved an inch she could have lunged it in. Her daughter had been deliberately defiant and she just couldn't take it any longer. The experience left the mother feeling weak, frightened and full of remorse.

Hostility, Depression, and Suicide Attempts

Attention has recently been drawn to the depressed patient who is overtly hostile to the therapist, especially during the initial treatment interviews. There are suggestions that this patient may be a special risk for suicide attempt. A number of clinical reports have commented on the hostility of suicide attempters and consider the eruption of rage in a depressed patient to indicate potential risk (Sarwer-Foner 1969; Shein and Stone 1969; Seiden 1969; Lesse 1967; Rosenbaum and Richman 1970; Birtchnell and Alarcon 1971; Philip 1970; Vinoda 1966). Two studies have actually compared depressed patients who made suicide attempts with those who did not and found that overtly expressed hostility at psychiatric interview was the most important distinguishing feature of the attempters (Paykel and Dienelt 1971; Weissman et al. 1973). These findings held up when other factors such as age and sex, which might have confounded the results, were controlled. Moreover, one study noted that the overtly expressed hostility of the depressed suicide attempter interfered with treatment, led to early discharge and high attrition and, by contrast, that the depressed patients who had not made a suicide attempt did not have the same high attrition (Weissman et al. 1973).

While the theory that "hostility turned inward" equals depression suggests that the depressed patient who begins to overtly express anger, especially to the staff, is improving, the results with depressed suicide attempters suggest a contrary interpretation—the eruption of angry, complaining behavior to strangers and staff in a depressed patient may be indicative of a risk for suicide attempt.

Clinical Implications

Studies have shown that the mobilization of hostility outward in depressed patients was not necessary for symptomatic improvement (Gershon et al. 1968; Klerman and Gershon 1970). While these studies rated verbal samples of hostility and may not be indicative of actual behavior, their findings, together with ours, suggest that the mobilization of additional anger outwards in depression has limited therapeutic value and might be disastrous to tenuous relationships. Treatment geared to helping the patient acknowledge and come to terms with his anger, its origins and consequences, rather than act it out might be effective in rebuilding relationships. Clinical experiences indicated that expression of overt anger was not impaired but that direct communication of needs, wishes, or feelings was, as evidenced by the impaired, inhibited communication discussed in the preceding chapter.

The discrepancies between the depressive behavior at interview and at home necessitates careful questioning about the patient's relationships with intimates and particularly her children. Even the most withdrawn depressed patient can be extremely hostile at home. This hostility is mixed with ambivalence and guilt. The patient may either not readily discuss it or may cloak it in socially acceptable terms such as "difficulty tolerating the children's noise" or "irritability," thereby minimizing the degree of actual violence. Direct questioning can lift the burden of secrecy from the patient and establish the treatment relationship on firm ground.

Lastly, we find no direct evidence to support the theory that "anger-in equals depression," which seems too simple in its original form. Depressed patients clearly are overtly hostile.

III.
THE RECOVERY

Part III shifts the study from the acute depressive episode to a longitudinal look at changes in the patients' social adjustment through eight months of treatment and a one-year follow-up. By comparing the patients' social adjustment during recovery with their acute state, and again with the normals, we can learn more about the nature of the impairments, their course, whether they are enduring or transient, and whether they respond to treatment. This enables us, in chapter 11, to answer questions about the existence and specificity of a depressive personality. Having established certain patterns, we then look, in chapter 12, at the relationship between the patients' social impairments and their symptoms, together with other important characteristics such as age, social background, and diagnosis. In chapter 13 we explore the effects of eight-months of psychotherapy in reducing the serious impairments characteristic of the acute episode. Up to this point the patients had been under the close care of the clinic. After eight months this care terminated, and in chapter 14 we revisit them one year later to learn what has happened in the interim. Our findings, in Part III, enable us to test more explicitly some of the hypotheses presented earlier about the origins of the social maladjustments in depression.

11
Social Adjustment, Improvement, and Recovery

The previous chapters have dealt with a small portion of time in the patient's lives, a cross section at the height of the acute depression. In this chapter we will follow the patients' longitudinal course and their patterns of change over eight months. The patterns of change and the amount of social impairment remaining in recovered patients will give clues to the factors underlying the social disturbance and to the need for treatment.

As discussed in chapter 3, there are two broad sets of theories regarding the origins and nature of the social dysfunction in depression. The first is that they are secondary consequences of the symptomatic disturbance of depression. The second view is that the social impairments reflect persistent character abnormalities which are exaggerated during the depressive episode. This theory is consistent with the psychoanalytic hypotheses that depression-prone individuals have certain specific character traits. It is also consistent with the more general pattern of neuroticism suggested by some nonpsychoanalytic writers.

We would predict different patterns of change over time with these different hypotheses. If the social disturbance is entirely secondary to depressive symptoms, it should subside quickly and completely, since these were patients who showed rapid symptomatic remission. They should be well-adjusted when their symptoms resolve. If, however, the social disturbance reflects character more than symptoms, we would expect slow and incomplete social recovery. The end state might show specific abnormalities in keeping with one or another psychoanalytic hypothesis; even when well, patients may be dependent and hostile. Alternatively, if the abnormality is a general neuroticism, there might be an overall impairment in all areas of function without any specific patterns.

Procedure of Follow-up

After the acute episode, the patients remained in treatment with the research team. Their social adjustment was evaluated at the end of two, four, and eight months, using exactly the same rating instrument with which they were initially interviewed.

The majority of patients remained both symptomatically well and accessible for interview during these eight months. Only three patients were lost to the study due to noncooperation. Ten patients developed clinical relapses at some point during the eight months. Relapse was defined as a return of symptoms, lasting one month, at the level that would have initially qualified the patient for inclusion in the study, or a return of more severe symptoms for a shorter period that made an alternative course of treatment imperative. Patients who relapsed were withdrawn from the therapeutic study and a social-adjustment rating was made within two weeks of withdrawal. Since we were primarily interested in the pattern of social recovery in symptom-free patients, in this chapter we will focus on the twenty-seven patients who did not relapse and continued to remain available for interview. The ten subjects who relapsed, as well as the three who refused to cooperate, will be described separately.

The procedure for the normals was different in that they were interviewed only once. This single interview was used as a base line throughout the study since there was no a priori reason to expect them to change systematically in one direction.[1]

In presenting the results we will make use of the individual variables, but we will concentrate on the derived factor scores discussed in chapter 9 since these factor dimensions offered the most useful framework in which to view changes.

Depressed and Recovered Patients and Normals

Individual variables. We first examined findings using the forty-eight individual ratings. Table 11.1 shows mean scores for the twenty-seven depressed patients at initial and eighth-month ratings, and for the single rating of the forty normals. Three sets of differences were tested for significance, using the t test: between patients' depressed status and normals; between patients' depressed and recovered status (this analysis used the test for paired data); and between patients' recovered status and normals. The acutely depressed patients were found to be significantly more maladjusted than normals on most variables. Essentially these findings recapitulate those already extensively presented for the acute episode. However, they were important to check since we were dealing here with a slightly different sample, twenty-seven of the original forty patients.

Over the eight months from acute depression to the recovered rating, most variables tended to show some improvement (table 11.1). The improvement reached statistical significance for twenty-six variables; no variable showed significant worsening. Only three showed even any nonsignificant worsening—diminished frequency of dating, reticence in social and leisure activities, and domineering behavior towards extended family. The first of these was rated only in single subjects, who were very few, and the last was only present to a very low degree in any group. Thus the answer to one important research question has

1. The forty normals were retained as a single group to compare with the depressives in the main analyses, rather than being reduced to twenty-seven. As a preliminary check, patients who relapsed were compared with those who did not, using sociodemographic variables. No significant differences were found so that there did not appear to be any systematic sociodemographic biases requiring correction by rematching.

TABLE 11.1. SOCIAL ADJUSTMENT OF DEPRESSED PATIENTS, RECOVERED PATIENTS, AND NORMALS

Variable†	Depressed N = 27	Recovered N = 27	Normals N = 40	Depressed vs. Normals	Depressed vs. Recovered	Recovered vs. Normals
Work:						
Time lost	2.96	1.48	1.28	5.70***	4.96***	1.03
Impaired performance	2.96	1.41	1.15	7.34***	5.29***	1.83
Friction	1.48	1.37	1.10	2.83**	0.68	2.30*
Distress	3.26	1.85	1.59	8.82***	6.98***	1.38
Disinterest	3.37	1.93	1.67	7.78***	5.38***	1.17
Feelings of inadequacy	2.67	1.22	1.15	7.20***	6.32***	0.55
Social and Leisure:						
Diminished contact with friends	3.41	2.89	2.55	3.18***	2.27*	1.25
Diminished social interactions	3.44	2.78	2.38	3.19**	2.08*	1.19
Impaired leisure activities	3.56	3.04	2.40	4.12***	1.86	2.00*
Friction	1.52	1.30	1.13	2.77**	1.30	1.48
Reticence	2.48	2.74	2.25	0.65	−0.79	1.31
Hypersensitive behavior	2.33	1.63	1.50	3.43**	2.82***	0.56
Social discomfort	2.52	1.39	1.38	6.34***	5.87***	0.06
Loneliness	1.89	1.59	1.40	2.38*	1.32	1.10
Boredom	2.82	1.70	1.48	5.79***	5.00***	1.05
Diminished dating	2.25	3.67	3.80	−1.46	−1.00	−0.15
Disinterest in dating	2.83	2.44	2.40	0.44	2.24	0.06
Extended Family:						
Friction	1.74	1.60	1.33	1.96	0.36	1.65
Reticence	3.46	3.42	2.68	2.35*	0.12	2.21*
Withdrawal	1.79	1.23	1.13	3.96***	2.72*	1.12
Family attachment	1.68	1.1†	1.45	1.17	3.12**	−1.61
Rebellion	1.24	1.00	1.03	2.17*	2.01	−0.80
Guilt	1.69	1.23	1.18	2.69**	1.85	0.50
Worry	1.46	1.31	1.65	−1.00	0.85	−2.11*
Resentment	2.19	1.42	1.38	3.12**	2.87**	0.26

Table 11.1—Continued

Variable†	Depressed N = 27	Recovered N = 27	Normals N = 40	Depressed vs. Normals	Depressed vs. Recovered	Recovered vs. Normals
Marital:						
Friction	2.18	2.00	1.77	1.70	1.31	0.95
Reticence	2.47	2.11	1.77	2.30*	1.28	1.15
Domineering behavior	1.18	1.50	1.44	−1.12	−1.29	0.24
Dependency	2.65	1.78	1.94	−2.78**	3.00**	−0.69
Submissiveness	2.53	1.83	1.65	3.07***	1.56	0.75
Lack of affection	2.12	1.83	1.65	1.92	1.81	0.77
Diminished intercourse	3.06	3.06	2.32	1.93	0.42	2.01
Sexual problems	1.73	1.73	1.27	2.52*	0.00	1.64
Disinterest in sex	2.77	2.33	1.56	5.24***	2.28*	2.82**
Parental:						
Lack of involvement	2.83	1.82	1.63	5.76***	4.14***	0.86
Impaired communication	2.32	1.86	1.67	2.90**	1.79	0.99
Friction	3.13	2.18	1.93	5.16***	3.87***	1.40
Lack of affection	2.22	1.36	1.19	4.46***	3.70**	1.28
Family Unit:						
Guilt	2.96	1.67	1.33	7.15***	5.46***	1.75
Worry	2.52	1.85	1.83	2.89**	2.59*	0.08
Resentment	2.00	1.78	1.39	2.70**	1.10	2.21*
Economic inadequacy of family unit	1.74	1.85	1.15	2.87**	−0.55	3.33**
Overall Evaluations:						
Work	4.11	2.07	1.46	10.90***	7.15***	3.49***
Social and leisure	4.22	3.26	2.43	6.65***	4.74***	3.35**
Extended family	3.50	2.69	2.25	4.81***	3.04**	2.31*
Marital	3.41	3.17	2.53	3.26**	2.22*	2.05*
Parental	3.87	2.64	2.11	7.68***	6.01***	2.23*
Overall adjustment	4.67	3.07	2.48	11.51***	8.89***	3.33**

* Significant at $< .05$
** Significant at $< .01$
*** Significant at $< .001$
† Ranges for all items were 1–5, except overall evaluations, where the range was 1–7.

already emerged. Social maladjustment in depressives is not a long-term, static phenomenon. There is a general tendency for adjustment to improve over the months following symptomatic recovery. For most rating assessments this improvement was moderate in extent.

What of residual defect? The recovered depressives at eight months tended to be more socially impaired (higher scores) than the normals. The differences were not statistically significant on many variables—twelve in all—but these included all the overall evaluations of role areas. On only five variables were patients less impaired than normals and on only one of these, worry over extended family, was the difference statistically significant. Thus we find that on the whole there is some residual deficit. Although the patients improved a good deal, they did not return to the level of the normals.

Although not all variables showed these improvements and residual deficits to the same extent, specific differentiating patterns were not very marked. As we will see in subsequent sections, patterns emerged much more clearly when different scoring approaches were examined.

The economic inadequacy of the family unit was one area with an exceptional pattern. It showed no improvement over the eight months, and there was a substantial residual difference between patients and normals, suggesting a harsh impact of the illness itself on the economic status of the family. This finding is particularly striking since treatment at the research clinic was free, and direct costs were not an important factor. Moreover the patients were women, and most were not the main family breadwinner. It would appear, nevertheless, that absence of their contribution to the family finances was sufficient to prevent improvement in the family's impaired economic status. Unfortunately, we cannot be sure of this conclusion. Patients were interviewed four times over eight months, normals only once. For most variables there was no reason to anticipate that systematic changes in the normals would occur. However, the assessment of financial status poses a particular problem since the time when the study data was collected (1968–69) was one of generally worsening economic conditions, and the normals might have shown a worsening over this period also.

Factor Scores. In order to explore specific patterns, a similar set of analyses was carried out using the derived scores by factors, roles, and qualitative categories discussed in chapter 9. Findings for the factors are shown in table 11.2. As with the individual items, the patterns for the depressed status closely resembled those found for the full sample. Initially, patients differed significantly from normals on all factors, the most striking differences being on work performance and anxious rumination.

Over eight months the patients improved significantly on all factors except inhibited communication, for which the change fell only minimally short of 5 percent significance. The greatest improvement was on work performance and anxious rumination, which had showed the greatest initial impairment.

When recovered patients were compared with the normals, there was still a general trend for patients to show more pathology. However, there was evidence of a differential pattern. The recovered patients still showed significantly more inhibited communication and more interpersonal friction than the normals. There was borderline abnormality, not far from significance, on work performance and anxious rumination. On submissive dependency and family attachment, patients and normals were closely comparable.[2]

Clinical Relapse

The previous findings all involved patients who were relatively symptom-free during the eight months. Ten patients relapsed

2. Findings for the role areas, qualitative categories, and the total score are shown in Appendix B in table B2. They showed similar trends, but less evidence of a differentiated pattern. The overall scores faithfully mirrored the general trend, showing significant patient abnormality compared to the normals, significant improvement over eight months, and significant residual deficit. Role areas showed a relatively nondifferentiated pattern. As for the full sample, all roles were initially impaired, the largest being for work. All roles improved significantly over eight months but tended to show residual abnormality. The impairment was greatest in social and leisure activities and least for the extended family.

The qualitative categories showed a partially differentiated pattern. The greatest initial impairment was on instrumental role performance and satisfactions and feelings. The latter showed the greatest improvement. Residual abnormality, however, remained for three of the four categories, and not far short of significant for the fourth, quality of interpersonal relations.

TABLE 11.2. FACTOR SCORES IN DEPRESSED PATIENTS, RECOVERED PATIENTS, AND NORMALS

Factor	Mean Scores			t Values for Differences		
	Depressed $N = 27$	Recovered $N = 27$	Normals $N = 40$	Depressed vs. Normals	Depressed vs. Recovered	Recovered vs. Normals
Work performance	2.99	1.51	1.31	9.62***	8.21***	1.75
Anxious rumination	2.44	1.67	1.54	8.23***	8.67***	1.51
Submissive dependency	2.03	1.45	1.51	2.86**	2.89**	−0.49
Family attachment	2.54	1.99	1.81	3.44**	2.94**	0.92
Interpersonal friction	2.07	1.65	1.41	5.02***	3.27**	2.09*
Inhibited communication	2.57	2.31	1.97	3.65***	2.01	2.30*

* p $\bigvee$ .05
** p $\bigvee\bigvee$ .01
*** p $\bigvee\bigvee$ .001

during the eight months, and their social-adjustment course was examined separately. Before relapse their social adjustment was nearly identical to that of nonrelapsers. Additional social-adjustment ratings were made on these patients at the time of relapse and withdrawal from the study. Table 11.3 shows mean

TABLE 11.3.   CHANGES ON FACTOR SCORES IN PATIENTS WHO RELAPSED (N = 10)

Factor	Last Rating Prior to Relapse* Mean	Relapse Rating Mean	Difference	Significance of Difference
Work performance	1.55	2.13	0.58	<.05
Anxious rumination	1.69	1.88	0.19	NS
Submissive dependency	4.47	1.77	0.30	<.05
Family attachment	2.08	2.55	0.47	<.05
Interpersonal friction	1.74	1.84	0.10	NS
Inhibited communication	2.34	2.52	0.18	NS

* Scale range is 1–5. Higher score means more impairment.

factor scores for these ten patients at the last rating before relapse and at the height of relapse. Significance of change was tested by t tests for paired data. All six scores worsened with relapse, although for only three was the change statistically significant. The greatest worsening was on work performance. Family attachment and submissive dependency also worsened significantly. The change for anxious rumination was not significant. Neither were those for inhibited communication or for interpersonal friction, which worsened the least. Except for anxious rumination, which might have been expected to change more markedly, the factor dimensions behaved in relation to symptomatic relapse in the same way as they did for recovery in well patients. The worsening in these factors was sufficiently rapid for it to be detected shortly after relapse; it was therefore probably more rapid than the equivalent previous improvement.[3]

3. Findings for the role areas and qualitative categories are set out in Appendix B, table B3. For roles, the pattern was less consistent. The least change was for the parental area, which actually showed minimal improvement after relapse. The pattern for qualitative categories was more consistent,

Patterns of Change and Specific Impairments

So far the findings do not reveal how rapidly or slowly these different dimensions changed. The time course of social adjustment was now examined by plotting graphically the patients' adjustment at the beginning of the study and at two, four, and eight months. Findings for the factors are shown in figure 11.1. For ease of interpretation all scores were reduced

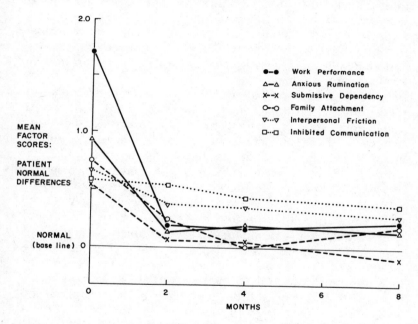

FIG. 11.1.   Dimensions of social adjustment: depressed patient-normal differences over eight months.

to the same base line, that of the normals, by subtracting from each the appropriate mean score for the normals. Therefore, plotted values reflect mean differences between patients and normals over eight months.

---

the greatest worsening occurring on the two categories which previously appeared most closely related to symptomatic course, instrumental role performance and feelings and satisfactions.

Two factors showed rapid remission, the most pronounced changes having occurred in the first two months. This pattern was shown most strikingly by work performance, and secondly by anxious rumination. Both these factors remained essentially static thereafter, at a level a little more abnormal, although not significantly so, than the normals. Submissive dependency also improved rapidly in the first two months, eventually to the normal level, at which it remained. Family attachment improved more slowly, over four months, to the normal level, and worsened a little over the next four months. The disturbances summarized by inhibited communication and interpersonal friction showed a different pattern. They improved quite slowly and gradually; both were still significantly worse than normal level at eight months.

Taken together, the patients' initial impairments, course of remission, and residual deficits showed different patterns. At one extreme were the patients' work performance and anxious rumination, both of which seemed closely related to symptomatic illness. These two factors showed the greatest initial impairment, the most rapid remission, and the greatest worsening on relapse, although their levels were still slightly worse than those of the normals. Submissive dependency and family attachment were also closely related to symptom course. However, they were initially less impaired. They improved the most, and worsened considerably with relapse. At the other extreme were interpersonal friction and inhibited communication. Less strikingly abnormal to start with, they showed the slowest and most incomplete remission and the least change with relapse. They were most closely related to the underlying personality of the depressive.[4]

We can transpose these findings into clinical terms. An acutely depressed woman will be almost completely unable to do her work and will ruminate about her failures. Her ruminations are characteristic of the hopelessness and worthlessness felt by the

---

4. Similar graphs for role areas and qualitative categories are contained in Appendix B, figures B1 and B2. Differentiated patterns were less clear cut. For role areas, the most rapid remission was in work, parenthood, and in the family unit. For qualitative categories, rapid improvement took place in feelings and satisfactions, and instrumental role performance.

depressive. She will be withdrawn from social activities, dependent on her family and submissive to their wishes. As she recovers from her depression, much of this impairment will disappear. She will resume her work, stop ruminating, be more independent and assertive. These social impairments can be considered as symptom-related.

On the other hand, she will experience increased friction with others and an inability to communicate openly and freely, both at the height of illness and to a lesser but still serious extent after her recovery. These two areas, interpersonal friction and impaired communication, may represent more enduring personality features that can be considered potential targets for psychological intervention.

Rate of Improvement

The most rapid remission of social impairments occurred in the first two months. There was slower improvement in the next two months, following which, to a total of eight months, the average course was relatively static, with some residual impairment.

How does this course compare with that of symptoms? Since each assessment concerned the prior two months, some time-lag in improvement was inevitable. Nevertheless the social recovery was a good deal slower than that for symptoms. These were all patients responding to initial treatment with amitriptyline and remaining well. When symptom ratings made by psychiatrists were examined, symptomatic improvement was found ιo be virtually complete at the end of one month and to remain essentially stationary thereafter. This was in sharp contrast to social functioning, which did not improve for at least four months and often showed residual impairment. The patient was still likely to be considerably impaired in social function at a time when she was symptom-free.

These findings have important implications for treatment. Although antidepressants can have a marked impact on reducing the symptoms of depression in a relatively brief time, social recovery is slower (at least four months) and incomplete. The patient may be "feeling better" after a month of pharmacotherapy, but psychological support and intervention may need to continue well beyond that time.

Mrs. P., a 33-year-old married woman suffering her second depression, illustrates the distinction between symptomatic and social remission.

Mrs. P.'s depression developed over a period of three months following a move from another state due to her husband's job change. A viral infection, fatigue from making a move she resented, and the care of two children in new surroundings without familiar friends gradually led to increasing depressive symptoms. She lost 15 pounds, was unable to sleep through the night, was frequently on the verge of tears, and had thoughts of suicide.

Her marriage had been going steadily downhill since the birth of her two children, aged 10 and 4. Her husband was possessive of them, critical of her, and his mother, who lived with them, had taken over their care, making the patient feel like a stranger in her own home. The patient felt completely unable to change the course of events. She began weekly treatment with antidepressants and over the course of five weeks her appetite returned and her weight increased. Her sleep became regular and she felt renewed energy and confidence in herself. At the end of three months she had taken a job as a secretary, and over the course of the next few months she worked herself into the job so that she was well-liked by her associates and gained much satisfaction from her work.

Despite her good response to medication, nothing changed much at home. Her mother-in-law was still in the house and she continued to have marital friction. She and her husband rarely communicated with each other and she continued to feel like a stranger in her own home. Despite these problems, she was almost completely free of symptoms, and her lessened irritability reduced some but not most of the family tension.

Residual Deficits

Some of our aims in this chapter have been to attempt to answer fundamental questions about the origins and nature of the social dysfunctions in depression. Are these dysfunctions primarily consequences of depressive symptoms and epiphenomena? Are they primarily manifestations of the long-standing personality disorders which predispose to depression?

The findings indicate that overall, in the eight months after the depressive episode, considerable improvement in social function occurs. Although the improvement is substantial, it is incomplete and there is some residual dysfunction. Relapse of depressive symptoms is associated with rapid worsening of social function.

The social function of the patients does not reach that of normals. The possibility must first be considered that a portion of this deficit could be spurious. Practical considerations in designing the study forced us to make compromises. While the patients were interviewed four times, the normals were interviewed only once. Increasing familiarity might have suggested subtle dysfunction to the raters. The raters were not blind as to which subjects were patients or normals, and they might have tended as a result to have rated even recovered patients as worse. Moreover, the normals were not entirely representative of the general population. They were "normals" in the sense that those with psychiatric symptoms were excluded. These factors might have contributed to the residual impairment. However, it is unlikely that they were responsible for all of it. The impairment was of moderate degree and showed a specific pattern that would be hard to attribute to methodologic bias. It seems likely that much of the residual deficit was real.

We are thus led to a conclusion intermediate between the two extremes of symptomatic consequence and personality disturbance. Much of the social impairment appears symptom-related, subsiding with symptom reduction and returning with relapse. A smaller but definite portion reflects underlying personality disturbance. The relative magnitude of residual deficit and symptom-related portion can be roughly estimated from the ratings, although any such estimate must be treated cautiously since we have little evidence that our ratings form a perfect tape measure in which the successive numbers correspond to equal intervals. If, however, we examine the overall evaluation of adjustment (table 11.1), the initial mean rating was 4.67, the recovered rating 3.07, the normal rating 2.48. The symptom-related improvement (1.60) thus spanned 73 percent of the original patient-normal difference of 2.19: the residual deficit was 27 percent of the original difference.[5]

5. These percentages were obtained by taking the normals' overall adjustment score of 2.48 and subtracting that from the patients' score at the height

In these terms, three-quarters of the original disturbance might be regarded as symptom-related, and one-quarter personality-related. Looked at another way, the improvement over eight months was impressive. As shown in the previous case of Mrs. P., following the patient's recovery, she was able to obtain a job, make friends, and enjoy herself at work. She was getting along somewhat better with her husband and mother-in-law and was caring for the children. However, her marriage still remained a serious problem, and she and her husband had poor communication.

Equally important, the symptom-related and the persisting aspects of social maladjustment were to some extent separable. Impaired work performance, anxious rumination, submissive dependency, and family attachment are particularly related to symptomatic course. We have already in chapter 9 discussed the relationship of these functional disturbances to depressive symptoms. The persistent disturbances tended to be in other aspects: interpersonal friction and inhibited communication.

The Depressive Personality

These residual deficits provide an indirect way of testing hypotheses about the depressive personality. Since there are relatively few direct studies which have used rating methodologies or comparisons with normals in order to examine these issues, the findings of the recovered depressives are of interest. We found that the residual impairments were a good deal less in amount and different in pattern than those at the height of illness. Therefore, it is unwise to conclude much about the depressed woman's lifelong social and personality patterns from her depressed state. Clinical writings, including some by psychoanalytic authors, which extrapolate a depressive personality

---

of illness, which was 4.67. This gave the acutely depressed patient-normal differences. In the same way the normal score was subtracted from the recovered patients' score of 3.07 to get the recovered depressive-normal differences. The illness difference, which was 1.60, was divided by the recovery difference, which was 2.19, to obtain a mean percent of recovery in the patients in relation to the normals. This amount of recovery was equal to 73 percent. The difference between 73 percent and 100 percent, or 27 percent, was considered the patients' residual deficit.

type from experience with acutely symptomatic patients are subject to such error.

There were a number of important negative findings. First, those theories which postulate dependency as a central and enduring feature predisposing to depression, as discussed in chapter 3, were not supported. Although dependency was characteristic of the depressed state, it is the dimension which returns most convincingly to normal on recovery.

Second, we might use work performance as an index of obsessionality. Obsessive personalities as described in the psychoanalytic literature show traits such as conscientiousness and ambition (Lazare et al. 1970) that we would expect to see reflected in good work performance. The inference is somewhat indirect but appears justified. The recovered patients could not be regarded as obsessional, as had been postulated by the classical work of Abraham and Cohen. Although work performance improved strikingly as the depression remitted, it tended to remain worse, not better, than that of the normals.

Third, not only was hostility increased during the acute depression, but there was no evidence of any inhibition of hostility after recovery. Interpersonal friction remained substantially increased rather than decreased. Once again those simple formulations which relate depression in a direct way to the internalization of hostility and the inability to externalize it receive no support.

In addition to these negative findings, positive personality abnormalities were found. To some extent, we found a rather general residual disturbance in the recovered patient. This would be in keeping with the theories of the English writers who have proposed a general tendency to neuroticism or personality vulnerable to stress.

There were, however, specific features to the abnormalities. The two maladjustments characteristic of the recovered depressive were interpersonal friction and inhibited communication. An inability to communicate freely, directly, and appropriately to family and friends is combined with pathological communication through friction and resentment. These abnormalities were not postulated as central in the classical psychoanalytic writings. They do correspond closely to one set of theories—those of Spiegel—and similar abnormalities were noted by Mabel Blake Cohen et al. Both described the potential depressive as showing patterns of defective communication and an inability to deal with aggression directly.

In general, the findings of this chapter show that most of the widespread dysfunctions of the acute depression subside on recovery, but somewhat slowly and incompletely. The remaining impairments are partly specific and can best be described as a difficulty in having open and harmonious intimate relationships.

12
Symptom Intensity, Diagnosis, and Social Background

In a study of social maladjustment we must at some time ask to what degree the impairments are universal and homogeneous and to what degree they vary among patients and are colored by extraneous factors such as social background. In this chapter we will examine the relationship of social adjustment to additional information about the patients from four areas—symptom patterns, diagnosis, sociodemographic status, and previous history. These four areas are somewhat disparate, and our aims in examining each are different. For symptoms, we will refine the findings of the last chapter by directly examining the relationship between the intensity of the patients' symptoms and social function. For diagnosis, we are concerned with how social maladjustments may differ according to the type of depression. Regarding sociodemographic status and previous history, we will see how social impairments are tinged with cultural expectation and patterns as reflected in the patient's social class, marital status, and age.

In these comparisons we will make use of social adjustment ratings at two points—when the patient is acutely depressed and when she is recovered. The recovery will tell us something about normal patterns of behavior. However, findings may still be tinged with the effects of illness. To exclude this as much as possible, in the ratings after recovery we will be concerned only with the twenty-seven patients who experienced no relapse during the eight months.

Symptom Patterns

In the previous chapter we implied that there was a relationship between social maladjustment and the acute symptoms of depression. We showed that patients were more socially impaired when acutely ill than when recovered. However, we made no direct comparisons between the intensity of the symptoms and social adjustment. Here we will directly look at the degree to which social maladjustment and symptom disturbance parallel each other. In other words, does the most symptomatic patient have the worst social adjustment, during illness and after recovery? Symptoms were rated on the forty depressed women by psychiatrists responsible for the patients' treatment, but without knowledge of the social adjustment ratings. Four rating scales were used to assess symptoms: Clinical Interview for Depression (Paykel et al. 1970); The Brief Psychiatric Rating Scale (BPRS) (Overall and Gorham 1962); Raskin Three Area Scale of Depression (Raskin et al. 1971); Overall Illness Scale.[1]

1. *Clinical Interview for Depression* (Paykel et al. 1970). This modified version of the Hamilton Rating Scale for Depression (Hamilton 1960) contains ratings of specific depressive symptoms, all rated on seven-point scales with closely defined anchor points, and interview cues for a semistructural interview. Initial ratings were made on a thirty-item scale, subsequent ratings on a shortened version with fourteen items. Only the fourteen items will be reported here.

The Brief Psychiatric Rating Scale (BPRS). This instrument was originally described by Overall and Gorham (1962), and has since been widely used in psychiatric research. It was employed in a more recent eighteen-item version. The items, also rated on seven-point scales, cover a wide range of psychopathology.

Three Area Depression Scale. As previously described, all patients were rated on the thirteen-point three-area scale of severity and depression used as criterion for entry to the study and relapse, and derived by summing separate 1–5 ratings for verbal report, behavior, and secondary symptoms of depression (Raskin et al. 1971).

Overall Illness Scale. Ratings were also made on a seven-point global scale in which the rater was asked to assess the overall illness of the patient.

For each, the time period was the week prior to interview.

Symptom ratings were made at the time of the patient's initial entrance into the study, weekly for the first four to six weeks, and monthly over the next eight months. Since symptoms were rated for one-week periods and social adjustment for two months, it was necessary to select an appropriate symptom-rating time for comparison with each social adjustment rating. The ultimate choice was empirical, on the basis of whichever set of ratings showed the highest correlation. Initial ratings of symptoms were used for the comparisons at the height of illness; eighth-month ratings for recovery.

We first examined, at the height of illness, product-moment correlations between the social adjustment dimensions and two ratings of overall illness pathology—the three-area depression scale and the overall illness scale. Findings are shown in table 12.1. Unexpectedly, there were no significant correlations be-

TABLE 12.1. CORRELATIONS BETWEEN SOCIAL-ADJUSTMENT FACTOR SCORES AND OVERALL SYMPTOM RATINGS DURING THE ACUTE DEPRESSIVE EPISODE (N = 40)

Social-Adjustment Factor Scores	Symptom Ratings	
	Three-Area Depression Scale	Overall Illness Scale
Work performance	−.004	−.070
Anxious rumination	−.006	−.183
Interpersonal friction	−.121	−.144
Inhibited communication	.085	−.109
Submissive dependency	.114	−.061
Family attachment	.257	−.054
Total Scale Score	.079	−.168

tween the two sets of variables, indicating their virtual independence.

Although overall assessment of symptoms and major dimensions of social maladjustment appeared unrelated, it was nevertheless possible that specific symptoms and aspects of social functioning might be closely related. In order to explore this possibility, correlations were examined between the six social adjustment factors and total score and twenty-six individual ratings of symptoms, fourteen from the clinical interview for depression and twelve from the BPRS. Six additional items from the latter scale could not be utilized because there was little or no variance. These correlations are set out in table B4 in Appendix B.

Correlations were still sparse. The total social adjustment score correlated significantly with three symptom ratings. Patients who were more maladjusted showed more guilt on both symptom scales: they showed less evidence of emotional withdrawal on the BPRS. These specific correlations suggest that patients who were maladjusted showed more depressed mood, although it is hard to say why these specific symptom ratings should be picked out, and not others.

Correlations were also weak for the factors. Work performance showed only one significant correlation—less than chance expectation. This correlation was with guilt feelings on the BPRS. It is important that the psychiatrist's rating of impaired work and interests was not significantly related to this more detailed assessment of work. Anxious rumination showed one positive correlation—with guilt at the clinical interview—and three negative correlations—with emotional withdrawal and blunted affect, with two related indices of emotional deficit, and with anorexia. Interpersonal friction related significantly to three symptoms—negatively with anxiety on the BPRS, positively with irritability rated on clinical interview, and with hostility on BPRS. The latter two might be expected to relate to overt friction; moreover, a similar rating of uncooperativeness just failed to relate significantly. Inhibited communication correlated positively with only two ratings, but they were consistent, being assessments of guilt in both instruments. Submissive dependency showed no significant correlations. Family attachment correlated with two symptoms, depressed feelings and initial insomnia.

The major finding here was once again the weakness of relationships. There was some specificity in keeping with expectation. Interpersonal friction did appear correlated with similar behaviors (irritability and hostility) assessed in the symptom scale. Anxious rumination appeared greatest in patients whose affective expression was preserved. Otherwise, relationships

were neither strong nor easily interpretable. It was striking that
the psychiatrist's interview assessment of work impairment failed
to relate to the assessment of work on the social adjustment
scale. The latter was much more detailed and likely to be the
more accurate. The validity of the more simple overall evaluations made at interview by psychiatrists would appear open to
question.

Thus far the relationship between social adjustment and
symptoms appeared quite weak. We now turned to the eight-
month ratings, after recovery, and carried out a similar set of
analyses. Table 12.2 shows the correlations between overall

TABLE 12.2.   CORRELATIONS BETWEEN SOCIAL ADJUSTMENT FACTOR
SCORES AND OVERALL SYMPTOM RATINGS AFTER RECOVERY (N = 27)

Social Adjustment Factor Scores	Symptom Ratings	
	Three-Area Depression Scale	Overall Illness Scale
Work performance	.402*	.381*
Anxious rumination	.675***	.700***
Interpersonal friction	.531**	.557*
Inhibited communication	.263	.339
Submissive dependency	.020	—.016
Family attachment	.528**	.449*
Total Scale Score	.709***	.703***

* p < .05
** p < .01
*** p < .001

symptom assessments and social adjustment factors and total
score. Correlations were now substantially higher, mostly significant, and closely comparable in the two symptom assessments. Both correlated about .70 with the total social adjustment score. Among the factors there appeared to be specific
patterns. Correlations were highest with anxious rumination,
and were almost as high as with the total score. Correlations
with the other factors were moderate, except for inhibited communication and submissive dependency, which consistently
failed to show significant relationships.

Correlations between the individual symptom assessments

and social adjustment were also examined. Significant correlations were now plentiful. Work performance, anxious rumination, and interpersonal friction, in particular, showed numerous correlations with individual symptoms: inhibited communication, submissive dependency, and family attachment showed relatively few statistically significant correlations. For the three factors that showed plentiful correlations, their detailed patterns did not suggest any particular specificity. All tended to relate to the same symptoms, particularly such central aspects of depression as depressed mood, guilt, and hopelessness. Interpersonal friction, however, showed its expected relationship to irritability and hostility, and work performance now correlated significantly with the psychiatrist's assessment of impaired work and interests and was the only social adjustment factor to do so.

The relationship of social adjustment to symptom intensity can be summarized simply. During the height of illness there is an absence of correlation between ratings of symptom intensity and of degree of social maladjustment. This absence is not quite complete: there is a relationship between the assessment of overt interpersonal friction with others in the social sphere and ratings of hostility and irritability similar in content but made in the symptomatic sphere. There is no such relationship for similar assessments of work performance, and there is a virtual absence of other relationships between symptoms and social function during acute illness. After eight months, when most patients are well, the situation is different. There is a good deal of overlap between the two domains.

The most striking finding is the absence of correlation during the acute illness. It bears on the findings of the previous chapter. There we concluded that a good deal but not all of the social maladjustment was a consequence of acute illness and subsided with recovery. Here we find the relationship is by no means a close one. Symptom intensity and degree of maladjustment do not parallel each other. If the maladjustments are consequences of illness or epiphenomena, they are somewhat remote ones.

We cannot be certain from this data of the reason for the low relationship. The ratings were of demonstrated reliability, were adequate to demonstrate relationship between friction and hostility during illness and a variety of relationships after recovery. The one-week period of symptom assessment overlapped with only a small part of the two months covered by social adjustment assessments, but we have already seen that the rate of change of the latter was quite slow. We may presume that a host of additional elements mediate between the illness and its social consequences. These elements might include the patients' previous personality, length of illness, culturally induced patterns, and the nature of the immediate social environment. We will examine some of these issues in subsequent sections of this chapter.

Why then should correlations have been substantially higher eight months later? The situation regarding degree of pathology was very different at that time. Initially all patients showed at least a moderate degree of symptomatology in terms of selection criteria and most showed at least moderate social malfunction. However, after eight months patients were on the average asymptomatic and functioning moderately well. There was still some variation, but it was within a different range. At the height of illness the variation, both for social adjustment and symptoms, was within degrees of impairment. After eight months it was within a limited range of minor impairment, and the correlations reflected the contrast between the unimpaired majority and a minority showing mild impairment. Under these conditions it has previously been found, for the relationship between interview symptom ratings and self-reports, that correlations tend to be higher and pathology tends to be a more unitary phenomenon (Prusoff et al. 1972). The same would appear to apply for social function.

Some specificity regarding the factor dimensions was also present under these conditions of residual impairment. In general, it was consistent with the patterns found in the previous chapter. In particular, work performance, anxious rumination, and family attachment were correlated with symptom intensity, as might be predicted from their course in relation to illness and recovery. Moreover, inhibited communication, as expected, was not significantly related to symptoms. However, the correspondence was not perfect. Submissive dependency was not correlated with intensity of depression; interpersonal friction was.

Diagnosis

If social maladjustment at the height of illness is not clearly related to symptom intensity, to what does it relate? One possibility is the type of depression. As we discussed in chapter 1, recently there has been considerable emphasis placed on the heterogeneity of depressives and the value of classifying them into different types. Yet so far we have regarded our depressed patients as suffering from a single entity, and have ignored any differences between depressive subtypes. We will now proceed to examine these.

The traditional diagnostic categories were examined first. All the patients received clinical diagnoses at the end of the first month's preliminary treatment. These diagnoses were made by the treating psychiatrists, using the criteria of the American Psychiatric Association Diagnostic and Statistical Manual, II (1967). The majority of patients (thirty-one) were diagnosed as neurotic depressives. Only nine patients were diagnosed in one of the three psychotic categories (two bipolar manic depressive, two involutional melancholia, five psychotic depressive reaction). When the social adjustment of these nine patients was contrasted with the thirty-one neurotic depressives, no significant differences were found between the two groups, either at the height of illness or after recovery. Evidently both groups of depressives show similar patterns of social dysfunction.

One problem with this analysis is the small number of psychotic depressives. Our sample was predominantly neurotic, and there could be further differences among the neurotic depressives. To explore this possibility we turned to another classification of depressives into four groups—psychotic depressives, anxious depressives, hostile depressives and young depressives with personality disorder. This classification was originally derived by application of a special computer classification procedure to a varied sample of depressed patients (Paykel 1971; 1972). Three of these four groups are diverse kinds of neurotic depressives. Anxious depressives are a group of middle-aged, somewhat chronic depressives showing a symptomatic admixture of anxiety. Hostile depressives were originally described as a group showing undue self-pity and hostility at interview, although in subsequent samples, including the present one, they have tended to be a rather nonspecific group in whom hostility is less marked (Paykel et al. 1973). Young depressives with personality disorder are a relatively young group who show mild depression overall, but with marked fluctuations of mood and a previous history suggestive of personality disorder.

The forty patients were assigned to these groups by computer procedures based on discriminant functions (Rao 1952; Paykel et al. 1973). Differences in social adjustment were examined, and once again no differences were found. Although this sample is too small for definitive conclusions to be drawn from it, the data do suggest that diagnostic type is not an important element in determining social maladjustment. With respect to social function we find the different diagnostic groups to be homogeneous. In this regard social adjustment is quite different from symptoms. The latter have been found to distinguish both psychotic and neurotic depressives (Kendell 1968) and the various groups of the four-group classification (Paykel 1971).

Previous History

A further area which might be expected to influence social function is the patients' previous history and premorbid adjustment. We therefore examined the relationship of our social-adjustment factor scores and total score to a number of ratings of previous history which had been made by the psychiatrist at his first interview with the patients. These included length of illness, number of previous depressions, past neurotic symptoms, previous suicide attempts, foreign or native birth, occurrence of neurotic traits such as enuresis in childhood, childhood relationships with parents, education, premorbid work, marital and sexual adjustment, number of children, habitual friendship patterns, intelligence, and a rating of premorbid stability. Degree of neuroticism and extroversion were also assessed by scores on the self-report Maudsley Personality Inventory (Eysenck 1959).

Few correlations between the patients' background and premorbid adjustment were found. Those that did emerge were expected, for example, patients with outgoing social relationships prior to illness were less impaired in their social activities during the acute illness. The one dimension of functioning that showed the most correlation with social functioning during the acute illness was that of friction. Patients' display of overt friction with the family at the acute illness was related to being married, American-born, neurotic, young, having a poor relationship with parents as a child, a poor premorbid marital relationship, higher intelligence, premorbid unstable personality.

A few other significant relationships are of interest especially with regard to social activities and relationships with friends. Impairment in outside social activities during the acute depression were related to having decreased social activities prior to the depression and to premorbid personality problems.

After recovery, the relationship between interpersonal friction and personality observed during the acute depression had disappeared. A few relationships were found which were expected and interpretable. Work performance correlated directly with intelligence. Impaired social and leisure activities were related to the patient having a longer length of illness and more neurotic personality. Impaired marital relations during recovery were related to poor premorbid marital relations.

Overall relationships between previous characteristics of the patient and current social adjustment, although not strong, were stronger than relationships to symptoms or diagnosis. In particular, the degree of interpersonal friction during the acute illness bore a strong relationship to the patient's background. This finding supports the view that the depressed woman's degree of interpersonal friction is as closely related to personality as to her depressive episode.

Sociodemographic Characteristics

Last, we examined the relationship of social function to sociodemographic characteristics—age, marital status, social class, race and religion. We used the data on the depressed patients during illness and after recovery in the same way as before. Individual rating variables were used for this analysis. Since these sociodemographic data were available on the normals, we could look at similar relationships in them at their single interview. This enabled us to step outside the frame of depression to examine a broader issue: to what extent do patterns of social function vary according to the social group? (Alternatively, we might ask to what extent our techniques for measuring these patterns are biased by cultural or other expectations based on the particular group from which the individual is drawn.)

Age. There were very few relationships between age and social adjustment in either acutely ill patients or the normals. In the patients, age was related to increased friction, in that the younger patients generally showed more friction with a variety of people—friends, the extended family, spouse, and children. This relationship disappeared when the patient recovered, probably because fewer recovering patients were overtly hostile. In the normals only friction with children was slightly increased in the younger persons.

Social class. Contrary to expectations, social class also showed few relationships to social functioning in either the patients or normals. The depressed persons from the higher social classes showed somewhat more distress at work, more interest in sex, more worry about the family. During the recovery these relationships disappeared, and only one remained. Patients from higher social class had more impaired relations with their extended family. In the normals, the persons from the lower social classes had somewhat more marital friction, worried more about their families, and were rated by the interviewer as having decreased social activities.

Marital status. The twenty-eight currently married and twelve unmarried depressed patients were compared. The unmarried group included widowed, divorced, and single women. Again, few differences in social functioning between married and unmarried patients were found. The unmarried persons had slightly more friction at work, were more hypersensitive with friends, worried more about the family. During the recovery, the married patients with poor premorbid marriages, as expected, tended to continue to have impaired marriages. In the normals thirty-four persons were currently married and six were not married. Again, few differences between these groups were found. The non-married persons, as contrasted with the married, lost slightly more time from work, were somewhat more lonely and more tied to their extended family.

Race and religion. No significant relationships between social adjustment and race or religion were found in depressed patients during illness or in the recovery, and few were found in the normals. The nonwhite normals were slightly more impaired in performing their work, had more economic and less sexual problems.

An Overview

The partial independence of symptoms and social adjustment has several important implications. First, it suggests that the impaired social functioning of the acutely depressed woman is not entirely a product of her illness but may reflect features of her personality. For example, while hostility is increased in depressives, there are variations in the amount of hostility that may depend on the woman's background, personality, and age rather than entirely on her symptoms. More important, the findings suggest that the intensity and pervasiveness of the patient's symptoms and even her diagnostic grouping are at best a weak guide to her social disability. In general terms this means that patients who show relatively mild depressive symptoms may nonetheless have considerable social maladjustment, and, conversely, the acutely symptomatic patient may not necessarily be as severely impaired socially.

The weak association with social background found in both patients and normals shows that social adjustment is relatively independent of cultural expectations and can be measured with stability across different social groups. The fact that few associations were found in normals confirmed this finding as one that is not merely a peculiarity of the ill state. Contrary to popular belief, a woman's social adjustment cannot readily be predicted from her income, education, family background, race, or religion. The one minor exception is age. Younger persons, when ill, do seem to have more relations that are filled with tension and friction.

13
The Effects of Treatment

There is little doubt from this research that an acute depressive episode is associated with serious disruptions in the patient's life and that these effects linger even after the symptomatic recovery. These observations should encourage practitioners to include in the treatment of depression a psychological intervention which might alleviate the social dysfunction. Theoretical and clinical reports about the benefits of such treatment have been numerous (Spiegel 1960; Jacobson 1954; Stuart 1967; Lorand 1937; Walzer 1961; Levin 1965; Cohen et al. 1954; Bonime 1962). In light of these reports it is surprising to learn that there is not one published, controlled trial of psychotherapy in a homogeneous sample of depressed patients.[1] Interest in the use of psychotherapy or other psychological treatments in depression has been somewhat diverted by the introduction of various effective psychotropic drugs during the last two decades. Controlled clinical trials with a number of antidepressants have confirmed that therapeutic effects occur in a significant portion

---

1. For an excellent review of psychotherapy outcome studies, see L. Luborsky et al., "Factors influencing the outcome of psychotherapy: A review of quantitative research," *Psychological Bulletin* 75: 146–85, 1971.

of acutely depressed patients.[2] Furthermore, promising results which underscore the efficacy of antidepressants in reducing clinical relapse during maintenance treatment have recently been presented (Mindham et al. 1972).

The efficacy of psychological treatments has not been established. They are costly, time-consuming, and have been considered inappropriate for certain types of patients (Weissman et al. 1973). Moreover, psychotropic drugs are often prescribed by nonpsychiatric physicians who are less interested in psychological treatments and therefore less inclined to suggest their combination with pharmacotherapy (Stolley 1969; Klerman 1973).

Despite the positive results of antidepressant trials, there are also many unanswered questions regarding drugs. It is unclear if the initial advantages of symptom-reducing drugs have long-term value in the posttreatment phase, if they improve the patients' social functioning, and if their combination with psychological treatments provides additional benefit.

These questions cannot be resolved in a study of forty patients. After three months of drug treatment, approximately one-third of our patients continued receiving medication, one-third were withdrawn double blind onto placebo, and one-third were withdrawn overtly onto no medication for an additional six months of treatment. These numbers are too small to examine drug-treatment effects. Numbers were slightly higher for psychotherapy effects: twenty patients received psychotherapy and twenty did not. Although these numbers are also small, we will use them to report preliminary results of psychotherapy with depressed patients and our experience with the patients' interest in and use of this treatment. The results will be reported elsewhere in the full-maintenance treatment study when available. Our main purpose in reporting this small sample is to examine the impact of a psychological treatment on the patients' social adjustment, using the patients who did not receive psychotherapy and the normals as comparison groups.

2. For a detailed discussion, see J. O. Cole, "Therapeutic efficacy of antidepressant drugs—a review," *JAMA* 190: 448–55, 1964; or G. L. Klerman, "Drug therapy of clinical depression: Current status and implications for research on neuropharmacology of the affective disorders," *Journal of Psychiatric Research* 9: 253–70, 1970.

Pharmacotherapy in Acute Treatment: Impact and Adjustment

In chapter 11 we showed that the patient's social improvement did not parallel her symptomatic recovery during the first three months of treatment when all patients were receiving pharmacotherapy. After one month of preliminary treatment with pharmacotherapy before entrance into maintenance treatment, patients were almost completely asymptomatic on two measures of symptom status (the Raskin Three Area Scale and the Overall Illness Assessment). All were maintained on medication for an additional two months. During this time their improved clinical status remained unchanged. This provided an opportunity to examine the changes in the patients' social functioning after symptomatic improvement with drug therapy, and to compare the social functioning of the recovered depressed patients with that of the normals.

We found that effective treatment with antidepressant medication could have a remarkable impact on the reduction of acute depressive symptoms during one month of treatment and did produce improvement in the patient's social dysfunctions associated with the illness. However, there was a lag in the effect of medication on the social functioning. We concluded that symptomatic and social recovery did not parallel one another. The recovering depressed patient may superficially appear quite well. She will have resumed her housework or job and appear to be carrying on as before the illness. Her social impairments may take considerably longer to remit, or may never remit, predisposing her to relapse. Clinical experience would suggest that psychological interventions would enhance recovery, especially the impairments in communication and interpersonal friction. Therefore, our research question concerns the efficacy of psychotherapy in reducing these lingering impairments.

Psychotherapy

Twenty of the forty depressed patients were randomly assigned to receive psychotherapy for eight months. The psychotherapy consisted of one to two weekly sessions of at least forty-five minutes each, with one of three psychiatric social workers. At least one of the weekly sessions was an interview with the patient alone. The second hour was with the patient or family member, or could be eliminated.

The purpose of the psychotherapy was to help the patient cope with the personal and social consequences of the illness; to improve the quality of her role performance, interpersonal relations and satisfactions; and to prevent relapse. The focus of the treatment was on the patient and her current functioning. Familial and social causes of dysfunction were recognized, and, where appropriate, social intervention such as arranging welfare and child-care was undertaken. The patient entering psychotherapy was told at the first interview that therapy would continue for eight months, that two hours a week were set aside for her. In addition she continued to see the psychiatrist monthly for assessment of symptoms.

The social workers were qualified graduates of accredited schools and were judged to be skilled on a variety of criteria considered important to outcome (Cartwright 1966; Traux 1967). For example, each caseworker had a minimum of ten years of clinical experience in a comparable psychiatric setting and was judged to be empathetic by previous record and personal interview.

Low Contact

The other twenty patients were randomly selected not to receive psychotherapy (low contact). They received low contact for eight months, which consisted of the same monthly sessions with the psychiatrist as received by the psychotherapy patients. These were brief sessions (fifteen to twenty minutes) used for the assessment of symptoms.[3]

3. Although patients were randomly assigned to psychotherapy and low contact, there was a possibility that differences between the groups, which might effect their outcome, inadvertently existed at the beginning of treatment. Therefore, patients in both groups were compared on age, race, religion, social class, marital status, past psychiatric history and treatment, premorbid work, marital and sexual adjustment, childhood history, family history, premorbid personality, precipitation, attitude towards treatment, clinical status, and social adjustment. No significant differences were found on any of these indices except one, length of present episode of depression, which was slightly longer in patients assigned to low contact ($p < .05$). This single difference was not in excess of chance expectation.

Attrition and Relapse

Patient attrition from treatment is not a clear-cut outcome measure. A patient might drop out of treatment if she perceives no need for further treatment because she is so well, or if she becomes dissatisfied with treatment because it does not seem to help.

Relapse, on the other hand, is a clear outcome. In this study it was defined as a persistent return of clinical symptoms, enough to warrant the patient's readmission for acute treatment. Relapse was not, however, defined in terms of the patient's social adjustment. Completion of the eight months treatment is a general measure of the patient's perseverance and satisfaction with the treatment, as well as absence of symptoms.

Comparing attrition and relapse rates in the two treatment groups, we found that none of the patients in psychotherapy dropped out of eight months of treatment, whereas two patients in low contact did. Seven low-contact patients (35 percent) relapsed as compared with four psychotherapy patients (20 percent). Overall, only 55 percent of low-contact patients, as compared with 80 percent of the high-contact patients completed the study. Our findings indicate that there was little difficulty in retaining patients in treatment and that relapse was slightly but not significantly lower in the psychotherapy patients.

Relapses were distributed evenly over treatment months. Three patients (two low-contact and one psychotherapy) relapsed at the month treatment was due to terminate. Interestingly, psychological treatment was arranged for the two patients receiving low contact when they refused to come for monthly interviews. These patients wanted social or psychological treatment. One patient was a forty-six-year-old divorced woman with many social problems, including a teenage son who was delinquent and physically abusive to her. She perceived no benefit from coming to the clinic after her depression lifted. She stated that difficulty with her son was still her main problem, and she did not feel medication was going to help that situation. She was withdrawn from the study after five months and casework treatment was begun.

The second patient was a thirty-three-year-old woman recently separated from her spouse. After six months of treatment she had only mild symptoms and felt that her main problems were marital. She was withdrawn from the study and referred to group therapy.

The Effects of Psychotherapy: Comparison with Low-Contact Patients

Most patients were asymptomatic or had only mild symptoms after the initial four to six weeks of treatment with antidepressants. Symptom differences between the psychotherapy and low-contact patients were rare over the course of eight months of treatment.

The effects of psychotherapy on social adjustment were examined after two, four, and eight months of treatment. To overcome the problem of attrition, final ratings were included at subsequent points for those patients withdrawn from the study early because of poor cooperation or relapse. There had been no difference between the social adjustments of the groups at the initiation of treatment, as previously noted. We used the factor dimensions and role areas of adjustment to summarize treatment effects. As samples were small, the 10 percent level of significance was accepted. After two months those patients receiving psychotherapy showed significantly less abnormality at the 10 percent level than those receiving low contact on the factor dimensions of interpersonal friction, family attachment, and anxious rumination, and the role areas of family unit and parenthood ($p < .05$). They were however a little more impaired in the work role ($p < .10$). The general trend for the psychotherapy patients to show better adjustment was continued at four months, with significant differences at the 10 percent level on the factor of inhibited communication and the family-unit role, and at the 5 percent level on the factor of work performance and the total score for the scale. At eight months only the difference for the factor of work performance reached the 10 percent level of significance. On all other scores except submissive dependency, both at four months and at eight months, the patients receiving psychotherapy showed nonsignificant trends to better adjustment.

The Effects of Psychotherapy: Comparison with Normals

The social adjustment of the psychotherapy and the low-contact patients who did not relapse after eight months of treatment was compared with that of the normals. Since the purpose was to determine whether psychotherapy produced a return to normality, eight-month ratings were used of those patients who did not relapse. These results are presented in figures 13.1 and 13.2.

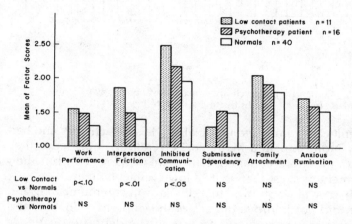

FIG. 13.1. Comparison of psychotherapy and low contact patients, and normals after eight months treatment (by factors).

Looking first at dimensions of social adjustment (fig. 13.1), the low-contact patients were significantly more impaired than the normals in three out of six dimensions: work performance, interpersonal friction, and communication. The psychotherapy patients did not differ significantly from the normals on any dimension. For all dimensions except submissive dependency there was a clear gradation from low-contact patients, who were most impaired, through psychotherapy patients to normals.

In the role areas this gradation was found in all roles. The patients receiving low contact were still significantly more impaired than the normals in all roles but extended family (fig. 13.2). The patients receiving psychotherapy did not differ significantly from the normals in their work, with their extended families, in their marriages, or with their children. They were

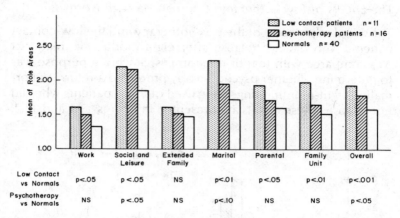

FIG. 13.2.   Comparison of psychotherapy and low contact by patients, and normals after eight months treatment (by roles).

still significantly impaired in social and leisure activities and had slightly more impaired marriages. Overall on total score they were a little more impaired than normals (p < .05), but their impairment was less than that of low-contact patients.

In chapter 11 we showed that difficulty in communicating and friction did not improve directly with symptom reduction and represented more enduring aspects of the depressed patient's personality. The answer to another important research question now emerges. Psychotherapy appears to lessen the residual social impairments in depression and to hasten a return towards normality. It is particularly in improving the recovering depressed patient's interpersonal friction and impaired communication that psychotherapy has its most marked effects. The small sample size of this study means that conclusions can only be tentative. However, preliminary results of studies under way seem to confirm these findings.

There are three ongoing studies on long-term treatment in depression. The forty depressed women are part of a larger maintenance-treatment study of antidepressants and psychotherapy being conducted in New Haven and Boston (Klerman et al. 1973a; Paykel et al. 1972; DiMascio and Klerman 1973; Klerman et al. 1973b).

Preliminary results based on 150 depressed women randomly

assigned to psychotherapy and low-contact support the efficacy of psychotherapy. This larger study has found that psychotherapy does not produce further improvement in symptoms in recovering depressives. However, patients who remain in psychotherapy for eight months, as contrasted with patients receiving low contact, have considerably less social impairments of the kind we have described in the forty patients.

Friedman and associates in Philadelphia have studied combinations of randomly assigned drugs and marital therapy in the maintenance treatment of outpatient depressives (Friedman 1972). About 170 depressed outpatients, predominantly neurotic depressives, were studied and treated for twelve weeks with either drugs or placebo, plus marital therapy or minimal contact. While marital therapy was not as effective as active drug in relieving symptoms or in overall clinical improvement, the patients receiving marital therapy, as compared with minimal contact, had considerably more satisfaction in their family roles, were better able to manage the children, handle family emergencies, and solve family disagreements.

Covi and associates in Baltimore are studying the effects of drugs and group therapy in the outpatient treatment of depression (Covi 1973). The study is a double-blind placebo controlled design with patients randomly assigned to one of three drug groups, plus group therapy or minimal contact. One hundred forty-nine patients are included in eighteen weeks of intensive weekly treatment and maintenance treatment of ten months at four-week intervals, preceded by two months of two-week intervals. The results of this study are not yet available.

These three well-controlled studies with their varying psychological approaches, supportive psychotherapy, group and marital therapy should provide important answers on the efficacy of these interventions. While a definitive answer is not completely available, thus far the evidence points to the potential benefit of psychological treatment in reducing social impairments during the postacute phase of depression. We will next look at the nature of the treatment used in this study.

The Content of Psychotherapy

A systematic record was kept of the patient's attendance and what was discussed during each therapy hour (Weissman et al.).[4] Patients were seen on the average of once a week and their attendance was good. Most interviews were with the patient alone. Family members were not highly involved, although this varied widely and most families were seen on several occasions. Interestingly, we found that most of the time was spent by the patient describing her current daily life and not in reconstruction of past experiences. In other words, her current social adjustment occupied most of the therapy. Discussions revolved around practical problems such as work, finances, recreation, as well as relationships with husband, children, and close friends. Little time was spent discussing physical symptoms and the current treatment. The least time was spent on discussions of early experiences or sexual problems. Therapy discussions were primarily descriptive accounts of daily life and not reflective insights or childhood developmental material. These findings were not surprising since the recovery of the other material would have required an increased frequency of interviews and adoption of a passive, neutral stance in contrast to the reassuring, active one usually adopted by the therapist. Thus the study findings were consistent with the way in which the therapy was structured and the nature of the contact between the clinic and the patient. This form of treatment, primarily supportive in nature with emphasis on current adjustment, seemed more appropriate to the treatment of depressed patients recovering from an acute symptomatic episode (Deykin et al. 1972).

The extensive case records kept by therapists, who were unaware of the research ratings, filled out the picture. They also enabled us to gain some insight into the mechanisms by which psychotherapy helped to reduce the tensions in the patients' lives.

Therapy revolved around the major incidents of life—birth, courtship, maternity, companionship, enmity, and death—and their manifestations in the patient's daily life. These were presented as homely problems, not existential crises. One example of a typical problem was that of how to live on an inadequate

4. For a detailed description of the methodology used in collecting these data, see M. M. Weissman, B. A. Prusoff, and E. S. Paykel, "Checklist quantification of a psychological therapy: Pilot studies of reliability and utility," *J. Nerv. Ment. Dis.* 154: 125–36, 1972.

budget that left the spouse angry at himself for being an inept provider; that reverberated in unreasonable demands by the spouse on his family as he tried to prove he was a man; and that resulted in the patient's irritation, loss of pride, and loss of love for him, and left her little energy for the care of the children. Others were the fatigue, anger, and sadness of full-time care of a dying father and resentment over the withdrawal of the other family members from their share; conflict over holding a job and catering to the family; feelings of inadequacy as a mother relating to children's poor progress in school; having too many children; not being able to conceive; meddlesome in-laws; boredom and loss when the children left home; feeling up-rooted and lonely in a new neighborhood; having a son arrested for draft evasion; fear of getting old and being alone; a daughter marrying out of the religion; conflict about remarrying and suffering another failure, or remaining single and leaving the children without a father.

As these glimpses indicate, the depressed woman, unlike the schizophrenic, is fully involved in the network of family friends. The content of the therapy dealt with a breakdown in this net-work and her helplessness in handling problems directly. Even-tually this frustration erupted, alternating between anger on the one hand and withdrawal and defeat on the other. The drugs were helpful in reducing the most debilitating symptoms, for example, helping her to sleep and eat again and become inter-ested in life. The psychotherapy allowed her to talk about the problems more directly and to find ways of solving them. As one patient graphically put it, "the drugs made me feel better and the psychotherapy helped me make my marriage better."

The Recovering Patient's Motivation for Psychotherapy

Obviously all patients did not have the same intensity of prob-lems or wish to talk about them when they got better. To gain an adequate picture of treatment effects, we must also consider the patient's interest in the treatment, since the intensity and direction of the treatment vary with the specific needs of each patient.

Interest in therapy was assessed by the caseworker during the first week of treatment. Patients were rated on a nine-point scale ranging from very interested to very disinterested. Patient interest was found to show wide variation. Of the twenty patients who received psychotherapy, 45 percent were quite interested in psychotherapy to explore social and interpersonal problems. Thirty percent of the patients were only mildly interested or were neutral toward psychotherapy, willing only to continue if the staff felt it might be beneficial. The remaining 25 percent were definitely not interested in psychotherapy but agreed to continue as part of the research.

Interested Patients. Patients who expressed the most interest recognized that the drugs had helped them to feel better so that they had renewed energy to explore what they felt were their real problems. These usually were family problems and, most often, overt marital conflict which they believed caused the depression. These patients tended to have the most serious marital difficulties as reflected in the ratings of marital adjustment at the initiation of treatment. They feared that failure to understand these problems would result in recurrence, and they saw psychotherapy as an opportunity to understand antecedents. The depression did not serve to win their families' attention and sympathy. Instead, the patients' increased dependency and irritability further alienated them from their families. These patients were eager to engage in eight months of psychotherapy and attended one to two times a week. Often their families were involved as well.

M.L., a 44-year-old, plump, vivacious woman, lived with her husband, who was a self-employed shopkeeper, and her two sons. One daughter was away at college. This was her second episode of depression, the first one having occurred after the birth of her last child, a number of years before. Her symptoms were characterized by apathy, sadness, loss of appetite, agitation, hostility towards her family. Marital conflict revolved around her husband's financial mismanagement. "Big bills and little income" were her chief complaints and her way of explaining what made life so discouraging. She felt her extra efforts to help out were unappreciated and resulted in the family, especially her husband, doing even less for her. She made a good symptomatic response to medication and after one month was more active, less dejected, but still quite angry at her husband. She welcomed the chance to talk and blamed her husband's unloving attitude towards her as the cause of her depression. In eight months of treatment she began to separate the real frustrations of her life which had been displaced onto her husband and which had contributed to her overreacting. She was better able to discuss her wishes directly with her husband. This resulted in a more reasonable attitude on his part and reduced the tension between them.

Neutral Patients. Patients who were less interested in psychotherapy felt that the antidepressant medication had made them so well that they did not want to think about problems. Usually these were the patients with a good marital adjustment and stable social situation. Family conflicts were covert, and the illness gained the patients a great deal of sympathy. They tended to blame their depressions on medical problems such as menopause, an operation, hormone injections. When asymptomatic, these patients often denied the extent of symptoms. For example, one woman who had been rather severely depressed, insisted upon recovery that she really had a stomach ailment. Therapy with these patients encouraged the reestablishment of former activities with friends and family, not confrontation with underlying conflicts. To show how well they were doing, the patients focused on their descriptions of daily routine, new activities, and increased enjoyment. They were encouraged to seek drug treatment again if they ever needed it and psychotherapy was used to reinforce their good progress.

F.P., a 34-year-old, neat, well-scrubbed single woman, lived in a small suburban home with her unmarried brother. She worked regularly as a seamstress, a job she held for many years. Her brothers and sisters lived nearby and she maintained regular and close contacts with all of them.

The patient had taken care of her ailing mother until her death a few years before and also devoted herself to the care of her younger siblings. She felt consoled by the fact that her mother fully appreciated all she did for her and she stated that she had never married because her mother needed her. Following her mother's death she moved from the old neighborhood because of city redevelopment. She missed the central location and closeness she felt with former neighbors. Loneliness-fatigue from her mother's care and grief over her death led her to become increasingly depressed.

In psychotherapy the patient was friendly and talkative, and gave copious information about her daily life. She believed that her depression was brought on by hard work and dwelled on health problems when she felt dejected. Her thinking tended to be along concrete

and naive levels of understanding. When feeling well, she was satisfied with her life style and discussed new outlets for social life such
as participating in a neighborhood club or family parties. While she
seemed to enjoy the attention of the therapist and came for interviews,
she did not particularly seek it out.

Negative Patients. A small number of patients were negative
toward psychotherapy. These patients were unable to deal
with emotions in verbal terms and unable to tolerate the intimacy of the relationship. Sometimes remarks might have a
paranoid flavor, and there were hints that ego dysfunction was
such that exploration could produce decompensation. Although
these patients received symptomatic benefit from antidepressants, at times they tended to be negative about the medication
as well. When seen by the therapist they preferred to focus on
increase or decrease of symptoms. They attended sessions
poorly.

D.R. was a 39-year-old mother of four children. She was described
as a conscientious and hard-working wife and mother when well. She
was referred for antidepressant treatment after a three-week history
of crying, social withdrawal, suicidal thoughts, and sleep disturbance.
She felt people were talking about her and saying that she was crazy.
She made some response to medication after one month but was
quite unwilling to see the social worker. She accepted the referral
with much resentment saying that the pills had done the job for her
and that no one could say what had caused her illness. In the presence
of the social worker she continued to praise the value of the pills,
while at the same time the physician found her to be rather uncooperative, taking less than 75% of the medication dose prescribed.
She attended both the social worker's and the physician's appointments poorly, although she did continue to see them for eight months.
Emotional and economic deprivation in the patient's early family
life, an ambivalent and harsh relationship with her father and lingering
traces of marital conflict all appeared to be areas for discussion. However, she said "no" to any of these. She hinted that it was important
for her to keep busy, as a way of warding off morbid thoughts.
Although she said she liked people around her, she avoided close
relationships. She tended to feel worse after discussing painful material, since she had been taught to solve problems alone. Nevertheless, she discussed termination with hesitancy, related to the fact that
she experienced the clinic as a crutch which enabled her to function
when minor symptoms recurred, and gave her assurance that she
would get treatment promptly if she needed it.

These experiences indicated that patients' use of psychotherapy, reflected in interest, emotional involvement, and attendance, varied widely. Further research is needed to document the characteristics of patients who might best benefit from longer-term intensive psychotherapy, those to whom brief supportive intervention might be more helpful, and those who should receive only antidepressant medication. Our findings on this small sample suggest that social adjustment may be an important determinant of interest in psychotherapy and of the need for it.

Implications for Outcome Studies

One theme of this book has been the need for appropriate measures of treatment outcome. When evaluating psychotherapy in long-term outpatient studies, social adjustment would seem to be an important measure. As we found and as will probably be confirmed in the larger maintenance study, psychotherapy does not have a major impact on reducing relapse or improving symptoms in the recovering depressives. For most patients, acute symptoms remit rather rapidly with drugs, and only mild symptoms linger. Had we used symptoms as the only criteria of efficacy, we would not have been able to demonstrate a psychotherapy effect or to document the lingering social impairments of depression.

In the past, the efficacy of psychotherapy has been difficult to establish. Many believe, and these data support the belief, that this may be due to the use of insensitive outcome criteria. In the 1950s Eysenck published a summary of the psychotherapy literature and drew the conclusion that patients treated with psychotherapy showed no more improvement than untreated patients (Eysenck 1952). Eysenck's work stirred intense attack and was successful in stimulating more precise questions about psychotherapy. In more recent years psychotherapy studies have moved from reports of global and undefined success to concern over achieving more carefully defined and theoretically relevant criteria of outcome (Fiske 1970; Strupp and Bergen 1969; Uhlenhuth 1969; Malan 1968), particularly through the use of multiple criteria which are reliable and valid (Waskow 1972).

The introduction of pharmacotherapy has sharpened the issue of outcome criteria, especially when combined treatments are employed. For example, it is clear that drugs are prescribed primarily for symptom relief. In depression this would mean the reduction of feelings of hopelessness, worthlessness, sadness, crying, anergia, anorexia, sleeplessness. While certain alterations of behavior and pathological thought may occur with symptom reductions, drugs would not be expected to cure bad marriages, loneliness, impaired communication, disturbed parent-child relations, or other problems in living. Since psychotherapy aims to improve interpersonal and social adaptation, outcome measures which may be sensitive to changes in social behavior are essential. This view has received increasing support (Malan 1968; Frank et al. 1961; Parloff 1954; Goldman 1969).

Conclusions

The evidence we have presented is fragmentary and incomplete, yet in the absence of contrary data it suggests that a psychological approach in the postacute phase of treatment for depression is important. Supportive psychotherapy can reduce the residual impairments of depressed patients, especially the irritability and the inability to communicate directly and freely with others. There are many forms of psychotherapy, and it is unlikely that intensive psychotherapy would be feasible or even desirable for many patients. As we have shown, a sizeable number of patients will not want to look for psychological antecedents to their illness. Perhaps they are correct that none exist. For these patients all that is necessary may be a rehabilitative model of treatment which will help them to recover and to repair their disrupted lives, weakened confidence, and alarmed families. This repair may require nothing more than a chance to share the experience of the illness and to have timely reassurance from the clinician about its course. Patients welcome this opportunity and spontaneously talk about their daily lives. The direction, intensity, and specific form of psychological intervention depend on the patient's needs. The results of research underway may throw further light on these. It is also possible that psychotherapy begun in the acute phase of the depression might have a greater impact. This question has not been touched by this research and requires separate study. There is little doubt that drugs have increased the possibility of rapid symptom-relief in depression. It is also clear from this research that the disruptions associated with the disorder do not entirely remit with symptom reduction and that the clinician's planning of treatment should include an awareness and a sensitivity to these social disruptions. Overall, these findings point to the importance of social adjustment as a target area for psychotherapy and as a measure of its efficacy.

14
The Follow-up

One year after patients had terminated treatment from the study clinic, or twenty months after treatment had begun, we returned to find out how they were progressing. A larger number of persons are required to fully sort out all the intervening effects, particularly as treatment during this time was uncontrolled. We will give a brief overview of findings.

The close patient surveillance during the course of the eight-month study had demonstrated that most had recovered from the acute episode and managed fairly well at home, although with the important deficits which we have described. Attending a psychiatric clinic and being part of research observations are artificial situations, and even those patients not receiving psychotherapy were provided with a certain amount of emotional support. By following up the patients we might see how they got along without the clinic. We allowed what we expected was sufficient time for the patients to have recovered and for the lingering effects of the illness to have subsided if they were going to.[1]

1. Patients were followed up at six months, as well as one year, after the eight-month treatment was terminated. Since our findings were nearly identical for both time periods, we will describe only the one-year follow-up

All forty patients were followed and their response was excellent. Thirty-nine of the forty patients agreed to participate, thirty-six agreeing to a two-hour personal interview and three to answering a mail questionnaire. One patient had moved out of the state and could not be found. The same interviewers and rating assessments were used.

As has been found in other follow-up studies with different time periods, diagnostic classifications, and criteria, symptomatic recovery from the depressive episode was on the average, moderately good (Beck 1967; Robins and Guze 1972). After one year 45 percent of the patients were completely asymptomatic. Another 45 percent had only mild symptoms. However, the remaining 10 percent (four patients) were as depressed as when they had first come for treatment. Over the year there were no suicides, but two patients did make minor attempts and one patient was hospitalized for depression.

Social Adjustment

Figures 14.1 and 14.2 compare the social adjustment of all patients at the beginning of the study (0), the termination (8), the follow-up (20), with the normals. On the average, the patients' social adjustment at one year follow-up was not greatly different than it had been at the termination of the eight-month study. It was considerably better at follow-up than it had been during the acute illness, but had not reached the levels of the normals. Looking at the factor scores, work performance and communication were the only dimensions which showed a slight improvement from the termination of the study.

Work, social and leisure activities, and parental performance had improved somewhat between eight and twenty months. Marital relations, which at eight months had not improved markedly from the acute episode, showed no further improvement and were still quite impaired. Despite the marital dishar-

---

(which was twenty months from the time the patient began the maintenance treatment study). For an excellent discussion of the purpose, values, and pitfalls of follow-up studies, see L. N. Robins, "Follow-up studies investigating childhood disorders," in *Psychiatric Epidemiology*, eds. E. H. Hare and J. Wing (Oxford University Press, London, 1970), pp. 29–90.

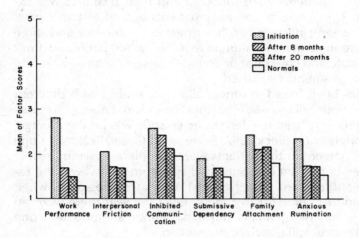

FIG. 14.1.   Depressed patients at initiation, eight, and twenty months, and the normals (by factors).

mony, only one patient had separated from her spouse and no divorces had occurred.

Work

The patients' capacity to maintain or to find new jobs outside the home was excellent. Many women were holding at least half-time jobs in addition to keeping up with housework. During the acute episode 27 percent of the depressed women as contrasted with 40 percent of the normals were working. At follow-up 44 percent of the depressed women were working.

Seven of the thirty-nine (18 percent) had maintained their jobs throughout the twenty months. A few women who were not working were in the process of seeking employment. Although no differences were found at follow-up in the social adjustment of working and nonworking women, many women strongly felt that their jobs were important to their adjustment.

As Mrs. L., a 57-year-old former nurse, reported, she needed the stimulation of getting out of the house and meeting different people. A full-time nursing job was too taxing for her, but she had found a good part-time job.

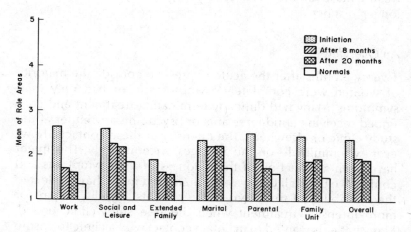

FIG. 14.2. Depressed patients at initiation, eight, and twenty months, and the normals (by roles).

Symptoms and Adjustment

Since minor relapse was common, did the return of symptoms again produce further impaired functioning? A group of seventeen patients who were asymptomatic over the year was compared to the remaining nineteen patients who had mild-to-severe symptoms. Similar patterns to those observed during the course of the study were found. A return of symptoms was generally associated with impaired social functioning in nearly all areas.

Interestingly, marriage and the ability to communicate were equally impaired in both the symptomatic and asymptomatic groups. Earlier relapse did not, however, produce persistent effects. Most of the ten patients who had relapsed before completing the eight-month study were asymptomatic or had only minor symptoms at one year follow-up, and their social adjustment was no different from that of patients who had not relapsed during the study. Unfortunately, the effects of the psychotherapy could not adequately be examined. They were confounded by the fact that many patients sought different treatments over the year, so that treatment groups were no longer distinct.

An Overview

Twenty months after the acute depressive episode the majority of women were completely asymptomatic or had only mild symptoms. Many had difficulty terminating treatment and continued receiving antidepressants or psychotherapy either at the study clinic or elsewhere. The intensity of these contacts, however, was minimal—on the average, twice monthly. This might have been a reflection of the mildness of their symptoms and could have been all that was required, or it might have reflected the availability of treatment or the patients' inability to pay for more intensive treatment when the free study-clinic ended. Many patients wanted to maintain contact with a clinic to ensure they could get more intensive treatment should their symptoms return. The depressive episode had dampened confidence and left many frightened that it might recur. As one patient said, "I like to know I can get help quickly if I ever feel I am going downhill." Patients often needed reassurance that a sleepless night or a minor argument did not necessarily herald the beginning of a depression.

Despite the mild symptoms and insecurities, the social impairments were real but not severe. The serious impairments of the acute episodes had vanished, especially the parental discord. Many women were working, managing their families, taking care of their children and getting along with them. They were not grossly impaired. Marriages often, but not always, remained seriously vulnerable, filled with tension, unhappiness, and emotional distance. Most marriages did not improve greatly from the acute episode but, despite this, were not terminated; separation or divorce was rare. The inability to get jobs, the lawsuits, or the divorces noted by Winokur and Cassidy were not found in this group (Winokur 1969; Cassidy 1957). This may be due to the relative absence of manic-depressives or severely ill hospitalized or psychotic patients in our study, as contrasted with theirs.

Freedom from symptoms, while not the only measure of successful outcome, is an important one. Failure to remain free of symptoms unquestionably interfered with the patients' functioning at home. A short-term relapse, however, did not have any special negative effect on the patients' long-range outlook. Patients who had relapsed early in their treatment were progressing about as well as those who had not.

The follow-up study supports the contention that depressions remit but require intermittent treatment over time. While the formerly depressed women were not floridly impaired and had made marked gains, they were not functioning as well as their normal neighbors. They were vulnerable to the recurrence of symptoms, and, with this recurrence, to the social disruptions they experienced when acutely ill. It was not surprising that they wanted to maintain continuity with the clinic for early treatment. The attention received by these patients in a controlled research study is not representative of all clinical care. The support of the clinic may have helped to reduce the impairment, and the addition of weekly psychotherapy may have had a further positive impact on their lives.

The tenacity with which such patients maintain clinic contact, have mild symptoms and accompanying impairments reinforces the need for ongoing treatment programs past the acute phase of depression.

IV.
CONCLUSIONS

15
Synopsis and Implications

The main theme of this book has been the social relationships of depressed women. Previous research has given considerable attention to the symptoms of depression, leaving largely unexplored what depressed people are like in their daily lives. The findings leave little doubt that depression produces far-reaching and lingering impairments and that specific problems remain even during the symptom-free periods. Before discussing the overall implications, we will present the salient findings of the study, many of which confirmed common sense, while others challenged old theories and presented in detail new observations.

This study of depressed women set out to investigate how acute depression effected social, family, and community adjustment; how long the maladjustments associated with an acute episode remained during treatment and recovery; to what degree they reflected symptomatic illness or underlying personality. Growing out of a general shift from hospital to community psychiatry, the research was prompted by the dearth of such study in depressed patients. The first studies reflecting the new trend of community psychiatry had been with schizophrenic patients discharged from the mental hospital. The large number of persons with depressive symptoms coming for outpatient treatment to community facilities convinced us that it was time for similar studies with depressives.

Over the course of twenty months we followed the social adjustment of forty depressed women and compared them with forty women of similar social class, place of residence, race, religion, and marital status, who had no major physical or emotional problems and had never received psychiatric treatment. These women were, in general terms, the patients' normal neighbors.

In summarizing the findings we will present a composite of depressed patients during the acute episode and the recovery.

The acute depressive episode. As might be expected, women suffering from an acute depressive episode are considerably impaired in their daily lives and interpersonal relationships. The impairment is of moderate degree, is quantitatively rather than qualitatively different from that in normals, and falls short of the grossly aberrant patterns described in schizophrenics. Also, unlike schizophrenics, depressed women are not personally isolated; most often they are housewives and mothers living with their families.

The social impairments of the acutely depressed patient reach into all roles, as wife, mother, worker, and member of the community. The impairments are most marked in work and in the intimate relationships of marriage and parenthood. They are less marked in the less emotionally charged and distant relationships with friends, acquaintances, and the extended family. Consistent with the guilt and self-negation of depression, the patient's subjective distress about her performance within each role tends to be more marked than her actual objective impairment. As examples, dissatisfaction and distress in doing work are greater than actual work impairment. Despite this discomfort, and unlike schizophrenics, a reasonable portion of depressed women remain at work during the acute depressive episode. Interestingly, women who work outside the home show less impairment in work than do housewives. While it is possible that this difference reflects a tendency for the most impaired patients to give up work, there is a suggestion that an outside occupation has a protective effect.

Social and leisure activities and relationships with extended families show many similarities. Although the depressed women are more impaired than the normals in both these areas, the differences are not very striking. Social relationships with the wider community are somewhat impaired for both patients and normals who show rather limited participation. The pattern for the depressives is one of further disengagement and withdrawal. For relationships with extended family, neither patients nor normals show much evidence of serious maladjustment. The cultural pattern in housewives of Italian background is one of fairly close relationships with extended family. These are accomplished without unusual dependency or friction. When these relationships are disturbed by depression, the characteristic pattern is one of withdrawal and reduction of communication coupled with feelings of resentment and guilt. The resentment is largely unexpressed, and overt friction is not significantly increased.

This relatively harmonious withdrawal contrasts with the friction and tension that characterize the depressed woman's intimate relationships with her spouse and children. Marital relationships become an arena for the depression and are characterized by friction, poor communication, dependency, and diminished sexual satisfaction. The depressed woman feels a lack of affection towards her husband, together with guilt and resentment. Communication is poor and hostility overt. Although she is submissive and dependent, and overtly domineering behavior is absent, the depressed woman may exercise covert control through symptoms and sex. She continues to have sexual relations with the spouse, although with reduced frequency. Moreover, she tends to have physical difficulties and to be disinterested.

Acutely depressed women show increased rather than decreased hostility. This hostility is directed particularly towards the husband and children and least towards the more distant relationships with work associates and friends. As might be expected, women with premorbid adaptive marriages have somewhat less impaired marriages during the depression. They withdraw from the spouse in an effort to protect him from the effects of depression, and the husbands in turn are more protective towards them. On the other hand, the depressed patients with premorbid maladaptive marriages view the spouse as having caused the depression, and the marital conflict is intimately involved with the patient's symptoms.

Relationships with children are also markedly impaired, although the precise details vary with the stage of the family life-cycle. Depressed mothers of infants tend to be overconcerned, helpless, guilty, and sometimes overtly hostile. With young school-age children, the mothers' attitude varies from irritability to emotional uninvolvement and withdrawal. With adolescent children, there is often intense conflict. The adolescent appears to exploit the mother's helplessness rather than give her sympathy. Finally, the children's departure from home precipitates feelings of loss and depression in the mother.

The role framework by itself does not entirely describe the social dysfunctions of depression, since there are consistent patterns of malfunction which cut across roles. These can be summarized in six dimensions: impaired work performance, interpersonal friction, emotional dependency, inhibited communication, family attachment, and anxious rumination. The most marked impairments are in work performance, and there is considerable anxious rumination.

The recovery. As symptomatic recovery occurs, there is a general tendency for social adjustment to improve considerably. The improvement is, however, slower than that of symptoms. It is most rapid in the first two months and continues more slowly for the next two months. Thereafter, it is more or less static; it may even worsen over the next year. Although the improvement is considerable, it is not complete and does not quite reach the levels of normals.

The most rapid remission is seen in those abnormalities which were greatest to start with—work performance and anxious rumination. This would suggest that these dimensions are most clearly related to symptomatic illness. Family attachment and submissive dependency also show fairly rapid and relatively complete remission. Interpersonal friction and inhibited communication show a slow and incomplete remission, suggesting that these are more enduring personality features largely independent of symptoms. Symptomatic relapse is accompanied by a rapid worsening of social functioning. In particular, the patient's work performance worsens and her dependency and family attachment increases. This supports the specific relationship of these dimensions to symptomatic illness.

After eight months those patients who are asymptomatic still have mild residual social impairments. Even after recovery, free communication with close family and friends is inhibited. Instead, there is a pattern characterized by friction, resentment, and argumentative behavior.

Although much of the social disturbance subsides with recovery from symptomatic illness, the relationship between symptoms and social disturbance is not close. At the height of illness social disability and symptom severity are virtually independent of each other. At eight months the two are only moderately related. Apparently many other factors mediate between symptomatic illness and social consequence, but it is not entirely clear what these other factors are. Social adjustment is unrelated to the patients' diagnostic type and only weakly related to previous history or cultural background, such as race, religion, and social class. This lack of sociocultural relationship applies to normals also. The one exception can be found in the patients who are overtly hostile at the height of the depression. These patients tend to be younger, more neurotic, and to have had more precipitants preceding the depression.

The trends which are evident during eight months of treatment are confirmed at follow-up, twenty months after the acute episode. On the whole, the patients' social functioning tends to improve a little further. The general level of adjustment is fairly good, but it is not as good as that of the normals. Many patients seek further treatment, and a number of them have a return of depressive symptoms during the year. Such patients show worse adjustment than those who are well.

Although derived from a treatment study, the research we have reported here was not primarily designed to investigate effects of specific treatments. For that purpose a much larger sample is required. A preliminary look at treatment effects in this small sample, however, suggests that psychotherapy has effects in speeding a social remission after the acute phase of depression and in reducing the ultimate social disability. Patients who received psychological treatment, as compared with those who did not, were closer to the normals in functioning at the end of eight months of treatment. Psychotherapy has its greatest impact on improving social dysfunction—reducing friction and improving communications. Fortunately, motivation for psychotherapy appears greatest in the patients for whom it might therefore be most indicated—those with greatest social dysfunction.

The findings, taken together, suggest that many of the social disturbances of depression are a consequence of acute illness, that about three-quarters subside with recovery, and that many return with relapse. However, it is inadequate merely to regard the disturbances as epiphenomena, since they are pervasive and subside at a considerably slower rate than symptoms. More important, social disturbances correlate poorly with symptom severity at the height of illness; if the disturbances are a reflection of symptoms the reflection is a somewhat indirect one.

Personality

This study indirectly tested several common assumptions regarding the personalities of depressives, such as their dependency, obsessionality, and difficulties in handling their feelings. The residual impairments of recovered depressed patients are a great deal less in amount and are different in pattern to those at the height of illness, so that it is unwise to conclude much about the lifelong social patterns from the acute depressed state.

There were a number of important negative findings. Those theories which postulate dependency as a central and enduring feature predisposing to depression (Abraham 1968; Rado 1968) were not supported. Although dependency was characteristic of the depressed state, it returned most convincingly to normal on recovery.

In terms of work performance the depressed women could not be regarded as obsessional. Although work improved strikingly as the depression remitted, it tended to remain worse rather than better than that of normals, and the depressed woman's premorbid work adjustment did not show any particular tendency to obsessionality. The psychoanalytic literature on obsessionality is equivocal as to whether this is to be regarded as an attribute of all depressives or merely of manic-depressives. It is still possible that the latter group might show this trait.

One further unexpected finding involved hostility. Not only was this increased during the acute episode, but there was a small decrease rather than any increase after recovery. In general, recovered depressed women displayed more hostility than normals. Therefore, simple formulations which relate depression to an internalization of hostility and an inability to externalize it receive no support. Of course, the classical psychoanalytic formulations suggest something more complex than simply "depression equals anger turned inward." They do not posit a direct inhibition of external hostility but an increase of hostility directed inward on an introjected object. With respect to this, our data on overt hostility in the social field do not provide a crucial test. Comparisons with psychoanalytic reports are difficult because of their unclear diagnostic criteria, neglect of neurotic depressives, and absence of demographic data.

In addition to these negative findings, there were several positive ones. Recovered patients showed general residual impairments in many facets of their lives, which is in keeping with the theories of the English writers who have proposed a tendency to neuroticism in depressives. There were also specific features to the remaining impairments. Two maladjustments most characteristic of the recovered depressive were interpersonal friction and inhibited communication. The importance of interpersonal friction as a personality dimension was buttressed by the fact that it bore the greatest relationship to the patients' age and background. A theme central to both these impairments is that of communication: the patient's inability to communicate freely, directly, and appropriately to the family and friends is combined with pathological communication through friction and resentment. These maladaptive patterns would seem most likely to be revealed in intimate relationships such as marriage. It is quite plausible that the inability to communicate directly might be prior to the pathological friction and lead to it, ultimately even creating the precipitant stress that precedes the depressive episode.

The present findings do not establish these patterns of interpersonal friction and inhibited communication as linked exclusively with depression. The recovered patient's residual impairments were to some extent general. Moreover, without other control groups we cannot be sure that the same patterns do not characterize subjects with histories of other psychiatric disorders. They do, however, appear to be the most marked patterns among formerly depressed women.

In most of this study we have treated social adjustment as if it were an attribute of the person alone. This of course is not so; it concerns the person's interaction with the environment, and the nature of that environment may make a substantial contribution to the development of depression. The quality of the interpersonal environment is difficult to measure. We have preferred to operationalize social function and to avoid highly judgmental inferences as to the contribution of various individuals, such as the spouse, to difficulties in relationships.

The environment undoubtedly has an important influence and provides another hypothesis as to the origins of the social malfunctions. Some impairments may represent reflections of recent situational crises or long-standing stressful situations which have contributed to the development of the depression. The causative chain may be complex. For example, the personality abnormalities of the depression-prone person, in areas such as communication and friction, may put her in situations which precipitate depression, and may provide the link between personality and illness. The social consequences of the illness may themselves be stressful and tend to perpetuate the condition. We do not have data from this study on these important links.

One lack in many genetic studies of depression is any attempt to explore the means by which the morbid inheritance is translated into actual depression. It is often assumed that this is by some endogenous biological process. This is not the only possible mechanism. It is quite possible that what is inherited may be a vulnerable personality which interacts with stress to produce illness. The origins of the personality abnormalities which we infer from the persistent maladjustments observed in the formerly depressed patients can only be guessed in the present study. They might well be the consequences of genetic processes, in the same way as schizoid personality is believed by many to reflect the action of the gene associated with schizophrenia.

Normality

Our study was not designed primarily to investigate normality. We selected our normals to be free from a depressive psychiatric disorder and to match the patients in other respects, including absence of serious physical illness. Because of the exclusion of psychiatric or physical disorder, they cannot be regarded as representative of the general population, that is, the statistical norm. Moreover, they did not span adequately all sociodemographic groups. Because no attempt was made to exclude those with poor social function, they could not be regarded as approaching the ideal norm of perfect function.

With these caveats in mind, the study does provide an opportunity to describe social function in a group of selected women from a normal population. In general, although the level of functioning of these women fell short of the "ideal" in certain expressive roles, it was surprisingly good. The normal women experienced housework as satisfying, parent-child relations as warm and involved, marriages as affectionate and harmonious. These findings contrast with those from other studies that have reported a high degree of pathology in normal subjects. It is always possible that the normals were unreliable in reporting impairments. Precautions were taken by the interviewers to avoid this problem. The interview format was semistructured, and the interviewer was cautioned to probe for more information if it appeared that the answers were inaccurate. The interviewer's overall assessment of each area, based on all observations and suspicions, including what the subjects expressed indirectly, correlated quite highly with the structured ratings and added little more. Moreover, the fact that the normals were not consistently at the least-impaired end of the scale increases confidence in the findings.

The characteristic pattern for these normal women was of a low level of social interaction with the wider community. Their lives centered around nuclear family and a close-knit extended family, relations with whom were characterized by compliance and dependency. These patterns did not produce dissatisfactions, friction, or conflicted loyalties between nuclear and extended families, which might have been expected.

These patterns probably reflect the norm for the working-class, Italian, Roman Catholic women who were our principal but not exclusive subjects. Researchers and therapists working with patients like ours should beware of expecting wider social participation, assertiveness in marriage, and independence from extended family, which are norms of middle-class, upwardly mobile professionals but may not be appropriate for all patients. Participation in such middle-class behavior might be at variance from the expected norms, and treatment aimed at producing it might be disruptive rather than helpful.

Methodology

The principal tool for assessing social adjustment has been a rating scale based on interview with the patient. While we demonstrated this to be of satisfactory reliability, we did not assess its validity and cannot directly prove that it measures what it purports to measure.

In particular, the ratings were based entirely on interviews with the subjects only, and not with outside sources such as relatives or friends. Many investigators have recommended the use of information from relatives or other informants to avoid patient-induced biases. Relatives and informants have proved particularly useful in the assessment of schizophrenics after discharge from hospital.

We considered incorporating interviews with relatives in the design of our study. It would certainly have been possible to interview spouses of the married subjects. However, selection of reliable informants for patients and normals who were not currently married would have created problems. Our experience in other types of studies strongly suggested to us that informants who are not in close daily contact with subjects often lack adequate access to provide appropriate detailed information on intimate aspects of the subject's life. This may also apply to the nonperceptive or hostile spouse. Moreover, biases and misperceptions of the closely involved informant may be at least as potent as any that operate in the subject herself. In these circumstances, if the two sources of information do differ, reconciling them is by no means straightforward and may merely substitute one set of biases for another. The alternative of obtaining information from the subject alone, when carried out with careful attention to interview technique and training of raters, has been shown capable of obtaining accurate information (Spitzer and Endicott 1973). Moreover, schizophrenics, for whom information from relatives has particularly been advocated, are impaired and lacking in insight to a much more marked degree than we would expect in outpatient depressives.

Although we lack direct evidence of validity, we can cite indirect evidence. Relative-patient concordances were assessed in mixed neurotic subjects by Gurland et al. (1972), using the Structured and Scaled Interview to Assess Maladjustment (SSIAM) from which the main part of our scale was derived. They reached quite acceptable levels. Moreover, if biases were introduced into our data collection, we would expect them to be related closely to the distortions of self-perception resulting from the depressed mood of the patients at the height of illness. Were such the case, the patient ratings at the height of illness should show a large halo effect. In fact the evidence suggests they did not. We instructed our raters to assess, for the most part, actual behavior independent of the patient's perception and to confine the contribution of the patient's view to the ratings of feelings and satisfactions. The success of this method is attested by the results of factor analysis. Feelings and satisfactions emerged as a separate factor, quite distinct from the factors reflecting behavior. If there had been a sizeable contamination of one with the other, this separation would not have been possible.

There was, however, one aspect of the ratings in which we cannot be sure that bias may not have played a part. The raters were not blind as to whether subjects came from patient or normal samples. Preconceptions could have led to the depressives being rated as more impaired. Moreover, the patients were rated on several occasions, the normals only once. There was no reason to expect systematic changes in social function over a span of months in the normal group as a whole, and we did not consider it justified to submit them repeatedly to the rating procedure. However, it is possible that increasing familiarity with the patients might have led raters to perceive more abnormalities and patients to acknowledge them. The residual defects were not general, but showed specific patterns, which would be unlikely to be determined merely by bias. Information from other sources was of course used in describing the patients. This should not have biased the rating procedure since the information was all obtained by persons other than the social-adjustment raters and was not imparted to them.

In our sampling we depended on forty patients and forty normals. These are relatively small samples, although adequate for our statistical analyses and relatively large for an intensive study of this kind, over twenty months. However, we must be cautious in claiming universality for our findings. In particular our sample completely lacked males, almost completely lacked bipolar manic-depressives, and largely lacked severely ill psychotic depressives. In sociodemographic status both patients and normals tended to be married housewives in their thirties and forties. All our patients had initially responded to treatment with an antidepressant and were willing to participate in the study. This sample of cooperative drug responders represented over 70 percent of the depressed patients coming for treatment. We do not know the bias introduced by these characteristics, and future research will be required to extend the findings to a more heterogeneous sample of patients.

The process of obtaining normals from the general population is always difficult, fraught with refusals and potential biases. The largest proportion of our rejections was due to failure to meet our selection criteria for sociodemographic matching or absence of illness. However, a proportion was due to subject refusals. Persons who make such refusals are always likely to be a special segment, biased by such factors as covert disturbance. We should note also that our subjects were deliberately selected to be free of major psychiatric disorder; they were not intended to be an unselected sample of the general population. Social disability or its absence played no part in the selection process.

In order to set the social maladjustments of depressives in their full context, we would need in addition to normals other control groups, such as schizophrenics and patients with mixed neuroses other than depression. Without these, we cannot be certain that the dysfunctions we describe are specific to depression. However, we have used the literature on schizophrenia to make some comparisons.

Research Implications

For the researcher, studies such as this one might generate hypotheses to be tested or suggest new methodology. This research has shown the importance of evaluating social functioning independently of symptoms. Clinicians have sometimes observed that symptomatically recovered patients may not be functioning normally at home. In this research we made similar observations. It is important to assess social function separately when using rating measures to describe patient groups, measure change over time, and detect differences between treatments. This may be particularly crucial for studies of psychotherapy, where symptom measures alone may not be adequate.

Psychiatric diagnosis depends for the most part upon description of phenomena. Since biological criteria are usually lacking, there are problems of definition and classification. Psychosocial definitions introduce new problems. A common practice in the few studies assessing social functioning is to use global and subjective ratings of patient adjustment. Such judgments may have clinical utility but are difficult to replicate in research studies, since the criteria are not sufficiently precise and detailed. This study approached the problem by defining the specific behaviors to be assessed and five detailed anchor points for each behavior. This approach, while not without its problems, at least avoided the pitfall of more serious imprecision and provided us with detailed information. We were able to say not just that a marriage was impaired, but what characterized the impairment.

A few specific assessments deserve special comment. One such is the assessment of impaired work performance. This has long been recognized as a concomitant of depression and is included in various depression-symptom rating scales such as the Hamilton Scale (Hamilton 1960) from which our symptom-rating instrument was derived. However, the psychiatrists' initial assessment of work and interest on that scale did not correlate significantly with the social adjustment factor of work performance. The latter factor was derived by summing scores for detailed ratings of work and housework, such as time lost, degree of impaired performance, disinterest, and feelings of inadequacy, and is likely to have been more accurate than the psychiatrists' somewhat global assessment on a single seven-point scale. This finding calls into question the adequacy of psychiatric global interview ratings of this important area.

Another such special area was that of hostility. We have already commented on that. Broad assessments of hostility are unsatisfactory. The type of feeling or behavior must be closely defined. In our case it was overt friction, which we found depended primarily on the situation. In future studies it will be important to assess hostility separately and specifically with different members of the respondent's social field.

The differential and specific patterns of maladjustments found in this study confirmed for us an assumption which was important in our design of the study—that measures of social adjustment, especially in the areas of interpersonal relations, ought not to be limited to the concrete and easily quantified behaviors such as attendance at work. Although these assessments may be valuable in schizophrenics, by themselves they were unlikely to be adequate to measure the morbidity of the depressive or the effects of psychotherapy. Patterns of interpersonal relations and subjective distress may be harder to quantify, but, had we omitted them, most of the more important findings of this study might have been lost.

This study reaffirms the value of an adequate control group of nonpatients when measuring patient adjustment in the community. Realistically, it is against this index that the patient's normality in the community will be judged by others. Without this information, the evaluation of treatment or the patient's clinical course is incomplete.

In essence this was a descriptive study and, as such, belongs to a long tradition of clinical studies in psychiatry. Previous studies have been devoted mainly to symptoms. One of their aims has been the delineation of phenomena as an aid to diagnosis and classification. The social deficits we found bore no relation to traditional and newer symptom-based schemata of classification. It may be that a new classification could be derived on the basis of patterns of social dysfunction. Such a classification, however, would require a large heterogeneous sample of psychiatric patients for development.

Implications for Health of Children

There was little question that an acute depressive episode significantly impaired the woman's capacity as a mother. A major theme was her persistent difficulty in dealing with her affects, particularly her ambivalence towards affection and hostility. This occurred in her relationships with her children of any age and generated problems in the children. School-age children showed varying patterns of sibling rivalry, overactivity, and occasional overt symptoms such as enuresis or school problems.

Mental health personnel and family physicians treating the depressed mother should be alert to problems with the children. The patient who is withdrawn and weeping with a doctor can be irritable and hostile to her children. This hostility is often mixed with affection and guilt, and she may not readily discuss it in the first consultation. Inquiry as to the attitudes of the patient towards her child by using questions such as, "Do you find yourself picking on any one child?" may be helpful. This can open the topic for discussion, relieve the burden of secrecy, and may lead to alternative child-care plans to temporarily relieve the mother. Birth control measures are commonly recommended after a postpartum depression; they may also be considered with the patient during a depressive illness. Mental health professionals and pediatricians dealing with children should be fully aware of the nature of parental psychiatric problems—particularly maternal depression. Health workers treating disturbed families or "battered" children might consider the possibility of maternal depression. As Fabian and Donohue (1956) have noted, early maternal depression may solve the clinical puzzle of the apparently intact mother who seeks help with a severely disturbed child. The mother has recovered, while the child still shows evidence of contact with her during her depression. Inquiry into the mother's psychiatric history and mood disturbances might help unravel the child's problems.

The sensitive and astute clinician can thus facilitate major preventive work for the whole family. Early treatment of the mother's depressive illness may help break the cycle of mother-child impairments, since there were good indications that the mother's symptomatic relief improved her ability to care for her children.

Implications for Management

Unlike his earlier counterpart, the clinician today has a broad range of pharmacotherapies and psychological treatments available for depression, and he has the option to retain the patient at home while using these treatments. The emphasis on comprehensive care in psychiatric treatment further requires that the treatment goal should extend to the long-term effects of the disorder on the patient and family and on the prevention of recurrence.

The results of this study confirm that consideration must be given to both short- and long-term social disability. These findings come at a time when there are two divergent trends in psychiatric practice. The efficacy of pharmacotherapy in reducing symptoms raises the happy possibility that treatment will be brief. The mandate of community programs, however, suggests that it also be comprehensive. The widespread use of pharmacotherapy has resulted in a rapid turnover of patients. These data suggest that the social morbidity of the disorder must be taken into account in the treatment if rapid turnover is not to become rapid return.

Acutely depressed women usually are impaired wives, mothers, neighbors, and friends. Their impairments touch most areas of their lives. Unlike schizophrenics, depressives are not socially isolated, so that their impairments ultimately have an impact on many persons with whom they are in intimate contact. Since most depressives are treated as outpatients, they are not removed from their ongoing relationships or from the demands of their homes and families. Family members may be required both to assume some of the patient's responsibilities at home and to acquire understanding of the disorder. Active advice, practical suggestions, reasonable explanation by the treating clinician, and the use of community services may help the family to tolerate, support, and understand the patient throughout the treatment. The clinician should appreciate the practical implication of the finding that symptom intensity during the acute illness is only weakly associated with the degree of social pathology. Patients who show relatively milder symptoms may nevertheless show considerable degrees of social maladjustment. Therefore, it is essential that a diagnostic evaluation include inquiry into both domains.

Social maladjustment forms a large part of the acute depressive episode. Even with the successful alleviation of depressive symptoms, the social effects of the depression can continue for a considerable period of time. As we have shown, the improvement in social adjustment is much slower than in that of symptoms and, even then, is incomplete. Furthermore, antidepressants which produce rapid symptomatic remission may not be sufficient treatment for the social dysfunctions. The social disabilities were all present in our patients despite rapid and successful symptomatic remission with antidepressants. Psychological interventions seemed to have an additional value for the persisting social dysfunctions and did not conflict with drug therapy. Such intervention includes active help in the acute phase to enable patient and family to deal with the dysfunction and family to assume some of the patient's tasks. It also includes continuing treatment after symptomatic improvement to repair relationships and to cope with the problems of communication and interpersonal friction, which may predispose the patient to recurrence.

Progress

It was not until the middle of the twentieth century that new ideas and treatments supplanted those dominant in psychiatric practice for the previous century. The way was paved for these advances by the increase in facilities to treat large numbers of persons in the community, more enlightened attitudes towards mental illness, pharmacological therapies that made community treatment easier, and the availability of techniques to evaluate these new treatments. This study is a reflection and a result of all these trends.

Longitudinal descriptive information on this neglected area of depression seemed a prerequisite to understanding the course and consequences of the disorder, planning treatment, and modifying long-range effects. Such descriptive studies represent only one, perhaps limited, but nonetheless essential, piece of information. It is our hope that this information will contribute towards further understanding of the nature and consequences of depression.

APPENDICES

APPENDICES

Appendix A
Letter to Normals

Dear _____:

We would like you to know that you have been selected from the street listings of the City Directory, to see if you meet certain requirements to take part in a research survey we are conducting on 'Health and Everyday Activities.'

I will be calling you in one or two weeks to explain these requirements and the nature of the survey, and to find out if you are willing to take part.

If you can take part, we would like to ask you some questions in your own home about everyday matters in your work, family and social life. This will take from one-half to three-quarters of an hour. At the end of the interview you would be paid $10.00 in cash, as we realize this may involve some inconvenience for you.

We would like to stress that all information will be treated confidentially and that we will not trouble you again following the interview.

I shall look forward to speaking with you.

229

Appendix B
Supplementary Tables and Figures

TABLE B1. RELIABILITY OF RATINGS BY TWO RATERS

Items	N	Actual Value Range	Agree Com- pletely	1 Apart	2 or More Apart	Pearson r
WORK						
Time lost	18	1–5	15	3		.96
Impaired performance	18	1–5	12	6		.87
Friction	18	1–2	12	6		.33
Distress	18	1–4	9	8	1	.62
Disinterest	18	1–5	10	8		.89
Feelings of inadequacy	18	1–5	15	3		.95
SOCIAL AND LEISURE						
Diminished contact with friends	18	1–5	15	3		.89
Diminished social interactions	18	1–5	13	5		.94
Impaired leisure activities	18	1–5	10	7	1	.74
Friction	17	1–3	12	5		.68
Reticence	17	1–4	9	8		.84
Hypersensitive behavior	17	1–4	14	2	1	.86
Social discomfort	17	1–4	12	4	1	.73
Loneliness	18	1–5	13	4	1	.85

230

Table B1 cont.

Items	N	Actual Value Range	Agree Com-pletely	1 Apart	2 or More Apart	Pearson r
Boredom	18	1–5	14	4		.93
Diminished dating	6	1–5	4	1	1	.91
Disinterest in dating	8	1–5	6	1	1	.86
EXTENDED FAMILY						
Friction	16	1–3	11	5		.72
Reticence	17	1–5	9	6	2	.82
Withdrawal	17	1–3	12	4	1	.58
Family attachment	16	1–5	11	4	1	.64
Rebellion	16	1–2	14	2		—*
Guilt	18	1–4	15	3		.92
Worry	16	1–3	13	3		.75
Resentment	18	1–4	16	2		.95
MARITAL—AS SPOUSE						
Friction	9	1–4	3	6		.61
Reticence	9	1–4	7	1	1	.82
Domineering behavior	9	1–3	7	2		.76
Dependency	9	1–2	7	2		.55
Submissiveness	9	1–4	6	3		.86
Lack of affection	9	1–4	7	2		.92
Diminished intercourse	9	1–4	5	3	1	.61
Sexual problems	9	1–4	4	2	3	.96
Disinterest in sex	9	1–3	8	1		.91
MARITAL—AS PARENT						
Lack of involvement	15	1–4	9	5	1	.76
Impaired communication	15	1–4	9	6		.85
Friction	15	1–4	6	9		.69
Lack of affection	15	1–4	11	4		.90
FAMILY UNIT						
Guilt	15	1–4	11	3	1	.87
Worry	15	1–3	11	3	1	.72
Resentment	15	1–3	11	3	1	.73
ECONOMIC						
Economic inadequacy	18	1–4	17	1		.97
		PERCENTAGES:	67.1	29.0	3.9	
		Corrected Mean Correlation:				.83

* 95% of the time raters agreed on absence of rebellion.

TABLE B2. SOCIAL ADJUSTMENT IN ROLES, QUALITATIVE CATEGORIES, AND TOTAL SCALE SCORE

Factor†	Depressed N = 27	Recovered N = 27	Normals N = 40	Depressed vs. Normals	Depressed vs. Recovered	Recovered vs. Normals
AREA MEANS						
Work	2.78	1.54	1.33	11.41***	8.85***	2.31*
Social and Leisure	2.66	2.18	1.85	7.18***	5.06***	2.95**
Extended Family	1.94	1.55	1.48	4.70***	3.73***	1.17
Marital	2.31	2.04	1.72	5.06***	2.75*	2.41*
Parental	2.62	1.81	1.60	6.16***	5.86***	1.73
Family Unit	2.51	1.78	1.52	8.02***	6.41***	2.12*
QUALITATIVE CATEGORIES						
Instrumental Role Performance	2.91	2.29	1.86	7.38***	4.30***	3.16**
Quality of Interpersonal Relations	2.24	1.85	1.69	5.10***	4.63***	1.71
Satisfaction and Feelings	2.54	1.64	1.46	10.58***	8.42***	2.37*
Friction	1.97	1.66	1.39	4.34***	1.95	2.49*
TOTAL SCORE	2.44	1.85	1.61	10.72***	8.43***	3.66***

* Significant at $< .05$
** Significant at $< .01$
*** Significant at $< .001$
† Range is 1–5 for all scores.

TABLE B3. CHANGES IN ROLE AREAS AND QUALITATIVE CATEGORIES IN PATIENTS WHO RELAPSED

Variable	Last Rating Prior to Relapse Mean	Relapse Rating Mean	Differences	Significance of Difference
ROLE AREAS*				
Work	1.63	2.03	—0.40	.01
Social and Leisure	2.21	2.42	—0.21	.05
Extended Family	1.49	1.73	—0.24	.05
Marital	2.13	2.49	—0.36	.05
Parental	1.94	1.89	0.05	NS
Family Unit	1.80	2.03	—0.23	NS
QUALITATIVE CATEGORIES				
Instrumental Role Performance	2.12	2.55	—0.43	.01
Quality of Interpersonal Relations	1.95	2.06	—0.11	NS
Satisfactions and Feelings	1.75	1.99	—0.24	.01
Friction	1.77	1.79	—0.02	NS
TOTAL SCORE	1.83	2.12	—0.29	.000

* Range is 1–5 for all scores.

TABLE B4. CORRELATIONS BETWEEN INDIVIDUAL SYMPTOMS AND SOCIAL ADJUSTMENT FACTORS DURING THE ACUTE DEPRESSIVE EPISODE (N = 40)

Symptoms	Work Performance	Anxious Rumination	Interpersonal Friction	Inhibited Communication	Submissive Dependency	Family Attachment	Total Scale Score
Clinical Interview							
Depressed Feelings	−.189	.168	.054	.155	−.017	.376	.191
Guilt	.244	.420**	.276	.352	.247	.248	.522***
Pessimism and Hopelessness	.163	.207	.145	.111	.084	.188	.090
Suicidal Tendencies	−.055	−.208	.150	.071	−.055	−.040	.036
Impaired Work and Interests	.191	−.109	−.050	.134	.081	−.139	.016
Energy and Fatigue	.017	−.105	−.106	−.051	−.080	−.087	.083
Anxiety	.044	.235	−.182	.121	−.048	−.065	.035
Anorexia	.098	−.334*	−.117	−.159	.065	−.146	−.177
Irritability	.120	−.136	.491**	.185	−.118	.082	.213
Initial Insomnia	.024	.170	.120	.086	.050	.330*	.205
Delayed Insomnia	.267	−.017	−.285	−.126	.072	.035	−.080
Retardation	.191	−.074	.047	.192	.018	.086	.147
Agitation	.291	−.055	.004	−.096	.190	.181	.107
Depressed Appearance	.201	.165	.062	.070	.221	.288	.234
B.P.R.S.							
Somatic Concern	.113	−.237	−.252	−.400*	.028	.147	−.268
Anxiety	.166	−.037	.321	.061	.040	−.310	−.268
Emotional Withdrawal	−.216	−.457*	−.267	−.149	−.152	−.173	−.453**
Guilt Feelings	.393*	.220	.269	.454	.258	.037	.525***
Tension	.185	−.156	−.014	−.106	.265	−.035	.037
Depressed Mood	−.021	.012	−.001	.292	.134	.225	.257
Hostility	.158	−.218	.408**	.039	−.175	.010	.140
Suspiciousness	.089	.111	.301	.086	.072	.086	.234
Motor Retardation	.211	−.183	−.021	.147	−.006	.088	.064
Uncooperativeness	−.031	.186	.266	−.061	−.084	−.117	.099
Blunted Affect	−.172	−.341*	.016	.087	−.185	−.296	−.197
Excitement	.045	−.114	−.143	−.165	.139	.077	−.057

* p $<$ .05
** p $<$ .01
*** p $<$ .001

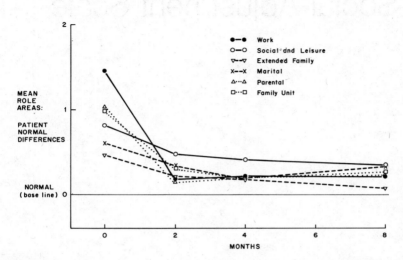

FIG. B1.   Social Role Performance: Depressed Patient–Normal Differences Over Eight Months

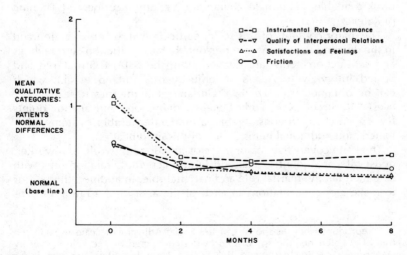

IG. B2.   Social Adjustment Categories: Depressed Patient–Normal Differences Over Eight Months

Appendix C
Social Adjustment Scale

This booklet* contains the interview format and scoring guide for the Social Adjustment Scales. Ratings for each subject are to be entered on a separate scoring sheet. In addition to this guide there is a handbook available, "Rationale, Reliability, Validity, Scoring and Training of Raters."

The major contents of this scale, particularly in its organization and in the detailed content of interpersonal behavior, friction, and feelings and satisfaction items, are derived from the SSIAM (Structured and Scaled Interview to Assess Maladjustment; Gurland et al.), which can be obtained from Dr. B. J. Gurland at Biometrics Research, 722 West 168 Street, New York. Detailed definitions and anchor points have been changed considerably, a moderate number of items eliminated, and additional items added in this modification.

The scale covers five major areas of functioning: work, as a worker, housewife or student; social and leisure activities; relationships with extended family; marital role and parental role. In addition the rater is to make global evaluations in each of the areas and a rating of eco-

* Reproduced here is the text of the Social Adjustment Scale used in the trial of maintenance-therapy of depression conducted by the Yale University Department of Psychiatry and the Boston State Hospital. The text is by Myrna M. Weissman and Eugene S. Paykel. Janis Tanner assisted in the revision.

nomic inadequacies. In general, the questions in each area fall into four major categories—the patient's performance at expected tasks, the amount of friction he has with people, finer aspects of his inter-personal relations, and his feelings and satisfactions. The first three categories have to do with the patient's actual behavior and the fourth with his inner feelings and satisfactions.

The scale is set out in the form of a semistructured interview. The initial questions should follow the general outline but may be suitably modified. In general, they should be followed up by questioning to enable exact assignment to a scale point. Suggested probing questions are provided after each question. For all items, except those specifically asking for the patient's feelings (the feelings and satisfaction items), the rating is made as to the actual behavior on the basis of all the in-formation available rather than purely on the patient's perception, especially if patient gives clues that his perception is unrealistic (e.g. "good" relationship with family when there is no contact on account of indifference). However, in those items which rate the patient's feelings and satisfactions, only the patient's perceptions of the situa-tion are used. Each of these feeling items is marked with an asterisk on the scoring sheet and is indicated on the interview format. In the global ratings, which are a general assessment of adjustment, the rater can use all available information and personal judgment in making a rating.

The scale for the individual items ranges from 1 to 5 and that for globals from 1 to 7. In all cases higher scores reflect poorer adjust-ment. The period to be rated is in each case the last 2 months (8 weeks). If marked changes have occurred during the segment of this time the rater should make a judgment as to the average score for the item in the period.

INTRODUCTION

"We are interested in finding out how you have been doing in the last two months. I'd like to ask you some questions about your work, your leisure time and your family life. This will take about three quarters of an hour. There are no right or wrong answers to these questions. We want to know the answer that best describes how you have been getting on. If any question does not make sense to you, let me know. Please try to answer all the questions for the last two months—that would be from (date) to today. Since then have you been in the hos-pital? on a vacation? living away from home? Has anything unusual happened to you? Do you have any questions before we begin?"

WORK

"The first set of questions has to do with your work."

Male—"What is your usual job? Have you been working continuously
since (date)?"

Female—"Do you work full or part-time outside your home?"

Both—"Have you been taking any classes in the last two months?"

WORKER	HOUSEWIFE	STUDENT	NOT APPLICABLE
–all subjects working over half time –male part-time worker	–full time housewife –woman working less than half time or going to school less than half time	–all subjects going to school at least half time (8 credits)	–male subjects unemployed for two mo. –retired subject (A woman is retired if she is no longer doing housework because of advanced age.)

If subject shares two roles equally, ask

"What do you see as your main role (choice)
or (choice)?"

The predominant role over the last two months is to be rated.
If the role changes during the two month period, rate the role
held the majority of time only. If not applicable, skip to social
leisure section.

1 = worker outside home, turn to page 2
2 = housewife, turn to page 3   cc. 16
3 = student, turn to page 4
4 = not applicable, turn to page 5

FOR WORKER ONLY

1. TIME LOST—"Have you missed any time from work in the last two
months?"
"How many days did you miss?"

This includes time lost due to many causes; physical illness, mental
illness, days laid off, days unemployed.

Do not rate paid vacations unless taken because of illness.
For less than full time workers, rate by work weeks.

In days	In work weeks	
1 = none to two days	1 = less than a half week	
2 = three to five days	2 = up to one week	
3 = six to ten days	3 = over one to two weeks	cc. 17
4 = eleven to twenty days	4 = over two to four weeks	
5 = more than twenty days	5 = over four weeks	

2. IMPAIRED PERFORMANCE—"Have you been doing your job well
   during the last two months?"
   "Have you fallen behind in your work?"
   "Has anyone had to speak to you about your work?"

—Do not rate the subject's feelings of inadequacy or time lost.

—This item implies some understanding of the norms for the particular type of work being done. Rate for the community norm,
not for the subject's normal performance.

1 = no impairment	
2 = adequate with some impairment	
3 = moderate impairment or needed help	cc. 18
4 = does poorly	
5 = does very poorly	

Skip to "Feelings of Inadequacy"

FOR HOUSEWIFE ONLY

1. TIME LOST—"Were there days in the last two months when you
   didn't do any housework?"
   "Could you tell me what those days were like?"

This includes days lost because of physical illness or mental illness.

1 = none to two days	
2 = three to seven days	
3 = eight to fourteen days	cc. 17
4 = fifteen to twenty-eight days	
5 = more than twenty-eight days	

2. IMPAIRED PERFORMANCE   RATE EACH ITEM AND AVERAGE
   "Now we are going to talk about how well you have been doing
   your work at home."

a) Meals—"Have you been making all the meals in the last two months?"
"Could you tell me what you cook on an average day?"
"Have you been using many convenience foods, such as frozen dinners?"
"Do you eat out often?"

b) Cleaning—"Have you been keeping up with the housecleaning?"
"How often do you do a thorough cleaning; bathrooms, floors, etc.?"

c) Washing—"Have you been keeping up with the laundry in the last two months?"
"Has anyone run out of clean clothes?"

d) Groceries—"How often do you go grocery shopping?"
"Do you have to make extra trips because you have forgotten things?"

e) Errands—"Do you keep up with other shopping and errands?—by this I mean clothes shopping, going to the post office, going to the drugstore?"

–Do not rate the subject's feelings of inadequacy or time lost.
–Rate for the community norm, not for the subject's normal performance.
–Rate as needed help only if the subject could not manage by herself (i.e., household help or family's help does not always mean impairment).

---

1 = no impairment
2 = does adequately but some impairment
3 = moderate impairment or needed help   cc. 18
4 = does poorly
5 = does very poorly or not at all

Skip to "Feelings of Inadequacy"

FOR STUDENT ONLY

1. TIME LOST—"How many classes have you missed in the last two months?"

---

1 = none or occasional
2 = up to $1/8$ of expected classes
3 = over $1/8$ to $1/4$ of expected classes   cc. 17
4 = over $1/4$ to $1/2$ of expected classes
5 = over $1/2$ of expected classes

---

2. <u>IMPAIRED PERFORMANCE</u>—"During the last two months, how
    have your grades been?"
    "Have you been able to complete assignments?"

—Do not rate subjects feelings of inadequacy or time lost.
—Rate for the community norm, not for the subject's normal per-
    formance.

1 = no impairment
2 = adequate with some impairment
3 = moderate impairment or needed help   cc. 18
4 = does poorly
5 = does very poorly or unable to complete assignments

FOR ALL SUBJECTS

3. <u>FEELINGS OF INADEQUACY</u>—"Have you felt that you might have
    done a poor job at any time in the last two months?"
    "Have you done your job as well as possible or could you do
    better?"
    HOUSEWIFE "Has unexpected company made you feel embar-
    rassed about the way the house looked?"

RATE SUBJECT'S FEELINGS

1 = feels quite adequate
2 = occasionally feels inadequate
3 = quite often feels inadequate   cc. 19
4 = usually feels inadequate
5 = never feels adequate

4. <u>FRICTION</u>—"Have you tended to argue with people you have come
    in contact with while doing your work?"
    "Have people gotten on your nerves or made you anrgy?"
    "Did you hold your feelings in? Did the other person know you
    were irritated?"
    "Could you give me an example?"

Rate overt behavior including arguing, overt annoyance, withdrawal due to tension. Do not rate inner feelings. Consider the
following individuals:

For worker—supervisors, other workers, customers
For housewife—salespeople, repairmen, neighbors (excluding
    close friends)

For student—teachers, administrators, other students (excluding friends)

1 = smooth relationships or no visible annoyance
2 = not provocative but overt difficulty with sensitive situations
3 = rather uneasy tense relationships or one major incident cc. 20
4 = moderate friction or friction with many people
5 = many furious clashes or is deliberately avoided by all others

5. DISTRESS—"Have you felt upset or worried for any reason while doing your work these past two month?"
"Do you ever have to stop doing your work because you are too upset to continue?"

Exclude distress due to disinterest but include tiredness, malaise or tension. Base ratings on frequency and severity. Explanation of distress includes being blue or crying, being tense or jittery, heart pounding, butterflies inside.
RATE SUBJECT'S FEELINGS

1 = no distress
2 = a little distress
3 = moderate distress   cc. 21
4 = very distressed
5 = feels absolute torture

6. DISINTEREST—"Have you found your work interesting during the last two months?"
"Do you feel satisfaction when your work is done?"
HOUSEWIFE "How do you feel about doing the housework and cooking?" "Do you like it? Do you hate it?"

RATE SUBJECT'S FEELINGS

1 = consistently interested
2 = interested
3 = some interest   cc. 22
4 = disinterest
5 = actively dislikes it

SOCIAL LEISURE

"Now I am going to ask you about your friends and about what you have been doing in your spare time since (date)."

7. <u>DIMINISHED</u> CONTACTS—"How many close friends do you have?" "By close friends I mean people you have regularly seen or telephoned during the last two months?"
   "Are you including couples? Are you close to both the people or just one?"

—Exclude as friends siblings, parents, children, close aunts and uncles, spouse's siblings and parents; exclude co-workers, unless there is contact outside of work; exclude friends of the opposite sex if dating; exclude old friends with no recent contact.
—Include as friends other relatives such as cousins or spouse's siblings.
—Regular contact is defined as contact about once a week during the two month period.
—Exclude second member of couple unless subject is close to both.

1 = nine or more
2 = five to eight
3 = two to four   cc. 23
4 = one
5 = no close friends

8. <u>RETICENCE</u>   DO NOT ASK IF SUBJECT DOES NOT HAVE CLOSE FRIENDS
   "Have you been able to talk about your feelings openly with your friends?"
   "What types of things do you discuss?"
   "What types of things do you hold back?"

—The subject should not be asked to determine the degree to which the communication was appropriate.
—The rater should not confuse satisfaction and level of communication (e.g. what is quite satisfying to one person may not be open communication and vice versa).
—Reasonably open includes subjects that withhold appropriately private matters (i.e. sex life with spouse).
—Use examples of problems known to be bothering the subject.

1 = reasonably open with at least one person
2 = mildly reticent
3 = moderately reticent or occasionally unable to discuss   cc. 24
4 = usually unable to discuss feelings
5 = unable to discuss feelings at any time

9. DIMINISHED SOCIAL INTERACTIONS—"How many times have you done something socially with friends in the last two months?" "What kinds of things have you been doing socially?"

—Include entertaining or visiting friends (not family excluded as close friends, page 7); going out in company of others (not just spouse, date or family) including movies, sports events, restaurants, shopping with friends, etc.
—Include weddings, showers, other parties; club meetings attended.
—Include attending church if subject socializes with people at the service.
—Ask subject to recall activities, asking specifically about each type of situation. The subject will not necessarily know which activities the rater wants to include.
—If subject went alone to an activity, rate only if he was an active participant rather than audience.

In number of interactions
1 = sixteen or more
2 = eight to fifteen
3 = four to seven   cc. 25
4 = two or three
5 = zero to one

10. IMPAIRED LEISURE ACTIVITIES—"Do you have any hobbies or special interests?"

"Have you been interested in them during the last two months?" "What have you been doing in your spare time?"

—Include hobbies, sports, political activities, gardening (not yard work), sewing (not mending), special baking (not routine), crafts, needlework, decorating for some women if it is a hobby, avid reading.
—For those with none of the above interests ask about casual reading (newspaper column daily followed, favorite magazine always read), television program to which the subject looks forward, etc.

1 = well developed, specific interests or activities which the subject participates in more than once a week
2 = definite interests or activities to which the subject devotes regular but less frequent time
3 = some specific interests but these are sporadic   cc. 26

4 = some interests but these are superficial or indiscriminating (e.g. watching television with little regard to programs)
5 = absence of any interests or activities

DO NOT ASK THIS PAGE IF SUBJECT HAS HAD NEITHER FRIENDS NOR CONTACTS

11. FRICTION—"How have you been getting along with friends during the last two months?"
   "Have people gotten on your nerves or made you angry?"
   "Have you held your feelings in? Did the other person know you were irritated?"

−Rate overt behavior including arguing, overt annoyance, withdrawal due to tension.
−Do not rate inner feelings.
−Include close friends and social acquaintances.

---

1 = smooth relationships or no visible annoyance
2 = not provocative but overt difficulty with sensitive situations
3 = rather uneasy tense relationships or one major incident cc. 27
4 = moderate friction or friction with many people
5 = many furious clashes or is deliberately avoided by all others

---

12. HYPERSENSITIVITY—"Have any of your friends offended you or hurt your feelings in the last two months?"
   "Tell me about what happened."
   "How long did it take you to get over this?"
   "Do you act the same now toward that person as you did before he (she) offended you?"

−Exclude family members
−Rate actual behavior change, not inner feelings

---

1 = behavior reasonable or unaffected, or subject does not remember taking offense
2 = behavior affected but returns to normal within hours
3 = behavior affected but recovers in days   cc. 28
4 = behavior altered requiring a week or more to recover
5 = behavior altered toward others as well as individual, behavior has not recovered in a month

---

13. SOCIAL DISCOMFORT—"Have you felt ill at ease, tense or shy

when you have been with people during the last two months?"
"Did you feel anxious to get away or to be alone when with people?"
"Did you avoid being with people because you felt uncomfortable?"

—Include general distress which interferes with the enjoyment of company.
—If necessary average as subject may feel tense only with certain situations or for only a part of the interaction.
—Do not rate situation unless there were several people present.
—Do not rate question unless subject has been in social situation.
—RATE SUBJECT'S FEELINGS

---

1 = enjoys company
2 = occasionally uncomfortable but can relax
3 = often distressed but can enjoy company at times   cc. 29
4 = mostly distressed
5 = always very distressed in company

---

14. LONELINESS—"Have you felt lonely and wished for companionship these last two months?"
"Have you felt this way when you were around people too?"

—Do not include fear of being alone, loneliness when with others or "cosmic" loneliness ("I'm all alone in the world").
—Loneliness must be a desire for human companionship.
—RATE SUBJECT'S FEELINGS

---

1 = has not felt isolated
2 = feels a little isolated or isolated occasionally
3 = feels moderately isolated or isolated often (i.e. every weekend)
4 = feels a great need for people   cc. 30
5 = feels totally alone, or feels lonely every day

---

15. BOREDOM—"Have you felt bored in your free time in the last two months?"
"Did you stay bored very long or could you find something to do?"

—Do not rate boredom while working.
—Do not rate inactivity unless subject reports feeling bored.
—RATE SUBJECT'S FEELINGS

1 = not usually bored
2 = occasionally bored but able to find activity or pass time
3 = frequently bored   cc. 31
4 = bored most of free time
5 = feels bored every day

ASK BOTH QUESTIONS FOR ALL UNMARRIED ONLY INCLUD-
ING SINGLE, DIVORCED, SEPARATED, WIDOWED
"Are you currently married?"
"Are you dating any person in particular?"
"Does your friend live with you?" IF YES ASK SPOUSE, NOT
DATING QUESTIONS

---

16. <u>DIMINISHED DATING</u>—"How often have you dated in the last
two months?"

—Rate any face to face contact other than accidental meetings.
—Include visiting as well as "going out."

---

1 = more than twice weekly (16 times)
2 = once or twice weekly (8 to 15 times)
3 = once every two weeks (4 to 7 times)   cc. 32
4 = once a month or less (1 to 3 times)
5 = not at all

---

17. <u>DISINTEREST IN DATING</u>—"How much interest have you had in
dating during the last two months?"
THOSE DATING "Did you enjoy dating?"
NOT DATING "Would you have been interested in dating?"

—Do not rate how much the subject liked the individuals but how
much one liked dating itself.
RATE SUBJECT'S FEELINGS

---

1 = pleasurable or interested
2 = usually pleasurable or interested
3 = variable or some interest   cc. 33
4 = little or no interest
5 = active dislike

"The next questions are about your outside family, your relatives, <u>not</u>
your husband or children at home. How have you been getting along
with your relatives?"

1. "Let's start with your parents."
   "Have you seen or heard from them in the last two months?"
   "How have you been getting along with them?"
   "Have there been any arguments?"

Continue asking these three basic questions
about: 2. siblings
                                                    3. spouse's parents
Consider in rating the friction and reticence   4. married children
only those family members seen or heard   5. children living
from during the two month period.   away from home
If the subject has no living extended family,   6. spouse's siblings
do not rate this area. Turn to extended fam-   (only if no other
ily guilt and resentment, questions 24 and 25.   family in area)

18. FRICTION

–Do not rate warmth, affection or other inner feelings.
–Rate behavior occurring during interactions in the last two
 months with the above relatives. Include friction in phone or
 letter contacts.

1 = harmonious family relations
2 = fairly harmonious family relations
3 = indifferent or a few disagreements or one major argument
4 = moderate friction involving more than one person   cc. 34
5 = very discordant family relations

19. RETICENT—"During the last two months, have you been able to
    talk about your feelings and problems openly with any of these
    relatives?"
    "What types of things do you discuss?"
    "What types of things do you hold back?"

–The subject should not be asked to determine the degree to
 which the communication was appropriate.
–The rater should not confuse satisfaction and level of communication.
–Reasonably open includes subjects that withhold appropriately
 private matters.

1 = reasonably open with at least one person
2 = mildly reticent
3 = moderately reticent or occasionally unable to discuss   cc. 35

4 = usually unable to discuss feelings
5 = unable to discuss feelings at any time

20. <u>WITHDRAWN</u>—"In the last two months, have you made an effort to keep in touch with family members or have you waited for them to contact you?"
"Who usually arranges getting together?"
"Is there anyone in the family you have avoided seeing?"

—Do not exclude relatives because of long standing friction.
—Include contact in person and by phone or letter.

1 = initiates some contacts regularly
2 = initiates some contacts
3 = relies on family to initiate contacts   cc. 36
4 = avoids family contacts
5 = no contact with family at all

21. <u>DEPENDENCY</u>—"Do you depend on your family for help or advice? for baby sitting? for financial help?"
"When you go visiting or go out is it usually with family or with friends?"

—Include dependence on family for friendship.

1 = quite independent
2 = a few dependent relationships
3 = mostly dependent but has other resources   cc. 37
4 = almost totally dependent
5 = completely dependent

22. <u>REBELLIOUS</u>—"Did you do things just to make your family angry or annoyed or just to go against their wishes?"
"Did you want to make them angry but didn't do it?"

—Focus on whether the subject could make more effective decisions if he did not need to defy the family.
—Rate effect on actions and behavior.

1 = feels no urge to defy family
2 = a little inhibited by need to defy family
3 = some decisions and values determined solely by a need to defy
4 = many important decisions and values determined solely to defy
5 = goes out of way to defy family continuously   cc. 38

23. WORRY—"Have you worried about things happening to members of your outside family during the last two months?"
"What kinds of things have you been worrying about?"

—Include living family only. Rate feelings during the last two months.
—RATE SUBJECT'S FEELINGS

1 = shows reasonable concern
2 = frequently uneasy
3 = worries a fair amount   cc. 39
4 = very often worried
5 = crippled by unreasonable fears

24. GUILT—"In the last two months, have you been feeling that you have let your relatives down at any time?"
"How did you let them down?"
"Have you felt guilty?"

—Include absent or deceased family members.
—Include feelings experienced in the period about events or relationships which occurred anytime in the past.
—RATE SUBJECT'S FEELINGS

1 = no guilt
2 = some slight misgivings
3 = moderate guilt   cc. 40
4 = very ashamed of his behavior
5 = constant distressing feelings of guilt

25. RESENTMENT—"In the last two months, have you been feeling that your relatives have let you down at any time?"
"How did they let you down?"
"Have you felt bitter?"

—Include absent or deceased family members.
—Include feelings experienced in the period about events or relationships which occurred anytime in the past.
—RATE SUBJECT'S FEELINGS

1 = reasonably satisfied with family
2 = appreciative but some grievances
3 = disappointment but some appreciation   cc. 41
4 = mostly bitter or disillusioned
5 = consumed by bitterness or resentment

MARITAL

"These questions have to do with marriage or a partnership between two people. Are you married? Do you live with a member of the opposite sex? Have you ever been separated or divorced? When?"

—It may be necessary to reassure welfare subjects of the confidentiality of the interview and that the rater is not part of welfare.
—The term partner may be substituted for husband/wife or spouse.
—Rate section if subject fits in any of the three following categories.

1 = Legally married or remarried and living with spouse at any time during the period
2 = Living with a person of the opposite sex in a permanent relationship (at least two months, but not legally married) (include even if still legally married to a past spouse)
3 = Separated, living alone but still has regular contact with spouse

26. FRICTION—"How have you and your husband/wife been getting along in the last two months?"
"Have there been any open disagreements?"
"Have you been arguing every day? How serious have the arguments been?"

—Rate subject's behavior, not inner feelings.

1 = smooth, warm relationship
2 = a few tensions and disagreements
3 = moderate friction or coolness   cc. 42
4 = marked friction
5 = constant friction, marriage may be breaking

27. RETICENCE—"Have you been able to talk about your feelings and problems with your husband/wife these last two months?"
"Could you tell me what kinds of things you talk about?"

1 = confides freely
2 = keeps back only a little
3 = moderate disability in communication   cc. 43
4 = marked disability
5 = completely unable to express themselves

The next two questions are used to evaluate the dominant-sub-missive balance in the marriage and are therefore asked at the same time. It is unusual, although not impossible for a subject to rate a high number on both items for the two month period.

28. DOMINEERING BEHAVIOR—"Who has been making most of the decisions at home in the last two months?"
"What decisions have you been making?"
"Do you take your spouse's wishes into consideration? Even when he's not there?"

29. SUBMISSIVENESS—"If you and your husband/wife have a dis-agreement on something, who usually gets his or her way? Who usually goes along?"
"Have you been pressured or bullied by your spouse during the last two months? Could you give me an example?"

DOMINEERING BEHAVIOR

1 = non-domineering
2 = mildly domineering
3 = moderately domineering   cc. 44
4 = little consideration given to spouse's wishes
5 = tyrannical

SUBMISSIVENESS

1 = can be firm when necessary
2 = firm enough except on unimportant issues
3 = cannot assert self against spouse's firm decisions   cc. 45
4 = cannot assert self against spouse's minor opposition
5 = cannot assert opinion even if invited to do so

30. DEPENDENCY—"During the last two months have you had to de-pend on your husband/wife to help you?"
"What kinds of things have you needed help with?"
"Do you lean on him for emotional support when you are upset?"

—Ask about specific types and instances of assistance as appropri-ate by sex. For women, driving, shopping, monetary decisions, helping with children, helping with housework, minor repairs (i.e. changing a light bulb or fuse, etc.), emotional support. For men, monetary decisions, driving, up-keep of house, emotional support.
—DO NOT RATE AFFECTION AS SUPPORT

1 = reasonably independent
2 = dependent in some ways
3 = moderately dependent   cc. 46
4 = markedly dependent
5 = depends on spouse in least things, cannot care for self

31. LACK OF AFFECTION—"What have your feelings been toward
      your husband/wife during the last two months?"
      "Have you felt affection? Have you disliked him?"
      "Did you love him when you were not getting along or did you
      sometimes wonder?"

—Do not rate friction
—RATE SUBJECT'S FEELINGS

1 = consistent feelings of affection
2 = mostly feels affection but some misgivings
3 = markedly ambivalent feelings   cc. 47
4 = mostly negative feelings
5 = none (turn to question 34)

32. DIMINISHED SEXUAL INTERCOURSE—"Have you and your hus-
      band/wife been using any form of birth control or rhythm
      method?"
      "About how frequently have you had sexual relations in the past
      two months?"
      "Has it been less frequent when you have been upset or not feel-
      ing well?"

—Careful questioning in a non-threatening way is required as subjects tend to overestimate. It is best to supply two or more
  choices in determining frequency. Subjects tend to agree to
  terminate the question.
—Different terms for intercourse may be used where appropriate
  as long as they cannot be misconstrued by the subject (i.e.
  sexual relations, marital relations, sexual intercourse).
—Couples using the rhythm method will have a lower monthly
  frequency depending on the length of time of abstinence.

1 = sixteen or more times
2 = eight to fifteen times
3 = four to seven times   cc. 48
4 = one to three times
5 = none (turn to question 34)

33. <u>SEXUAL PROBLEMS</u>—"Have you been having any problems during sexual relations—any pain, any difficulty reaching a climax?"

—It is important to use a term for orgasm or ejaculation that the
subject will understand and with which they feel comfortable.
—Do not ask or rate if the subject has not had sex with spouse.

1 = none
2 = frequent minor problems
3 = sometimes problems but can be normal   cc. 49
4 = significant difficulties
5 = difficulties always experienced

34. <u>DISINTEREST IN SEX</u>—"Have you enjoyed sexual relations during
the last two months?"
"Have you just gone along with your spouse's wishes sometimes?"
"Have you sometimes hated it?"

FOR SUBJECTS UNABLE TO HAVE SEX FOR A PHYSICAL REASON
"Though you and your husband/wife could not have relations in the
last two months, have you regretted not being able to have marital
relations or have you been relieved that it was not possible?"

—RATE SUBJECT'S FEELINGS

1 = pleasurable relations, interested
2 = pleasant but some disinterest
3 = merely tolerated, no interest   cc. 50
4 = unpleasant
5 = repugnant and disturbing

PARENT

"Do you have any children? step children? foster children?"
"These questions are about just your children living at home with you."
"What are your children's names and ages?"

—These questions apply to any children living with the subject
except for married children living at home. Exclude children of
the subject who have lived with a previous spouse or who were
placed in foster homes for more than six of the eight weeks of
the period (i.e. rate only if home at least two weeks).
—Discussing children by name prevents confusion for both the
subject and the rater.

35. <u>LACK OF INVOLVEMENT</u>—"What kinds of things have you been
    doing with the children during the last two months? Let's start
    with (name)."

—Ask about each child separately and average for rating.
—For pre-school children inquire about involvement with day to
 day care, child's play activities, pre-school learning.
—For older children inquire about school progress, child's inter-
 ests, friends and dates, special problems, chores, etc.
—Do note rate feelings, rate behavior.

---

1 = <u>active</u> involvement in children's lives
2 = good interest, knows children's lives well
3 = moderate interest   cc. 51
4 = little interest
5 = disinterest, totally uninvolved

---

36. IMPAIRED COMMUNICATION—"Have you been able to talk
    with your children during the last two months?" Starting with
    (name)."
    "Does he/she come to you with problems?"
    "Could you give me an example from the last two months?"

—Rate for each child and average
—Consider what is appropriate communication for the child's age
—Do not rate for children under two years of age
—By communication is meant discussion of feelings and problems
 and other overt forms of communication, not just the relating of
 activities
—DO NOT RATE FEELINGS

---

1 = communicates easily
2 = most times can communicate
3 = fair communication   cc. 52
4 = rarely able to talk
5 = never able to talk

---

37. <u>FRICTION</u>—"During the past two months how much friction has
    there been between you and the children?"
    "Have you had to discipline them much in the last two months?"
    "Do you tend to snap at them when you are tired or upset?"

—Rate friction by the actual incidents, amounts of friction and
 amount and severity of discipline.

—Include coolness or tension. Do not rate feelings, rate actual behavior.

1 = smooth relationships
2 = a little friction or tension
3 = moderate friction   cc. 53
4 = marked friction
5 = constant state of friction or children are intimidated and avoid parent totally

38. LACK OF AFFECTION—"What have your feelings been toward the children during the last two months?"
    "Have you felt affection for them?" "Did you dislike them?"
    "Did you wish sometimes that they weren't around or that they didn't live with you?"

—RATE SUBJECT'S FEELINGS

1 = consistently felt affection
2 = mostly loves the children
3 = moderate disaffection   cc. 54
4 = marked lack of love
5 = absolute lack of love and affection, dislikes children

FAMILY UNIT

Rate the next three questions for spouse, ex-spouses and children. Combine to get ratings. The term partner may be used in place of spouse.

39. WORRY—"Have you worried about things happening to your spouse or children during the last two months?"
    "What kinds of things have you been worrying about?"

—Include living individuals only.
—RATE SUBJECT'S FEELINGS DURING THE LAST TWO MONTHS.

1 = shows reasonable concern
2 = frequently uneasy
3 = worries a fair amount   cc. 55
4 = very often worried
5 = crippled by unreasonable fears

40. GUILT—"In the last two months, have you been feeling that you have let your spouse or children down at any time?"
    "How did you let them down?" "Have you felt guilty?"

–Include absent or deceased family members.
–Include feelings experienced in the period about events or relationships which occurred any time in the past.
–RATE SUBJECT'S FEELINGS

1 = no guilt
2 = some slight misgivings
3 = moderately guilty   cc. 56
4 = very ashamed of his behavior
5 = constant distressing feelings of guilt

41. RESENTMENT—"In the last two months, have you been feeling that your spouse or children have let you down at any time?" "How did they let you down?" "Have you felt bitter?"

–Include absent or deceased family members.
–Include feelings in the period about events or relationships which occurred any time in the past.
–RATE SUBJECT'S FEELINGS

1 = reasonably satisfied with family
2 = appreciative but some grievances
3 = disappointment but some appreciation   cc. 57
4 = mostly bitter or disillusioned
5 = consumed by bitterness or resentment

ECONOMIC

42. ECONOMIC INADEQUACY—"This last question has to do with your finances. In the last two months have you had enough money for your basic needs?"
"Have you had to go into your savings?"
"Have you had to put off important things, such as doctor visits?"
"Have you had trouble with bill collectors?"
"Are you receiving welfare?"

–This question covers the situation of the whole immediate family unit.
–Do not rate whether a husband gives his spouse sufficient money but whether the family unit has sufficient income and reserves to meet their basic needs.
–Do not rate a mortgage to buy a house as difficulties leading to a loan.

–This question is designed to measure the <u>amount of difficulties</u> the subject experiences with money, not their financial independence.
–Those with illegal income on welfare may or may not be rated 5.

---

1 = income adequate for needs (not necessarily adequate for wants)
2 = income and reserves adequate with minor problems
3 = income and reserves inadequate leading to major problems and/or small loans
4 = income and reserves inadequate necessitating supplements from outside resources. Subject is having major problems.
5 = severe financial problems, totally dependent with no income or reserves, on welfare   cc. 58

"Is there anything you would like to add that would help us to understand how you have been doing?"
"Thank you very much for your cooperation. It has been helpful to us. Do you want to ask me any questions?"

GLOBALS

Globals should be done immediately after the interview. Use all available information and own judgment in making these ratings. Unlike the items which must be based on the information supplied by the subject, the globals can take into <u>account suspected denial</u>. Also take into account <u>behavior that is maladaptive but not covered</u> in the items (i.e. the compulsive housewife, the parent that lives through her child with no life of her own, the subject with a social life so hectic that it interferes with the subject's health).
Do not use the average of the interview items!

<u>WORK</u> cc. 59   Do not rate the global for areas for which none of the interview items were rated.

---

1 = <u>Excellent</u>—no maladjustment, excellent adjustment and performance in main role, without deficiencies
2 = <u>Good</u>—no maladjustment, adequate adjustment with steady effective function, but on account of minor deficiencies cannot be rated as excellent
3 = <u>Mild maladjustment</u>—definite deficiencies, outside the range of adequate adjustment, but deficiencies limited in severity, pervasiveness, and proportion of time they manifest

4 = <u>Moderate maladjustment</u>—deficiencies moderate and manifest about half the period, or work adjustment about half its potential

5 = <u>Marked maladjustment</u>—poor functioning for most of the period but occasionally still displays adaptive behavior

6 = <u>Severe maladjustment</u>—very poor functioning most of the period

7 = <u>Very severe maladjustment</u>—complete inability to function in work role throughout the period

<u>SOCIAL LEISURE</u> cc. 60

1 = <u>Excellent</u>—no maladjustment, excellent adjustment with no deficiencies. Plentiful friendships and activities outside immediate family.

2 = <u>Good</u>—no maladjustment, adequate adjustment with friendship and activities appropriate to natural situation but not such as to warrant being described as plentiful

3 = <u>Mild maladjustment</u>—definite deficiencies in friendships, social participation and leisure activities, but limited in severity, pervasiveness and proportion of time manifest

4 = <u>Moderate maladjustment</u>—deficiencies moderate and manifest about half of the period or social adjustment about half its potential

5 = <u>Marked maladjustment</u>—marked deficiencies in friendships, social participation and leisure activities but occasionally still displays adaptive behavior

6 = <u>Severe maladjustment</u>—very poor social functioning most of the period

7 = <u>Very severe maladjustment</u>—completely isolated and socially maladjusted throughout the period

<u>EXTENDED FAMILY</u> cc. 61

1 = <u>Excellent</u>—no maladjustment, close and harmonious relationships with all living members of family of origin

2 = <u>Good</u>—no maladjustment, harmonious relationships with parents and siblings with minor deficiencies or insofar as geography permits

3 = <u>Mild maladjustment</u>—definite deficiencies outside the range of adequate relationships but limited in number of relatives involved and severity

4 = <u>Moderate maladjustment</u>—may be discordant relationships with several relatives or coolness to family in general

5 = Marked maladjustment—poor relationship with much of family, but some relationship retained

6 = Severe maladjustment—discordant relationship with entire family of origin, with minimal contact

7 = Very severe maladjustment—entirely out of social contact with family of origin for entire period due to severely discordant relationships or any interaction extremely limited and discordant

MARITAL cc. 62

1 = Excellent—no maladjustment, very good relationship in all respects, no deficencies

2 = Good—no maladjustment, stable and adequate marital relationship which on account of minor deficiencies, cannot be regarded as excellent

3 = Mild maladjustment—definite deficiencies, outside the range of adequate adjustment, but deficiencies limited in severity, pervasiveness, and proportion of time manifest

4 = Moderate maladjustment—deficiencies moderate and manifest about half the period or marital adjustment about half its potential

5 = Marked maladjustment—poor marital relationship with discord but some relationship remaining

6 = Severe maladjustment—relationship very poor in most respects. Separation may be impending or actual at time of rating.

7 = Very severe maladjustment—separation actual at time of rating and serious divorce proceedings impending

PARENTAL cc. 63

1 = Excellent—no maladjustment, very effective parent with good parent-child relationship with all children, no deficiencies

2 = Good—no maladjustment, adequate parent relationship which cannot be described as excellent on account of minor deficiencies

3 = Mild maladjustment—definite deficiencies in some areas with respect to at least one child but limited in severity, pervasiveness and time manifest

4 = Moderate maladjustment—deficiencies involving more children and manifest more consistently

5 = Marked maladjustment—consistent deficiencies involving most of parental function and relationships, but with some assets

6 = Severe maladjustment—very poor adjustment in most respects and manifest most of the period

7 = <u>Very severe maladjustment</u>—total neglect and lack of affection throughout the period. Children may be in the care of relatives or foster parents at time of rating

<u>OVERALL ADJUSTMENT</u> cc. 64   USE YOUR OWN JUDGMENT IN MAKING THE RATING, DO NOT USE THE AVERAGE OF THE GLOB-ALS SOLELY

1 = <u>Excellent</u>—no maladjustment, excellent rating in most areas. Handles problems well, good interpersonal relationships, happy with adjustment
2 = <u>Good</u>—adequate adjustment but because of deficiencies cannot be called excellent
3 = <u>Mild maladjustment</u>—definite areas of maladjustment, but limited in severity, pervasiveness, or time manifest
4 = <u>Moderate maladjustment</u>—greater deficiencies (moderate maladjustment includes subjects with good adjustment in some areas but marked maladjustment in others)
5 = <u>Marked maladjustment</u>—relatively persistent pervasive and severe difficulties
6 = <u>Severe maladjustment</u>—marked or severe maladjustment in <u>most</u> areas
7 = <u>Very severe maladjustment</u>—marked or severe maladjustment in <u>all</u> areas

First Name and Initial of Subject	Date	Surname of Rater

Yale University Department of Psychiatry
and
Boston State Hospital
Trial of Maintenance Therapy of Depression
SOCIAL ADJUSTMENT SCALE SCORING SHEET

- -
Enter score for each item. Items not scored or not applicable must be entered "X".
- -

<u>AREA 1—WORK</u>

	Role	cc.
Work role		16

		Score
1	Time lost	17
2	Impaired performance	18
3	Feelings of inadequacy*	19
4	Friction	20
5	Distress*	21
6	Disinterest*	22

AREA 2—SOCIAL & LEISURE ACTIVITIES

7	Diminished contacts	23
8	Reticence	24
9	Diminished social interests	25
10	Impaired leisure activities	26
11	Friction	27
12	Hypersensitivity	28
13	Social discomfort*	29
14	Loneliness*	30
15	Boredom*	31
16	Diminished dating	32
17	Disinterest in dating*	33

AREA 3—EXTENDED FAMILY

18	Friction	34
19	Reticent	35
20	Withdrawn	36
21	Dependency	37
22	Rebellion	38
23	Worry*	39
24	Guilt*	40
25	Resentment*	41

SCORE cc.

AREA 4—MARITAL

26	Friction	42
27	Reticence	43
28	Domineering behavior	44
29	Submissiveness	45
30	Dependency	46
31	Lack of affection*	47
32	Diminished sexual intercourse	48
33	Sexual problems	49
34	Disinterest in sex*	50

Parental

35	Lack of involvement	51
36	Impaired communication	52
37	Friction	53
38	Lack of affection*	54

Family Unit

39	Worry*	55
40	Guilt*	56
41	Resentment*	57

AREA 5—ECONOMIC

42	Economic inadequacy	58

AREA 6—GLOBALS

43	Work	59
44	Social and leisure	60
45	Extended family	61
46	Marital	62

		SCORE	cc.
47	Parental		63
48	Overall adjustment		64

* Feelings and satisfaction item—rate subject's feelings only.

References

Abraham, K. (1911) 1968. Notes on the psychoanalytical investigation and treatment of manic depressive insanity and allied conditions. In Gaylin and Willard, eds., *The Meaning of Despair*, pp. 3–26. Science House Inc., New York.

Ackerman, N. W. 1958. *The Psychodynamics of Family Life*. Basic Books, New York.

American Psychiatric Association. 1968. *Diagnostic and Statistical Manual of Mental Disorders*. Second edition. Washington, D.C.

Angrist, S., Lefton, M., Dinitz, S., and Pasamanich, B. 1968. *Women after Treatment*. Appleton-Century Crofts, New York.

Anthony, E. J. 1970. The impact of mental and physical illness in family life. *Amer. J. Psychiat.* 127: 56–64 (August).

Anthony, H. S. 1968. The association of violence and depression in a sample of young offenders. *British Journal of Criminology* 8: 346–65.

Axelson, L. 1963. The marital adjustment and marital role definitions of husbands of working and nonworking wives. *Marriage and Family Living* 25: 189–95 (May).

Bart, P. Depression in middle-aged women: Some sociocultural factors. Ph.d. dissertation, 1967. University of California, Los Angeles. University Microfilms, Ann Arbor, Michigan.

Beck, A. T. 1967. *Depression: Clinical, Experimental and Theoretical Aspects*. Harper and Row, New York.

Becker, J. 1962. Toward a comprehensive theory of depression: A cross-disciplinary appraisal of objects, games and meanings. *J. Nerv. Ment. Dis.* 135/1: 26–35 (January).

Becker, J. 1960. Achievement-related characteristics of manic depressives. *J. Abnorm. Soc. Psychol.* 60: 334–39.

Becker, J., Spielberger, C. D., and Parker, J. B. 1963. Value achievement and authoritarian attitudes in psychiatric patients. *J. Clin. Psychol.* 19: 57–61.

Bell, N. W. 1962. Extended family relations of disturbed and well families. *Family Process* 1: 175–93 (September).

Bell, N. W., and Vogel, E. 1960. *Modern Introduction to the Family.* Free Press, Glencoe, Ill.

Benedek, T. 1952. *Psychosexual Functions in Women.* Ronald Press, New York.

Bibring, E. 1953. In P. Greenacre, ed., *The Mechanism of Depression in Affective Disorder,* pp. 13–48. International University Press, New York.

Birtchnell, J., and Alarcon, J. 1971. Depression and attempted suicide. *Brit. J. Psychiat.* 118: 289–96.

Blueler, E. 1924. *Textbook of Psychiatry.* Translated by A. A. Brill. Macmillan, New York.

Bonime, W. 1962. Dynamics and psychotherapy of depression. In J. Masserman, ed., *Current Psychiatric Therapies,* vol. 2. Grune and Stratton, New York.

———. 1965. A psychotherapeutic approach to depression. *Contemporary Psychoanalysis* 2: 48–55 (Fall).

Bonjean, C. M., Hill, R. J., and McLemore, S. D. 1967. *Sociological Measurement, An Inventory of Scales and Indices.* Chandler Publishing Co., San Francisco, California.

Bowlby, J. 1951. *Maternal Care and Mental Health.* World Health Organization, Geneva.

Bowman, K. 1934. A study of the prepsychotic personality in certain psychoses. *Amer. J. Orthopsych.* 4: 473–98.

Briggs, P. F., Laperriere, R., and Greden, J. 1965. Working outside the home and the occurrence of depression in middle-aged women. *Mental Hygiene* 49: 438–42.

Brown, G. W. 1969. Some problems of family measurement. *Proc. Roy. Soc. Med.* 62: 22–24.

Brown, G. W., and Rutter M. 1966. The measurement of family activities and relationships: a methodological study. *Human Relations,* 19: 241–63.

Burdock, E. I., Hakerem, G., Hardesty, A. D., and Zubin, J. 1960. Ward behavior rating scale. *J. Clin. Psychol.* 16: 246–47.

Burgess, E. W., and Cottrell, L. 1939. *Predicting Success or Failure in Marriage.* Prentice Hall, New York.

Burke, L., Deykin, E., Jacobson, S., and Haley, S. 1967. The depressed woman returns. *Arch. Gen. Psychiat.* 16: 548–53.

Burks, H. L., and Harrison, S. I. 1962. Aggressive behavior as a means of avoiding depression. *Amer. J. Orthopsychiat.* 32: 416–22.

Burns, S. J., and Offord, D. R. 1972. Achievement correlates of depressive illness: A study of school records and social mobility. *J. Nerv. Ment. Dis.* 154: 344–51.

Buss, A. H., and Durkee, S. 1957. An inventory for assessing different kinds of hostility. *J. Consult. Psychol.* 13: 343–49.

Cain, L. D. J. 1964. Life course and social structure. In R. L. Fairs, ed., *Handbook of Modern Sociology*, pp. 272–309. Rand McNally, Chicago.

Carney, M. W. P., Roth, M., and Garside, R. F. 1965. The diagnosis of depressive syndrome and the prediction of ECT response. *Brit. J. Psychiat.* 111: 659–74.

Cartwright, R. D. 1966. A comparison of the response to psychoanalytic and client-centered psychotherapy. In L. A. Gottschalk, and A. H. Auerbach, eds., *Methods of Research in Psychotherapy*. Appleton-Century Crofts, New York.

Cassidy, W. L., Flanagan, N. B., Spellman, M., and Cohen, M. E. 1957. Clinical observations in manic depressive disease: A quantitative study of 100 manic depressive patients and 50 medically sick controls. *JAMA* 104: 1535–46.

Chodoff, P. 1972. The depressive personality: A critical review. *Arch. Gen. Psychiat.,* 27: 666–73.

Chwast, J. 1967. The depression reactions as manifested among adolescent delinquents. *Amer. J. Psychother.* 21: 574–84.

Chwast, J., and Lurie, A. 1966. The resocialization of the discharged depressed patient. *Canad. Psychiat. Assn. J.* 11: 5131–40.

Clayton, P., Halikes, J., and Maurice, W. 1971. The bereavement of the widowed. *Diseases of the Nervous System* 32: 597–604 (September).

Cohen, M. B., Baker, G., Cohen, R. A., Fromm-Reichmann, F., and Weigert, E. A. 1954. An intensive study of twelve cases of manic depressive psychoses. *Psychiatry* 17: 103–37.

Cole, J. O. 1964. Therapeutic efficacy of antidepressant drugs—A review. *JAMA* 190: 448–55.

Cooper, B., Eastwood, M. R. and Sylph, J. 1970. Psychiatric morbidity and social adjustment in a general practice population. In E. H. Hare and J. W. Wing, eds., *Psychiatric Epidemiology*. Oxford University Press, London.

Coppen, A. 1966. The Marke-Nyman temperament scale: An English translation. *Brit. J. Med. Psychol.* 39: 55–60.

Coppen, A., and Shaw, D. M. 1963. Mineral metabolism in melancholia. *Brit. Med. J.* 1439–44 (December).

Coppen, A., and Metcalfe, M. 1965. Effect of a depressive illness on M.P.I. scores. *Brit. J. Psychiat.* 111: 236–39.

Covi, L. 1973. *NIMH-PRB Treatment of Depression.* Johns Hopkins University School of Medicine Protocol. Personal Communication.

Department of Health, Education and Welfare Report. 1972. *Work in America,* as reported in the *New York Times,* Friday, December 22.

Deutsch, H. 1965. *Neuroses and Character Types: Clinical Psychoanalytic Studies.* International Universities Press, New York.

Deykin, E. Y., Jacobson, S., Klerman, G. L., and Solomon, M. 1966. The empty nest: Psychosocial aspects of conflict between depressed women and their grown children. *Amer. J. Psychiat.* 122/2: 1422–26.

Deykin, E. Y., Weissman, M. M., and Klerman, G. L. 1972. Treatment of depressed women. Therapeutic issues with hospitalized patients and outpatients. *Br. J. Social Wk.* 1/3: 277–91.

DiMascio, A., and Klerman, G. L. Long term treatment of depression with drugs and psychotherapy. *Psychopharmacology Bulletin.* In press.

Eisenstein, V. W. 1956. *Neurotic Interaction in Marriage.* Basic Books, New York.

Endicott, J., and Spitzer, R. L. 1972a. What! Another rating scale? The psychiatric evaluation form. *J. Nerv. Ment. Dis.* 154: 88–104.

————. 1972b. Current and past psychopathology scales (CAPPS)—rationale, reliability and validity. *Arch. Gen. Psychiat.* 27: 678–91 (November).

Evans, P. Infanticide. 1968. *Proc. Roy. Soc. Med.* 61: 36–68.

Eysenck, H. J. 1952. The effects of psychotherapy: An evaluation. *J. Consult. Psychol.* 16: 319–24.

————. 1959. *The Manual of the Maudsley Personality Inventory.* University of London Press, London.

Fabian, A. A., and Donohue, J. F. 1956. Maternal depression: A challenging child guidance problem. *Amer. J. Orthopsychiat.* 26: 400–405.

Feighner, J., Robins, E., Guze, S., Woodruff, R., Winokur, G., and Munoz, R. 1972. Diagnostic criteria for use in psychiatric research. *Arch. Gen. Psychiat.* 26: 57–63 (January).

Fenichel, O. 1968. Depression and mania. In W. Gaylin, ed., *The Meaning of Despair,* pp. 108–53. Science House Inc., New York.

Fiske, D. W., Hunt, H. F., Luborsky, L., Orne, M. T., Parloff, M. B., Reiser, M. F., and Tuma, A. H. 1970. Planning of research on effectiveness of psychotherapy. *Arch. Gen. Psychiat.* 22: 22–32.

Flach, F. L. 1964. Calcium metabolism in states of depression. *Brit. J. Psychiat.* 110: 558–93.

Fleck, S. 1966. An approach to family pathology. *Comprehensive Psychiatry* 7: 307–19.

Fox, R. E., Strupp, H. H., and Lessler, K. 1968. The psychotherapy experience in retrospect: Problems and potentials of an approach. In S. Lesse, ed., *An Evaluation of the Results of the Psychotherapies,* pp. 38–48. Thomas, Springfield, Ill.

Frank, J. D. 1961. *Persuasion and Healing.* John Hopkins Press, Baltimore.

Freeman, H. E., and Simons, O. G. 1963. *The Mental Patient Comes Home.* Wiley, New York.

French, N. H., and Heninger, G. R. 1970. A short clinical rating scale for use by nursing personnel: I. Development and design. *Arch. Gen. Psychiat.* 23: 233–40.

Freud, S. 1950. Mourning and melancholia. In *Collected Papers*, vol. 4. Hogarth Press, London.

Friedman, A. S. 1970. Hostility factors and clinical improvement in depressed patients. *Arch. Gen. Psychiat.* 23: 524–37.

―――. 1972. Drug therapy and marital therapy in outpatient depressives. Paper presented at the American College of Neuropsychopharmacology, San Juan, Puerto Rico, December 15.

Gallemore, J., and Wilson, W. 1972. Adolescent maladjustment or affective disorder? *Amer. J. Psychiat.* 129: 608–19 (November).

Gans, H. J. 1962. *The Urban Villagers.* Free Press of Glencoe, New York.

Garside, R. F., Kay, D. W. K., Roy, J. R., and Beamish, P. 1970. M.P.I. scores and symptoms of depression. *Brit. J. Psychiat.* 116: 429–32.

Gaylin, W., ed. 1968. *The Meaning of Despair.* Science House Inc., New York.

Gelder, M. G., Marks, I. M., and Wolff, H. H. 1967. Desensitization and psychotherapy in phobic states: A controlled inquiry. *Brit. J. Psychiat.* 113: 53–73.

Gershon, E. S., Cromer, M., and Klerman, G. L. 1968. Hostility and depression. *Psychiatry* 31: 224–35.

Gershon, E., Dunne, D., and Goodwin, F. 1971. Toward a biology of affective disorders. *Arch. Gen. Psychiat.* 25: 1–15 (July).

Gibson, R. W. 1957. Comparison of the family background and early life experiences of the manic depressive and schizophrenic patient. Final report on Office of Naval Research Contract (Nonr–751[00]) Washington, D.C. Washington School of Psychiatry.

―――. 1958. The family background and early life experiences of the manic-depressive patient. *Psychiatry* 21: 71–90 (February).

Glaser, K. 1967. Masked depression in children and adolescents. *Amer. J. Psychother.* 21: 565.

Goldberg, S. C., Cole, J. O., and Clyde, D. J. 1963. Factor analysis of ratings of schizophrenic behavior. *Psychopharmacology Service Center Bulletin* 2: 23–28.

Goldman, R. K., and Mendelsohn, G. A. 1969. Psychotherapeutic change and social adjustment: A report of a national survey by psychotherapists. *J. Abnorm. Soc. Psychol.* 74: 164–72.

Gould, R. E. 1965. Suicide problems in children and adolescents. *Amer. J. Psychother.* 19: 228.

Group for the Advancement of Psychiatry (GAP Report). 1966. Psychiatric research and the assessment of change. VI Report #63 (November).

Gurland, B. J., Fleiss, J. L., Cooper, J. E., Kendell, R. E., and Simon, R. 1969. Cross-national study of diagnosis of the mental disorders:

Some comparisons of diagnostic criteria from the first investigation. *Amer. J. Psychiat.* April Supplement, 30–39.

Gurland, B. J., Yorkstone, M. J., Stone, A. R., Frank, J. D., and Fleiss, J. L. 1972. The structured and scaled interview to assess maladjustment (SSIAM): Description, rationale and development. *Arch. Gen. Psychiat.* 27: 259–64.

Gurland, B. J., Yorkstone, M. J., Goldberg, K., Fleiss, J. L., Sloane, B., and Cristol, A. H. 1972. The structured and scaled interview to assess maladjustment: Factor analysis, reliability and validity. *Arch. Gen. Psychiat.* 27: 264–70.

Hamilton, M. 1960. A rating scale for depression. *J. Neurol. Neurosurg. Psychiat.* 23: 56–62.

Harman, H. H. 1960. *Modern Factor Analysis.* The University of Chicago Press, Chicago.

Heinecke, C. M. 1970. Parental deprivation in early childhood: A predisposition to later depression? Presented at the Symposium on Separation and Depression: Clinical and Research Reports. Annual meeting of the American Association for the Advancement of Science, Chicago, December 26–30.

Hill, R. 1955. A critique of contemporary marriage and family research. *Soc. Forces* 23: 268–77.

Hill, A. W., and Price, J. S. 1969. Childhood bereavement and adult depression. *Brit. J. Psychiat.* 115: 305–11.

Hogarty, G. E., and Katz, M. M. 1971. Norms of adjustment and social behavior. *Arch. Gen. Psychiat.* 25: 470–79.

Hogarty, G. E., and Ulrich, R. 1972. The discharge readiness inventory. *Arch. Gen. Psychiat.* 26: 419–26.

Hollingshead, A. 1957. *Two Factor Index of Social Position.* Yale University.

Honigfeld, G. 1963. Follow-up of depressed patients treated in a multi-hospital drug study. *Dis. Nerv. Sys.* 24: 160–61.

Honigfeld, G., and Klett, C. J. 1965. The nurses' observation scale for inpatient evaluation: A new scale for measuring improvement in chronic schizophrenia. *J. Clin. Psychol.* 21: 65–71.

Honigfeld, G., and Lasky, J. J. 1962. One-year follow-up of depressed patients treated in a multi-hospital drug study. *Dis. Nerv. Sys.* 23/10: 555–62.

Hordern, A., Burt, C. G., Gordon, W. F., and Holt, N. F. 1964. Amitriptyline in depressive states: Six months treatment results. *Brit. J. Psychiat.* 110: 641–47.

Horney, K. 1937. *Neurotic Personality of our Time.* W. W. Norton and Co., New York.

Isaacs, S. 1968. Physical ill-treatment of children. *Lancet* 1: 37–39.

Jackson, S. 1972. Unusual mental states in medieval Europe. I. Medical syndrome of mental disorders, 400–1100 A.D. *Journal of History of Medicine and Allied Sciences* 27: 226–97 (July).

Jacobson, E. 1954. Transference problems in the psychoanalytic treatment of severely depressive patients. *Journal of the American Psychoanalytic Association* 2: 595–606.

Jacobson, S., and Klerman, G. L. 1966. Interpersonal dynamics of hospitalized depressed patients' home visits. *J. Marriage and the Family* 28/1: 94–102.

Julian, T., Metcalfe, M., and Coppen, A. 1969. Aspects of personality of depressive patients. *Brit. J. Psychiat.* 115: 587–89.

Katz, M. 1970. The classification of depression: Normal, clinical and ethno-cultural variations. In R. P. Fieve, ed., *Depression in the 70's*. Excerpta Medica, October.

Katz, M. M., and Lyerly, S. B. 1963. Methods for measuring adjustment and social behavior in the community: I. Rationale, description, discriminative validity and scale development. *Psychol. Rep.* 13: 503–35.

Kaufman, E. M., and Zilbach, J. 1959. The impact of adolescence on girls with delinquent character formation. *Amer. J. Orthopsychiat.* 29: 130–43.

Kay, D. W. K., Garside, R. F., Roy, J. R., and Beamish, P. 1969. Endogenous and neurotic syndromes of depression: A factor analytic study of clinical features in 104 cases. *Brit. J. Psychiat.* 115: 377–78.

Kendell, R. E. 1968. *The Classification of Depressive Illnesses*. Maudsley Monograph No. 18. Oxford University Press, London.

Kendell, R. E. and DiScipio, W. J. 1968. Eysenck personality inventory scores for patients with depressive illnesses. *Brit. J. Psychiat.* 114: 767–70.

Kessel, A., and Holt, N. F. 1965. Depression—An analysis of a follow-up study. *Brit. J. Psychiat.* 111: 1143–53.

Kiloh, L. G., and Garside, R. F. 1963. The independence of neurotic depression and endogenous depression. *Brit. J. Psychiat.* 109: 451–63.

Klerman, G. L. 1970. Drug therapy of clinical depression—Current status and implications for research on neuropharmacology of the affective disorders. *J. Psychiat. Res.* 9: 253–70.

———. 1971. Clinical research in depression. *Arch. Gen. Psychiat.* 24: 305–19 (April).

———. 1971. Methodology for drug evaluations in affective disorders: Depression. In J. Levine, B. Schiele, and L. Bouthelet, eds., *Principles and Problems of Establishing the Efficacy of Psychotropic Agents*. U.S. Department of Health, Education and Welfare, P.H.S. Health Services and Mental Health Administration. P.H.S. Publication No. 2138.

———. 1972. Depression among Youths. Paper presented at Symposium on Man and His Moods at Taylor Manor Hospital, Ellicott City, Maryland, April 15.

———. Issues in the relationship between pharmacotherapy and

psychotherapy of depression. Paper presented for the GAP Committee on Research. Unpublished manuscript.

Klerman, G. L., and Barrett, J. The affective disorders: Clinical and epidemiological aspects. In *Lithium: Its Role in Psychiatric Treatment and Research*. Plenum Press, New York. In press.

Klerman, G. L., and Cole, J. O. 1965. Clinical pharmacology of imipramine and related antidepressant compounds. *Pharmacol. Rev.* 17: 101–41.

Klerman, G. L., and Deykin, E. *Inventory of Patients' Social Performance*, and *Interim History and Inventory of Patients' Social Performance*. National Institute of Mental Health, Collaborative Study I.

Klerman, G. L., and Gershon, E. S. 1970. Imipramine effects upon hostility in depression. *J. Nerv. Ment. Dis.* 150: 127–32.

Klerman, G. L., and Paykel, E. S. 1970. Long term therapy in affective disorders. *Int. Pharmacopsychiat.* 5: 80–99.

Klerman, G. L., DiMascio, A., Paykel, E. S., Prusoff, B. A., and Weissman, M. M. 1973a. Collaborative Study between Yale University Medical School, Department of Psychiatry (Connecticut Mental Health Center) and Tufts University School of Medicine (Boston State Hospital). Research Protocol. Personal Communication.

Klerman, G. L., DiMascio, A., Weissman, M. M., Prusoff, B. A., and Paykel, E. S. 1973b. Treatment of depression by drugs and psychotherapy. Paper presented at the American Psychiatric Association, Annual Meeting. Honolulu, Hawaii, May 8.

Kline, N. 1969. *Depression: Its Diagnosis and Treatment and Lithium: The History of Its Use in Psychiatry*. Brunner/Mazel, Inc., New York.

Koller, K. M. 1971. Parental deprivation, family background and female delinquency. *Brit. J. Psychiat.* 118: 319–27.

Komarovsky, M. 1967. *Blue Collar Marriage*. Vintage Books, New York.

Kraepelin, E. (1913) 1921. *Manic Depressive Insanity and Paranoia*. Translated by R. M. Barclay. Eighth edition, Edinburgh.

Kreitman, N. 1969. Scientific investigation of relationships and communication within the family. *Proc. Roy. Soc. Med.* 62: 895–98 (September).

Kreitman, N., Collins, J., Nelson, B., Troop, J. 1970. Neurosis and marital interaction: I. Personality and symptoms. *Brit. J. Psychiat.* 117: 33–46.

Kretschmer, E. 1925. *Physique and Character*. Translated by W. J. H. Sprout. Harcourt, New York.

Lansing, J. B., and Kish, L. 1957. Family life cycle as an independent variable. *Amer. Sociol. Rev.* 22: 512–19.

Lazare, A., Klerman, G. L., and Armor, D. J. 1966. Oral, obsessive and hysterical personality patterns. *Arch. Gen. Psychiat.* 14: 624–30.

Lazare, A., and Klerman, G. L. 1968. Hysteria and depression: The frequency and significance of hysterical personality features in hospitalized depressed women. *Amer. J. Psychiat.* 124: 48–56 (May Supplement).

Lesse, S. 1967. Apparent remissions in depressed suicidal patients. *J. Nerv. Ment. Dis.* 144: 291–96.

——. 1968. The multivariant mask of depression. *Amer. J. Psychiat.* 124: 35–40 (Supplement).

Levin, S. 1965. Some suggestions for treating the depressed patients. *Psychoanal. Quart.* 34: 37–65 (January).

Lewis, A. J. 1934. Melancholia: A historical review. *J. Ment. Sci.* 80: 1–42 (January).

——. 1934. Melancholia: A clinical survey of depressive states. *J. Ment. Sci.* 80: 277–378.

——. 1936. Melancholia: Prognostic study and case material. *J. Ment. Sci.* 82: 488–558.

Lidz, T. 1963. *The Family and Human Adaptation.* International Universities Press, New York.

——. 1968. *The Person: His Development Throughout the Life Cycle.* Basic Books, New York.

Lidz, T., Cornelison, A., Terry, D., and Fleck, S. 1957. The intra-familial environment of schizophrenic patients: II. Marital schism and marital skew. *Amer. J. Psychiat.* 114: 241–48 (September).

Lidz, T., Fleck, S., and Cornelison, A. 1966. *Schizophrenia and the Family.* International Universities Press, New York.

Linn, M. W., Sculthorpe, W. B., Euje, M., Slater, P. H., and Goodman, S. P. 1969. A social dysfunction rating scale. *J. Psychiat. Res.* 6: 299–306.

Lipman, R. S., Rickels, K., Covi, L., Derogatis, L. R., and Uhlenhuth, E. H. 1969. Factors of symptom distress: Doctor ratings of anxious neurotic outpatients. *Arch. Gen. Psychiat.* 21: 328–38.

Lorand, S. 1937. Dynamics and therapy of depressive states. *Psychoanal. Rev.* 24/4: 337–49.

Lorr, M., McNair, D. M., Klett, C. J., and Lasky, J. J. 1962. Evidence of ten psychotic syndromes. *J. Consult. Psychol.* 26: 185–89.

Lukianowicz, N. 1971. Infanticide. *Psychiat. Clin.* 4: 145–58.

Lundquist, G. 1945. Prognosis and course in manic depressive psychosis. *Acta Psychiat. Neurol.* 35: 59–61 (Supplement).

Lyerly, S. B., and Abbott, P. S. *Handbook of Psychiatric Rating Scales (1950–1964).* The National Institute of Mental Health, Bethesda, Maryland. Public Health Services Publication No. 1495. U.S. Government Printing Office, Washington, D.C.

Malan, D. H., Bacal, H. A., Heath, E. S., and Balfour, F. H. G. 1968. A study of psychodynamic changes in untreated neurotic patients. *Brit. J. Psychiat.* 114: 525–51.

Malmquist, C. P. 1971. Depressions in childhood and adolescence. *The*

New England Journal of Medicine 284: 887–93, 955–61 (April 22, April 29).

Mandel, N. G. 1959. Mandel Social Adjustment Scale. Department of Psychiatry, University of Minnesota. Minneapolis, Minnesota.

Maris, R. W. 1971. Deviance as therapy: The paradox of the self-destructive female. *J. Health and Social Behavior* 12: 113–24.

McDermaid, G., and Winkler, E. G. 1955. Psychopathology of infanticide. *Journal of Clinical and Experimental Psychopathology* 16: 22–41.

Mendels, J. 1970. *Concepts of Depression.* John Wiley and Sons, New York.

Mendels, J., and Cochrane, C. 1968. The nosology of depression: The endogenous-reactive concept. *Amer. J. Psychiat.* 124: 1–11 (May Supplement).

Mendham, R. H. S., Howland, C., and Shepherd, M. 1972. Continuation therapy with tricyclic antidepressants in depressive illness. *Lancet* 854–55, (October 21).

Metcalfe, M. 1968. The personality of depressive patients: I. Assessment of change; II. Assessment of premorbid personality. In A. Coppen and A. Walk, eds., *Recent Developments in Affective Disorders*, pp. 97–104. Royal Medico Psychological Association, London.

Miles, H. W., Barrabee, E. L., and Finesinger, J. J. 1951. Evaluation of psychotherapy: With a follow-up study of sixty-two cases of anxiety neurosis. *Psychosom. Med.* 13: 82–105.

Mueller, P. S., Heninger, G. R., and McDonald, R. K. 1969. Intravenous glucose tolerance test in depression. *Arch. Gen. Psychiat.* 21: 470–77.

Myers, J. and Bean, L. L. 1968. *A Decade Later: A Follow-up of Social Class and Mental Illness.* John Wiley and Sons, New York.

Nelson, B., Collins, J., Kreitman, N., and Troop, J. 1970. Neurosis and marital interaction: II. Time sharing and social activity, *Brit. J. Psychiat.* 117: 47–58.

Nye, F. I., and Berardo, F. M. 1966. *Emerging Conceptual Frameworks in Family Analysis.* Macmillan, New York.

Odegard, O. 1963. The psychiatric disease entities in the light of a genetic investigation. *Acta. Psychiat. Neurol. Scand.* 39: 94–106 (Supplement 169).

Ostow, M. 1970. *The Psychology of Melancholy.* Harper and Row, New York.

Overall, J. E., and Gorham, D. R. 1962. The brief psychiatric rating scale. *Psychol. Rep.* 10: 799–812.

Overall, J. E., Hollister, C. E., Johnson, M., and Pennington, V. 1966. Nosology of depression and differential response to drugs. *JAMA* 195: 946–48.

Palmer, H. D. and Sherman, S. H. 1938. The involutional melancholic process. *Arch. Neurol. Psychiat.* 40: 762–88.

Parloff, M. B., Kelman, H. C., and Frank, J. D. 1954. Comfort, effectiveness and self awareness as criteria of improvement in psychotherapy. *Amer. J. Psychiat.* 111: 343–51.

Parson, T., and Bales, R. F. 1955. *Family, Socialization and Interaction Process.* The Free Press of Glencoe, New York.

Pasamanich, B., Scarpetti, F., and Dinitz, S. 1967. *Schizophrenics in the Community.* Appleton-Century Crofts, New York.

Paykel, E. S. 1971. Classification of depressed patients: A cluster analysis derived grouping. *Brit. J. Psychiat.* 118: 275–88.

———. 1972. Correlates of a depressive typology. *Arch. Gen. Psychiat.* 27: 203–10.

———. Life events and acute depression. In E. Senay and J. P. Scott, eds., *Separation and Depression: Clinical and Research Aspects.* American Association for the Advancement of Science. In press.

Paykel, E. S., and Dienelt, M. N., 1971. Suicide attempts following acute depression. *J. Nerv. Ment. Dis.* 153: 234–43.

Paykel, E. S., Myers, J. K., Dienelt, M. N., Klerman, G. L., Lindenthal, J. J., and Pepper, M. P. 1969. Life events and depression: A controlled study. *Arch. Gen. Psychiat.* 21: 753–60.

Paykel, E. S., Klerman, G. L., and Prusoff, B. A. 1970. Treatment setting and clinical depression. *Arch. Gen. Psychiat.* 22: 11–21.

———. Prognosis of depression and the endogenous-neurotic distinction. *Psychological Medicine.* In press.

Paykel, E. S., Prusoff, B. A., and Klerman, G. L. 1971. The endogenous-neurotic continuum in depression: Rater independence and factor distributions. *J. Psychiat. Res.* 8: 73–90.

Paykel, E. S., Prusoff, B. A., Klerman, G. L., Haskell, D., and DiMascio, A. 1973. Clinical response to amitriptyline among depressed women. *J. Nerv. Ment. Dis.* 156 (3): 149–65 (March).

Paykel, E. S., Weissman, M. M., Prusoff, B. A., and Tonks, C. M. 1971. Dimensions of social adjustment in depressed women. *J. Nerv. Ment. Dis.* 152: 158–72.

Paykel, E. S., Klerman, G. L., DiMascio, A., Weissman, M. M., and Prusoff, B. A. 1973. Maintenance antidepressants, psychotherapy, symptoms and social function. In J. O. Cole, A. Friedhoff, and A. Freedman, eds., *Psychopathology and Psychopharmacology,* pp. 205–18. The Johns Hopkins Press, Baltimore.

Perris, C. 1969. The separation of bipolar (manic depressive) from unipolar recurrent depressive psychoses. *Biochem. Neuropsychiat.* 1: 17–24.

Phillip, A. E. 1970. Traits, attitudes and symptoms in a group of attempted suicides. *Brit. J. Psychiat.* 116: 475–82.

Post, F. 1962. The social orbit of psychiatric patients. *J. Ment. Sci.* 108: 759–71.

Post, F., and Wardle, J. 1962. Family neurosis and family psychosis, a review of the problem. *J. Ment. Sci.* 108: 147–56.

Poznanski, E., and Zrull, J. P. 1970. Childhood depression. *Arch. Gen. Psychiat.* 23: 8–15.

Prusoff, B. A., Klerman, G. L., and Paykel, E. S. 1972. Concordance between clinical assessments and patients' self-report in depression. *Arch. Gen. Psychiat.* 26: 546–52.

Rado, S. 1968. The problem of melancholia. In W. Gaylin, ed., *The Meaning of Despair*, pp. 70–107. Science House Inc., New York.

Rao, C. R. 1952. *Advanced Statistical Methods in Biometric Research.* John Wiley and Sons, New York.

Raskin, A., Schulterbrandt, J., Reatig, N., and Rice, C. E. 1967. Factors of psychopathology in interview, ward behavior, and self report ratings of hospitalized depressives. *J. Consul. Psychol.* 31: 270–78.

Raskin, A., Schulterbrandt, J., Reatig, N., and McKeon, J. J. 1969. Replication of factors of psychopathology in interview, ward behavior and self report ratings of hospitalized depressives. *J. Nerv. Ment. Dis.* 148: 87–98.

————. 1970. Differential response to chlorpromazine, imipramine and placebo. A study of subgroups of hospitalized depressed patients. *Arch. Gen. Psychiat.* 23: 164–73.

Resnich, P. J. 1969. Child murder by parents: A psychiatric review of filicide. *Amer. J. Psychiat.* 126: 325–34.

————. 1970. Murder of the newborn: A psychiatric review of neonaticide. *Amer. J. Psychiat.* 126: 1414–20.

Robins, L. N. 1970. Follow-up studies investigating childhood disorders. In E. H. Hare and J. K. Wing, eds., *Psychiatric Epidemiology.* Oxford University Press, London.

Robins, E., and Guze, S. 1972. Classification of affective disorders: The primary-secondary, the endogenous, and the neurotic-psychotic concepts. In *Recent Advances in the Psychobiology of the Depressive Illness.* D-HEW Publication #(HSM) 70–9053.

Robins, E., Munoz, R. A., Marten, S., and Gentry, K. A. 1972. Primary and secondary affective disorders: A classification for description, research and management of mood disorders. Preliminary report of 314 patients seen in an emergency room. In J. Zubin and F. A. Freyhan, eds., *Disorders of Mood.* The Johns Hopkins Press, Baltimore.

Rosenbaum, M., and Richman, J. 1970. Suicide: the role of hostility and death wishes from the family and significant others. *Amer. J. Psychiat.* 126: 128–31.

Rosenthal, S. H. 1968. The involutional depressive syndrome. *Amer. J. Psychiat.* 124: 21–34 (May Supplement).

Rosenthal, S. H., and Gudeman, J. E. 1967. The endogenous depressive pattern: An empirical investigation. *Arch. Gen. Psychiat.* 16: 241–49.

Rosenthal, S. H., and Klerman, G. L. 1966. Content and consistency in the endogenous depressive pattern. *Brit. J. Psychiat.* 112: 471–84.

Ruesch, J. 1969. The assessment of social disability. *Arch. Gen. Psychiat.* 21: 655–64.

Ruesch, J., and Brodsky, C. M. 1968. The concept of social disability. *Arch. Gen. Psychiat.* 19: 394–403 (October).

Rutter, M. 1966. *Children of Sick Patients. An Environmental and Psychiatric Study.* Institute of Psychiatry, Maudsley Monographs No. 16. Oxford University Press, London.

————. 1972. *Maternal Deprivation Reassessed.* Penguin Books, Middlesex, England.

Rutter, M., and Brown, G. W. (1966). The reliability and validity of measures of family life and relationships in families containing a psychiatric patient. *Social Psychiatry* 1: 38–53.

Sachar, E. J., Hellman, L., Fukushima, D. K., and Gallagher, T. F. 1970. Cortisol production in depressive illness: A clinical and biological classification. *Arch. Gen. Psychiat.* 23: 289–98.

Sampson, H., Messinger, S., and Towne, R. D. 1964. *Schizophrenic Women: Studies in Marital Crises.* Atherton Press, New York.

Sarwer-Foner, G. J. 1969. Depression and suicide—on some particularly high-risk suicidal patients. *Dis. Nerv. Sys.* 30: 104–10.

Schildkraut, J. J. 1965. The catecholamine hypothesis of affective disorders: A review of supporting evidence. *Amer. J. Psychiat.* 122: 509–22.

Schou, M. 1970. Use of Lithium. In W. G. Clark and J. del Guidice, eds. *Principles of Psychopharmacology,* pp. 653–65. Academic Press, New York.

Schwab, J. 1970. Coming in the 70's—an epidemic of depression. *Attitude* 1: 2–6 (January/February).

Seiden, R. H. 1969. *Suicide among Youth—a Review of the Literature, 1900–1967.* U.S. Government Printing Office, Washington, D.C. (December).

Shader, R. I. and Binstock, W. A. 1966. *Social Role Performance Evaluation Interview.* Mimeographed booklet. Massachusetts Mental Health Center.

Shein, H. M. and Stone, A. A. 1969. Monitoring the treatment of suicidal potential within the context of psychotherapy. *Comprehen. Psychiat.* 10: 59–70.

Silverman, C. 1968. *The Epidemiology of Depression.* The Johns Hopkins Press, Baltimore.

Slater, E. 1936. The inheritance of manic depressive insanity. *Proc. Roy. Soc. Med.* 29: 981–90.

————. 1943. The neurotic constitution. *J. Neurol. Psychiat.* 6: 1–16.

Speigel, J., and Bell, N. W. 1959. The family of the psychiatric patient. In S. Arieti, ed., *American Handbook of Psychiatry.* Vol. 1. Basic Books, New York.

Spiegel, R. 1960. Communications in the psychoanalysis of depressives.

In *Psychoanalysis and Human Values,* pp. 209–20. Grune and Stratton, New York.

——. 1967. Anger and acting out: Masks of depression. *Amer. J. Psychother.* 2: 597–606.

Spielberger, C. D., Parker, J. B., and Becker, J. 1963. Conformity and achievement in remitted manic depressives. *J. Nerv. Ment. Dis.* 137: 162–72.

Spitzer, R. L., Endicott, J., Fleiss, J. L., and Cohen, J. 1970. The psychiatric status schedule: A technique for evaluating psychopathology and impairment in role functioning. *Arch. Gen. Psychiat.* 23: 41–55.

Srole, L., Langner, T. S., Michael, S. T., Opler, M. K., and Rennie, T. A. C. 1962. *Mental Health in the Metropolis.* McGraw-Hill, New York.

Stevens, B. C. 1969. *Marriage and Fertility of Women Suffering from Schizophrenia and Affective Disorders.* Maudsley Monographs. Institute of Psychiatry, London.

Stolley, P. 1969. Prescribing patterns of physicians. *J. Chron. Dis.* 22: 395–405.

Strupp, H. H., and Bergin, A. E. 1969. Some empirical and conceptual bases for coordinated research in psychotherapy: A critical review of issues, trends, and evidence. *Int. J. Psychiat.* 7: 18–90.

Stuart, R. 1967. Casework treatment of depression viewed as an interpersonal disturbance. *Social Casework* 12/2: 27–36 (April).

Tait, A. C., Harper, J., McClatchey, W. T. 1957. Initial psychiatric illness in involutional women: I. Clinical aspects. *J. Ment. Sci.* 103: 132–45.

Titley, W. B. 1936. Prepsychotic personality of patients with involutional melancholia. *Arch. Neurol. Psychiat.* 36: 19–33.

Torgeson, W. S. 1958. *Theory and Methods of Scaling.* John Wiley and Sons, New York.

Traux, C. B., and Carkhuff, R. R. 1967. *Towards Effective Counseling and Psychotherapy, Training and Practice.* Aldine, Chicago.

Turner, R. J., Dopkeen, L. S., and Labreche, G. P. 1970. Marital status and schizophrenia: A study of incidence and outcome. *J. Abnorm. Psychol.* 76: 110–16.

Uhlenhuth, E. H., Lipman, R. A., and Covi, L. 1969. Combined pharmacotherapy and psychotherapy. *J. Nerv. Ment. Dis.* 1: 52–64.

U.S. Bureau of the Census Current Population Reports, Series P-20, #210. 1971. *Mobility of the Population of the United States: March 1969 to March 1970.* U.S. Government Printing Office, Washington, D.C.

Vernon, P. E. 1964. *Personality Assessment.* John Wiley and Sons, New York.

Vinoda, K. S. 1966. Personality characteristics of attempted suicides. *Brit. J. Psychiat.* 112: 1143–50.

Walzer, H. 1961. Casework treatment of the depressed parent. *Social Casework* 42: 505–12.

Waskow, I. E., and Parloff, M. B., eds. Psychotherapy change measures. Report of clinical research branch. NIMH Outcome Measures Project U.S. Government Printing Offce. In press.

Weissman, M. M., and Paykel, E. S. 1972. Moving and depression. *Society* 9: 24–28 (July/August).

Weissman, M. M., Prusoff, B. A., and Paykel, E. S. 1972. Checklist quantification of a psychological therapy: Pilot studies of reliability and utility. *J. Nerv. Ment. Dis.* 154: 125–36.

Weissman, M. M., Geanakoplos, E., and Prusoff, B. A., 1973. Social class and attrition in depressed outpatients. *Social Casework* 54/3: 162–70 (March).

Weissman, M. M., Paykel, E. S., French, N., Mark, H., Fox, K., and Prusoff, B. A. 1973a. Suicide attempts in an urban community, 1955–1970. *Social Psychiatry* 8: 82–91.

Weissman, M. M., Fox, K., and Klerman, G. L. 1973b. Hostility and depression associated with suicide attempts. *Amer. J. Psychiat.* 130: 450–55.

Winokur, G. 1970. Types of affective disorder. Paper presented at the annual meeting of the American College of Neuropsychopharmacology, San Juan, Puerto Rico.

———. 1973. Depression in the menopause. *Amer. J. Psychiat.* 130: 92–93.

Winokur, G., Clayton, P., and Reich, T. 1969. *Manic Depressive Illness.* C. V. Mosley Co., St. Louis.

Woodruff, R. J., Jr., Murphy, G. E., and Herjanic, M. 1967. The natural history of affective disorders: I. Symptoms of 72 patients at the time of index hospital admission. *J. Psychiat. Res.* 5: 255–63.

Woodruff, R. A., Robins, C. N., Winokur, G., and Reich, T. 1970. Manic depressive illness and social adjustment. Read at the 126th meeting of the American Psychiatric Association, San Francisco, California.

Zrull, J. P., McDermott, J. F., and Poznanski, E. 1970. Hyperkinetic syndrome: The role of depression. *Child Psychiatry and Human Development* 1: 33–40.

Index

Abbott, P. S., 25, 26
Abnormalities, neuropharmacological, 9
Abraham, K., 38, 39, 40, 41, 121, 139, 169, 212
Achievement, need for, 42–43; social, 43
Ackerman, N. W., 82
Adequacy, of patient, 19
Adolescent children: covert depression in, 118, 119; difficulties with authority, 116; disturbed behavior of, 117–18; emancipation of, 115–19; friction with, 105, 115; responses to mothers' recovery, 118, 212. See also Children; Parenthood
Affairs, extramarital, 97–98
Age: and incidence of depression, 16, 17; and social adjustment, 178, 181, 215
Agreement, indices of, 60
Alarcon, J., 147
American Psychiatric Association Diagnostic and Statistical Manual, II, 178
Amitriptyline, 13, 36, 49–50, 59, 165
Anergia, 198
Angrist, S., 29, 66, 89

Anorexia, 49, 174, 198
Antecedents, psychological, 198
Anthony, E. J., 87
Anthony, H. S., 118
Antidepressants: debate about, 14; and psychotherapy, 14, 18, 59, 183–84, 195; response to, 12, 13, 50, 165–66, 184–85, 195–96, 220. See also Pharmacotherapy
Anxiety, as symptom of depression, 4, 83, 178
Anxious depressives, 178–79
Anxious rumination, as factor of analysis, 129–33, 135, 137, 162, 164, 168, 174–77, 188, 212
Assessment: of hostility, 139–41, 143–45; of marital and sexual relations, 87–90; of parenthood, 105–6; of social adjustment, 19, 23–31, 36, 37, 55–58, 60, 135, 139, 140, 167–68, 212, 219, 222, 225; of work, 67–68. See also Rating scales and individual traits or areas
Attrition, rate of, 187–88
Australia, depression in, 16
Autonomy, 101–2
Axelson, L., 76

281

Feighner, J., 11
Fenichel, O., 39, 41
Financial problems, 68
Fiske, D. W., 30, 197
Flach, F. L., 8
Fleck, S., 107
Follow-up studies, 200–205; of acute
  depression, 35, 204–5; findings of,
  35, 46, 159, 201; procedure of, 155–
  56; relapses found in, 12, 155, 187,
  202–4; 213; response to, 201;
  trends confirmed at, 213
Fox, R. E., 30
Frank, J. D., 27, 28, 198
Freeman, H. E., 29, 66
French, N. H., 27
Freud, S., 38, 41, 139
Friction: amount of, 24, 29, 56, 68–69,
  115; assessment of, 24, 68–69, 88,
  130, 140; category of, 56, 125, 180;
  with children, 34, 105, 115, 120;
  with friends, 79; as factor of analysis, 127, 130, 133, 164–65, 168–69,
  174–77, 180, 188–89; and hypersensitivity, 80, 139; in intimate
  areas, 142–43; with spouse, 89, 94–
  95. See also Hostility
Friedman, A. S., 35, 191
Friendship, 78–81, 162. See also Social adjustment

Galen, 16
Gallemore, J., 16, 118
Gans, H. J., 85
Garside, R. F., 44, 45
Gaylin, W., 38, 39
Gelder, M. G., 38, 123
Gershon, E., 8, 16, 35, 82, 139, 148
Gibson, R. W., 43, 102
Glaser, K., 118
Goldman, R. K., 198
Gorham, D. R., 27, 30, 61, 140
Gould, R. E., 118
Group for the Advancement of Psy-
  chiatry, 25, 26
Gudeman, J. E., 45
Guilt feelings, 5, 6, 83, 97, 174, 176,
  211; and adultery, 97–98; about
  families, 88–89, 107; and masturba-
  tion, 97; and sexual fantasies, 97;
  and sexual satisfaction, 96–98
Gurland, B. J., 29, 30, 49, 130, 135
Guze, S., 11, 12, 201

Hamilton, M., 27, 132, 221
Hamilton Rating Scale, 61, 140, 221
Harman, H. H., 127
Harrison, S. I., 118
Headaches, 6
Heinecke, C. M., 8
Helplessness, forms of, 5, 6
Heninger, G. R., 27
Historical changes in psychiatric care,
  18, 227
Hogarty, G. E., 28, 29
Hollingshead, A., 54
Holt, N. F., 36
Honigfeld, G., 27, 36
Hopelessness, as symptom of depres-
  sion, 5, 119, 176, 198
Hordern, A., 36
Hospitalization: avoidance of, 18;
  importance of, 13
Hostile depressives, 178–79
Hostility: in acute depression, 41,
  68–69, 81, 83, 89, 94, 138–49, 215;
  assessment of, 35, 68–69, 138–42,
  143–45, 211; to children, 34, 104–5,
  107, 111, 114, 142, 146–47, 148–49,
  223; comparison with normals, 81,
  83, 89, 94, 138–39, 142–43; and
  diagnosis, 178–79; diminution of,
  139; expression of, 35, 139, 146,
  148–49, 222; externally directed,
  41, 139, 148, 149, 215; inhibition of,
  215; at interview, 140–41, 143, 145,
  146; internally directed, 40, 41, 148,
  169, 215; object choice of, 145–47;
  to parents, 146–47; rating of, 89,
  140–41, 143; after recovery, 215;
  social implications of, 41, 148; to
  spouse, 89, 141–42, 147; verbal, 35,
  148
Housewives, 68–70, 73–74
Housework: compulsive, 73–74; difficulty with, 68–70, 72–73
Husband. See Spouses
Hyperactivity, in children, 114
Hypersensitivity, 34, 80, 140. See also
  Friction; Hostility

Illness, medical, 51. See also Biologi-
  cal causes of depression
Imipramine, 13
Improvement: in individual variables,
  156–59; rate of, 165–66. See also
  Recovery; Remission

Psychotic depressives, 10, 104, 178–79, 220

Qualitative categories: conceptual framework of, 122; description of, 56–58; differential trends of, 131; overlapping of, 103, 137; scoring by, 125–27

Race, 182
Rado, S., 39, 121, 139, 214
Rage, expression of, 97–98. *See also* Hostility
Rao, C. R., 179
Raskin, A., 27, 30, 48, 62
Raskin Three Area Scale of Depression, 172, 185
Raters (for the study), 26, 58, 139, 140. *See also* Interviewers
Rating scales, 28–29, 61, 140, 170, 172, 174, 185, 221; anchor points of, 28, 29, 56; clinicians' objection to, 27; defined, 25; format of, 26, 218–29; for personality, 42, 44, 61–62, 179, 219; principles behind, 26; reliability of, 26–27, 60, 218; requirements of, 25–27; sensitivity of, 27; for social adjustment, 27–31, 37, 55–58, 60, 105–6, 130, 135, 138–45, 167, 172, 174; validity of, 27. *See also names of specific scales*
Religion, 182
Remission, 12, 13, 20, 35, 160, 164, 212. *See also* Recovery
Research, implications for, 221–23
Resentment, of families, 70, 83, 211
Residual deficit of depression, 159, 164, 166–69, 177, 213–14, 220
Resnich, P. J., 105
Resocialization program, 37
Richman, J., 147
Robins, E., 11, 12, 201
Robins, L. N., 104
Roles: ambiguity in, 71, 74; conflict in, 74–75; division into, 56, expectations, 34; expressive, 24, 72; framework, 65; instrumental, 24; and scoring, 123–25, 131, 137; separation of, 24
Rosenbaum, M., 147
Rosenthall, E. S., 10, 15, 44
Rosenthall, S. H., 45
Ruesch, J., 28

Rumination, anxious, 129–33, 135, 137, 162, 164, 168, 174–77, 188, 212
Rutter, M., 29, 103, 104, 105

Sachar, E. J., 9
Sadness, 6, 49, 198
Sampson, H., 87
Sarwer-Foner, G. J., 147
Satisfactions, category of, 56
Schildkraut, J. J., 9
Schizophrenics: comparison with, 42, 210; course of, 12, 19, 20, 49, 222; posthospital adjustment of, 29; studies of, 19, 44
School records, as testing tool, 42
Schou, M., 13
Schwab, J., 15, 17
Secondary disturbance, 11, 47, 49
Secrecy, burden of, 223
Seiden, R. H., 16, 147
Self-esteem, loss of, 39, 40
Self-perception: relation to behavior, 130
Separation, as precipitation stress, 7
Sexual relations, 8, 9, 16–17, 89, 96–97; adjustment, ratings on, 88; disturbances, 34; performance, 6, 33, 45, 95, 211
Shader, R. I., 28
Shaw, D. M., 8
Shein, H. M., 147
Sherman, S. H., 44
Silverman, C., 15
Simmons, O. G., 29, 66
Slater, E., 8, 42
Sleeplessness, 6, 49, 198
Social achievement, concern for, 43
Social activities, 79–81. *See also* Friendship; Social adjustment
Social adjustment: during acute depression, 33–35, 122–37, 214; assessment of, 19, 23–31, 36, 37, 55–58, 60, 83–90, 135, 139, 140, 167–68, 212, 219, 222, 225; and character, 155, 167; comparison with normals, 61, 80–81, 131–35; conclusions on, 45, 214; and cultural expectations, 182 (*see also* Roles); defined, 23, 24–25; and diagnosis, 179–80; evaluation of, 19, 23, 24, 28–31, 36, 37, 167–68, 212, 222, 225; follow-up studies of, 32–33, 35, 47, 159, 165, 201–2, 225; as index of disturbance,